GLQ

A JOURNAL OF LESBIAN AND GAY STUDIES

VOLUME 18   NUMBER 1   2012

Queer Studies and the Crises of Capitalism

edited by Jordana Rosenberg and Amy Villarejo

Books in Brief

QUEERNESS, NORMS, UTOPIA

Jordana Rosenberg and Amy Villarejo

Queer studies and the crises of capitalism. The title of this special issue begs a number of questions at once. The first is historical: which crises? The second is methodological: what has queer studies to do with the crises of capitalism? And the third is speculative: how might a methodology attuned to both sexuality and the specificities of capitalist crisis orient us toward a world other than the one in which we find ourselves currently mired?

As to the first question, we begin by noting that crisis is endemic to the functioning of capitalism and has been since its inception. By this we mean not just that capitalism typically produces speculative bubbles and crashes—though it has, at least since the seventeenth century.[1] More specifically, we emphasize the degree to which capitalism routinely experiences limits to accumulation in the form of resistance on the part of labor, technological and political hurdles, geographic challenges, and so on.[2] Such crises do not, in themselves, signal the death knell of capitalism. Quite the opposite. Anyone living through the last five (or forty) years knows well how the specter of crisis has resulted in the increased centralization of capital in the hands of the rich, the justification of brutal cuts to budgets and services, and the shifting of media attention from ten years of war and plunder to the minutiae of the market. "Crisis," then, is not new. Rather, it is a tried-and-true tactic of the consolidation of class power and imperialist nationalism that extends back at least to the Panic of 1893. As with our contemporary crisis, the capitalist classes reaped real benefits in 1893, interrupting the momentum of the thriving populist and labor movements in the United States and justifying a redoubled wave of imperial expansion.[3] Thus crises are both ideological and structural. As David Harvey puts it, "Financial crises serve to rationalize the

GLQ 18:1
DOI 10.1215/10642684-1422116
© 2011 by Duke University Press

irrationalities of capitalism. They typically lead to reconfigurations, new models of development, new spheres of investment, and new forms of class power."[4] "Queer Studies and the Crises of Capitalism" turns its attention to the set of crises defining the period we understand as neoliberal capitalism, the long wave of recessions and dispossessions stretching from the 1970s to the present.

In this focus, our special issue comes freighted with the woe of years of war, expropriation of the world's resources, and the crushing ongoingness of neoliberal capitalism's assault on humanity, both domestically and abroad. Yet, caught in the crosshairs of our contemporary moment, we are in good company. For even as neoliberal capitalism conscripts subjects to wage slavery, encloses commons, seizes resources, and consigns populations to death and dispossession, movements for resistance and liberation form and flourish in opposition to these depredations. And, informed by such activist interventions, there has been in recent years a wealth of work documenting, defying, and exposing the specificities of neoliberal capitalism and its various poisonous strategies. The dimensions of neoliberalism as an ideology, a politics, and an economic tactic have been eloquently and passionately analyzed in articles and in book-length studies both inside and outside queer studies. Lisa Duggan, David Eng, Jodi Melamed, Jasbir Puar, and Nikhil Pal Singh have shown how "neoliberal multiculturalism" masks capitalism's structural reliance on racism and imperialism in its seemingly endless quest to create and sustain profits.[5] Heterodox economists, historians, and critical geographers such as Gopal Balakrishnan, David Harvey, Anwar M. Shaikh and E. Ahmed Tonak, Gerard Dumenil and Dominique Levy, Chris Harman, and Giovanni Arrighi have charted how financialization, the permanent arms economy, falling profits, stagnant real wages, and the debt economy have convulsed the globe for decades. And, constellating the concerns of American studies, ethnic studies, and queer studies, critics like Roderick Ferguson, Kevin Floyd, Miranda Joseph, and José Muñoz have interrogated the historical lapses of political economy and Marxism in thinking gender, race, and sexuality.[6] Such work has initiated critical rapprochements between Marxism and queer studies, through readings of cultural texts marked by neoliberalism's inception and rise.

Thus burdened with the miseries of neoliberal capitalism — and buoyed by the uprisings, liberation movements, and thriving critical approaches that interrogate and resist neoliberalism's spoliations and havoc — "Queer Studies and the Crises of Capitalism" translates these contradictory castings into a robust engagement with the *capitalism* in "neoliberal capitalism." We take to heart Melamed's acute rendering of the forces of neoliberal multiculturalism, which, in "suturing liberal antiracism to U.S. nationalism," "depoliticizes capitalism by collapsing it with Americanism" (6). This special issue works to resist such depoliticization by specifying, along with Melamed, that neoliberalism is a qualifier for the more precise analytic and historical category of neoliberal capitalism. For, as Nikhil Pal Singh has argued, "liberalism insists on divorcing universal questions of individual rights from a historical context of unequal property relations and . . . primitive capital accumulation" (28). This is a divorce we must not repeat in our own work. Liberal ideology longs to veil the violence of capitalism from view, leaving only fantasies about nationalism and the naturalized fiction of a free market in its place. Our analytic response to such veilings must be to push capitalism always to the foreground as not simply an object of analysis but as the ground and condition of such analysis as well. To this end, "Queer Studies and the Crises of Capitalism" invokes quite specifically the Marxist, anticapitalist, and left lineages of thinking neoliberalism. Neoliberalism, that is, is always *neoliberal capitalism.*

On to the second, methodological question: what has all this to do with queer studies? Fortunately, this is a question that we do not have to answer alone. Marxist and historical-materialist methodologies undergird the foundational texts of the study of sexuality. From Michel Foucault's reflections on capital accumulation in *Discipline and Punish* to John D'Emilio's analysis of gay identity alongside wage labor and Gayle Rubin's "political economy of sex," sexuality studies has long deployed the matrices of Marxism and political-economic analysis to illuminate the sex/gender matrix.[7] This illuminative relation has become truly reciprocal with the interventions of queer of color critique, which ups the ante on traditional approaches to economic questions, turning the optic of queer theory onto political economy and historical materialism. Under such a lens, queer of color critique not only exposes the lacunae in historial materialist approaches but also recovers the force of those approaches that seem ever more relevant today. In weaving together questions of sexuality, critical race theory, and the psyche with economic history and capitalist development, recent work has revivified its engagement with historical materialism. This kind of methodological recovery is founded in Ferguson's reengagement with the Combahee River Collective and receives an exemplary extension in Muñoz's engagement with Ernst Bloch.[8] Melamed's weaving together of a conception of "race radical analysis" with Cedric Robinson's use of "black radicalism" also exemplifies the kind of recovery work that takes up the legacies of historical materialism to think through the relationship of racialization, imperialism, and neoliberalism. Although not explicitly written from a queer studies angle, Melamed's "Spirit of Neoliberalism" continues to be an important touchstone for queer studies and is vividly engaged with in Eng's *Feeling of Kinship*, for example.

What this burgeoning reencounter with historical materialism means for our special issue is an emphasis on the relationship between Marxist methodologies and queer studies. If, as we argued above, neoliberalism must be understood as a mode of capitalism, then the turn to analyzing neoliberalism finds a ready analytic tool in the history of Marxist critique. To our minds, the single most powerful methodological contribution of Marxism is its attention to contradiction in the form of dialectical critique. A dialectical approach to the problematic of neoliberal capitalism, then, is what we aim to provide and provoke here. As such, this special issue begins with one basic presumption: that the encounter between queer studies and Marxist and historical-material analysis, at its best, offers the possibility for analyzing capitalist culture in its dynamic, geographically diverse, and contradictory articulations. We invited authors to consider how queer methodologies illuminate the contradictions in current and historical economic patterns and advance our understanding of the complex structures of global capitalism.

In this focus on contradiction, the Marxist tradition we embrace most closely is Adorno's negative dialectic—a technique that distinguishes itself from the Hegelian idealist dialectic in its fundamentally aporetic quality: a negative dialectic does not posit a comprehensive account of the social world but points up the conceptual barriers to understanding the material conditions of that world. This analytic process is achieved through "thinking in contradictions": "To proceed dialectically means to think in contradictions, for the sake of the contradiction already experienced in the object, and against that contradiction."[9] The negative dialectical approach does not posit an alternative to the contradictions that score contemporary capitalism but reaches toward the possibility of overcoming those contradictions through overcoming the conditions of capitalism. This perspectival shift is praxical; it hinges on the existence of social movements working to overcome current conditions. This praxical viewpoint—a speculative moment necessary to the negative dialectic—is where Adorno invokes the utopian potential of his approach: negative dialectics that exposes the degree to which the conditions under which we live now are "false," or contingent. "In view of the concrete possibility of utopia," he says, "dialectics is the ontology of the false condition" (11).

The utopian component of negative dialectics is reliant on social movements. Just so, the encounter of queer studies and capitalist crisis showcased in this special issue also comes mediated by social movements—by the long history of queer resistance to the logic and demands of capitalist (re)production and by the movements for social justice that have come to define the 2000s and beyond in terms of coalition building between and among queer resistance, anticapitalist and antiracist work, immigrant rights, anticolonial struggle, and movements for national self-determination.[10] Such social movements have illuminated the character of American neoliberal capitalism as it seeks militarily to assert its economic dominance in Iraq, Palestine, Afghanistan, Pakistan, Venezuela, Bolivia, and beyond. In the essays within, and in the extended roundtable, authors consider the regulation and policing of sexuality—as well as the utopian or defiant aspects of queerness—as one critical optic in reconstructing various histories, including the American political landscape post–9/11, the legacies of the Cuban revolution, the militarization of the borders, deindustrialization and the dispossession of the commons, and the baleful conjuncture of slavery and capital accumulation.

The Roundtable: Queer Studies and the Spatial Character of Neoliberal Capitalism

In the pages that follow, the conjoined pressure of our authors' investigations and the dynamic collaborative work of the roundtable combine to illuminate the historical relationship between capital accumulation, racialization, and sexualization—a triumvirate of variously determinate forces whose interpenetration has been obscured by the deployment of "crisis" as a way to name the current conjuncture. In the roundtable, we invited authors to speculate on their own innovations on the relationship between political economy, Marxism, and queer studies. In responding, they have encapsulated our aims for the special issue as a set of vivid analytic provocations.

As Miranda Joseph reminds us in this issue, the loud decrying that capitalism is "in crisis" does not necessarily signal a long-term crisis for capitalism. For capitalism has long been fueled by recurrent crises: falling rates of profit, the bridging of gaps between production and consumption with ballooning credit and debt, the explosion of finance capital. Such crises have become occasions for capitalism to "revolutionize" itself—through imperialism, colonization, and increased rates of exploitation, the combined forces of which result in booms and the recuperation of the system, temporarily at least.[11]

Following the lead of recent queer theories of sensation and emotion, we might understand this latest "crisis" as, at least partly, an *affect* deployed in this moment to put into place and naturalize the intensification of exploitation, the systematic destruction of the gains of labor radicalism, and the unleashing of new, imperialist forms of violence. As Gopal Balakrishnan has explained, the faltering dominance of American neoliberal capitalism occasions an almost panoramic military theater in which the "rogue state" designation applies to an unprecedented number of nations and peoples now targeted for the use of violent force: "For the few remaining fully sovereign states, the use of military force is afforded cover by the 'international community,' while illegitimate 'rogue' states are subject to invasive, destabilizing qualifications of their nominal sovereignty in the form of sanctions, international supervision of their weapons programmes, no-fly zones, and regime change."[12] In representing the stumbling of certain sectors of finance capital as in "crisis," dominant media and political discourses legitimate — through the invocation of panicked affects — both assaults on domestic services and public programs and imperialist acts of violence as necessary steps toward restabilizing those sectors of profit. In interrogating such ideologies from the perspective of queer studies, we join other recent special issues of *GLQ* — notably "Sexuality, Nationality, Indigeneity" and "Queer Politics and the Question of Palestine/ Israel" — in bringing together accounts of such cruelty and violence with an analytics of sexuality.[13]

Such spikes of violence, moreover, reveal the degree to which, as Fred Moten argues in the roundtable, racism and racialization are not only currently but have long been "condition[s] of possibility" for capitalism itself. And, as Gayle Salamon suggests within the roundtable, it is also the case that this violence takes specifically spatial form. The relation between center and periphery, after all, is articulated not only globally but also domestically in a series of intensifying dyads, or what Raymond Williams describes as a relation of "interlocking exploitation."[14] For Harvey, this interlocking is both cause and result of capitalist "crises." In its quest to continually produce profit, territories are dispossessed and traditional social structures made insupportable, as capitalism moves within and between nation-states in an endless movement of de- and re-development. This movement wreaks havoc as it makes profit — a spatial logic vividly described by Mike Davis as a vast global network of sprawling "polycentric urban systems without clear rural/urban boundaries" — "megaslums" populated by a highly exploited informal workforce.[15]

This increasingly violent territorialization of new lands and resources is key to understanding how capitalism manages to reproduce itself as a system despite recurrent crises of overproduction and overaccumulation. Indeed, an understanding of this process may help us replace what Robert McRuer identifies as the problematic invocation of rhetorics of disability to describe the "terrain" of global capitalism, with a materially grounded and historically based language that describes the mechanisms of capital accumulation. And this hermeneutic of accumulation may also be key to understanding the ideological makeup of the current moment. For if the spatially deployed violence of capitalism exposes the fissures in the current mode of production, perhaps it is the case, as Tavia Nyong'o argues in the roundtable, that traditional ideological patches—such as marriage—no longer cover the wounds of capitalist profiteering. Nor do they cover the sheer brutality—analyzed dynamically here by Dean Spade—of the state.

Where does this leave us? Strangely, as Kevin Floyd points out, it seems to have left us turning to utopias. Floyd suggests that utopia—as it is currently debated within queer studies—is symptomatic of the limitations of capitalism. As we jut up against the impossibility of capitalist futures, we enact the negation of these futures in the name of another. So a hermeneutics of utopia is embedded in the dialectical nature of negation, the positive claims of which are inextricable from the conditions of suffering and misery that give rise to the negation in the first place. What are some sites on which to apply the analytic pressure of utopia/ negation? The contradictory and overdetermined nature of desire, as Lisa Rofel adds to the roundtable discussion, may be one crucial place to look for the dialectical mediation of capitalist contradiction. Or, as Christina Crosby responds, the fissures of capitalism may signal our necessary return to the question of form, and the contradictory character of the literary tropes that accompanied industrial capitalism as well as our own "post-Fordist nightmare." This nightmare, as Lisa Duggan forcefully reminds us, must be taken into account in all its global reach, and in the heterogeneity of its manifestations: not just "neoimperial plunder," "slaughter," "theft and exploitation," but the "affective roots" of the ideologies that are put in place to naturalize these acts.

Totalizing Affects: Queerness and Temporality

For all the potential in bringing Marxism and queer theory into a productive joint analytic, a number of hurdles still remain. One such hurdle is the question of totality. Indeed, we might say that, ever since the 1990s and the rise of identity politics, queer studies has counterposed totality-thinking with affect in a signature frisson.[16] Is there something that just *feels wrong* about conceptualizing totality within the ambit of queer studies—itself so finely tuned to the interstices, glimmerings, and fleeting connections that somehow miraculously seem to have escaped the thudding reductions and empty equivalences of capitalism and heteronormativity? Whether or not this antimony holds true, it has been the case that the beautiful, endangered details that flourish within queer studies have, for a number of reasons, been posed against a totalizing methodology, and this perceived conflict is the result, at least partly, of equating the Marxist tradition of totality-thinking with universalism. Yet this equation leans more on a commonsensical view of the "total-ness" of totality than it does on the richer theoretical heritage linking a world of uneven, contradictory particulars and uncovering the violence veiled by the patina of self-evident value attributed to commodities, regulatory ideals, and the state itself under capitalism. How can we reconcile this more fluid notion of totality-thinking with a queer studies ordinarily so suspicious of it? Perhaps it would be useful here to recall Fredric Jameson's investigation into the phenomenology of dialectical thought, which focuses on the moment at which the subject comes to understand himself or herself as an object—subject to and conditioned by the contradictions of the historical field he or she surveys. "There is a breathlessness," says Jameson, "about this shift from the normal object-oriented activity to such dialectical self-consciousness—something of the sickening shudder we feel in the elevator's fall or in the sudden dip in an airliner. That recalls us to our bodies, much as this recalls us to our mental positions as thinkers and observers."[17] Jameson's point here is not simply that the body is as much a mediator of the contradictions of capitalism as is the mind, and the concepts and objects it surveys. More specifically, the realization of the subject's position as an object conditioned by these contradictions occasions a shocking return to the body, one that might be explored more broadly by a dialectical queer methodology.

Furthering our rapprochement, it pays to remember, as Ferguson points out in the roundtable, that there are many totalities. Not only the "Eurocentric" universalism pointed to by Martin Jay but a tradition of "broad attempt[s] to appreciate social and epistemic heterogeneity." This latter sense of totality inheres in the work of Karl Marx and Georg Lukács, in Jameson's antitotalitarian totality, in Mikhail Bakhtin's "open totality," and in what Kenneth Surin describes as C. L. R. James's whole that is "an always displaced and decentered bundle of temporalities."[18] The conflation of totality and universalism has been attacked by activists working at the forefront of coalition politics. Indeed, this is a conflation that, as McRuer points out in the roundtable, may be remedied or unstrung by remembering that it is against "bourgeois universalism" precisely that activists, theorists, and all those who, as Rofel puts it, think "in the multiple," throw themselves wholeheartedly. And we do so with all the force that dialectical totalization—or, if one prefers, a *feeling* for (or shocking, bodily sense of) the contradictory interconnections between what McRuer calls the "bright new gay day" of homonationalist equality and the cuts to public services trumpeted by every politician from former California governor Arnold Schwarzenegger to President Barack Obama—has in its arsenal.[19]

We might see this "bright new gay day"—this hypersunny universalism—as a kind of "genre of identity politics." This is a formulation Ferguson counterposes, in the pages of this journal, to the "scavenger" nature of totalizing. As a scavenger methodology itself, queer studies might find itself surprisingly in tune with the disciplinary trespass endemic to totalizing thought in its best, most capacious versions. But even if we rehabilitate totality as a queering—or scavenging—of disciplines, we still need to address the sense that queer studies' attention to affect appears at odds with the potentials of a totalizing approach. Recent work by Sara Ahmed, Lauren Berlant, Ann Cvetkovich, Heather Love, and Salamon has emphasized the methodologically explosive force of an affect studies rooted in political and historicist orientations.[20] Here we could cite as inspiration Berlant's essay "Slow Death (Sovereignty, Obesity, Lateral Agency)," which displaces questions of sovereignty and agency from "bourgeois dramatics" (what a great term for the melodramas of crisis management!) to the realm of ordinariness. In her closing thoughts on the agency of self-interruption, Berlant offers a series of clauses that highlight with painstaking precision what a scavenger project might disclose. "In the scene of slow death," Berlant argues, "a condition of being worn out by the activity of reproducing life, agency can be an activity of maintenance, not making; fantasy, without grandiosity; sentience, without full intentionality; inconsistency, without shattering; embodying, alongside embodiment."[21] In "Slow Death," Berlant reframes crises of embodiment as ongoing; such a reframing could also be linked to the ongoingness of the economic crisis as the condition of capitalism's reproducing itself. In taking on the conjunctions of the body and the temporalities of capitalism, Berlant brokers a kind of rapprochement between queer studies, political-economic theories of development, and a rather traditional Marxist approach to temporality and embodiment—one we are inspired by and hope to have captured something of the spirit of in this issue.

Jasbir Puar's coda, "The Cost of Getting Better," builds on Berlant's conception of "Slow Death" to take on the intersection of disability studies with the spatial and temporal logics of neoliberalism and homonationalism. In her discussion of the "It Gets Better" project—in which queer teens are encouraged to emplot themselves within a *bildung* of capital accumulation, assimilation to a feel-good nationalism, and nuclear-family building—Puar exposes the implied (and denied) movements that score the logic of urbanization and immigration. Drawing on Nyong'o's observations about the narrative logic of "It Gets Better," Puar describes the demand to "get better" as "a call to upward mobility that discordantly echoes the now-discredited 'pull yourself up by the bootstraps' immigrant motto."[22] Adding to this analysis of the spatial injunction of "getting better," Puar argues that the migratory logic of "getting better" is married to a set of presumptions around capacity and debility. "It Gets Better," in other words, imagines spatial movement and nationalist assimilation in terms of the resuscitation of a debilitated body: "The subject of redress and grievance [in the "It Gets Better" project] . . . functions . . . as a recapacitation of a debilitated body." In highlighting capacity and debility as the conditioning registers of current debate around queer assimilation to the imperial nation-state, Puar brings together a queer studies perspective on bodiliness and disability with the problematic of finance capital. Given that "the latest phase of capitalism got an ersatz form of growth primarily through credit-card consumerism and asset bubbles" and that medical debt has been cited as the pre-eminent cause of credit card debt, the role of medical debt in growing the neoliberal state and supporting finance capital cannot be underestimated.[23] Puar's negative-dialectical assault on the commonsensical injunction to "get better" exposes the contradictory material and ideological undercurrents threading through the seemingly seamless articulation of queerness with an imperial nation-state producing and profiting from debility. Thus Puar models the sort of serious engagement with thinking about — and beyond — the neoliberal-capitalist state of which queer studies is capable.

Theorists of affect have asked how we can be attentive to the underdog emotions of queerness while still refining the tools of a queer critique that does not seek to affirm queer culture so much as analyze its historical articulations. It is this historicizing, critical impulse that drives the reconnoitering of totality and feeling — or negation and utopia — and that brings to the foreground the conditions in which, as Moten puts it here, "the question of totality becomes the question of utopia." Along these lines, scholars have interrogated the queer registration of the contradictions of temporality itself. In regarding these contradictions as the mediation of what Elizabeth Freeman has termed the queer "sensation of asynchrony" — or of what Molly McGarry describes as the "theories of embodiment" that stake themselves on a very queer investment in the enduring presence of the past in the present — queer studies takes on, with a kind of totalizing force, the historical arrangement and transformations of the very grounds of thought, feeling, and political action itself.[24]

If queer studies is now reencountering the question of utopia within the Marxist tradition, it is only through the kinds of concretizing negations made possible by a recent wealth of work that specifies the baleful cohabitations of queerness and nationalism, queerness and racialization, queerness and the neoliberalization of the globe. In Puar's words, queerness may be seen, in a number of important contexts, as "a process of racialization" deployed by the neoliberal nation-state to manage and control populations — to ensure ideological homogeneity in queers for whom an oppositional relationship to the state had once been paramount, and to legitimate neocolonial wars and plunder in the name of an empty "revitalization" of liberal subject-formations held to be the ideal citizens of the neoliberal state.[25] This trenchant analysis of the increasing violence endemic to the neoliberal state's quest for dominance shares a theoretical and future orientation with Muñoz's utopian casting of black radical traditions that highlights capitalism as the key framework against which radical futurity pits itself.[26]

Perhaps it is the force of both such angles—the "willfully idealistic" along with the spatiotemporal analytic—that creates the conditions for the turn to utopia within queer studies within these pages, and the rapprochement with Marxism more generally.[27] Taking as a guide not only the kind of call to horizonality issued by Muñoz but also the kind of spatiotemporal thought characteristic of Giovanni Arrighi's diagnosis of capitalism as having a cyclical motion that confounds even those notions of historical progression dear to capitalism's discursive heart—the participants in the roundtable take on utopia not simply as an unimaginable future but as a diagnostic methodology that zeros in on the uneven action of capitalism, the spatial differentiation of global production, and the prolonged, overlapping, and recursive temporal pulses of social contradiction itself.

Value, Perversion, Fantasy

If this special issue seeks to test the impact of economic analyses on queer theory—and vice versa—it resolutely does not seek to mark a new orthodoxy for cultural critique. At bottom, we propose that political philosophy and queer theory together offer powerful ideas for addressing problems of justice, redistribution, and recognition. A key idea that threads through this project—and one that links the above issues and points of departure—is that of the value form. As Gayatri Spivak has commented, "The question of value is everywhere. I mean, there is a value theory of everything, not just a value theory of labor. Because value, simple and contentless, is just a form in use when things are made commensurable."[28] The value theory of labor (as Spivak calls it, reversing the usual order of reference) or labor theory of value (which appears to restrict the latter by the former) suggests that human labor-power, the capacity to work, is what predicates the worker/subject; it is what workers/subjects are because it is what they have to sell. This is labor objectified, labor deadened. As people are reified, commodities come to life, and the world of things appears independent. But there is more to Marx's understanding of commodity fetishism than this: these outward appearances of commodities conceal their inner relations, but furthermore these mystifying appearances themselves also and crucially belong to the social realities they conceal.

Queer studies has established hermeneutics and methodologies that are particularly sensitive to the imbrication of these social bonds with the economic structures of capitalism. And the questions originally opened by theories of sexuality rooted in social and economic analysis — like Foucault's, D'Emilio's, and Rubin's — continually press us to reimagine and retheorize the conditions of capitalist modernity and the mediation of these economic structures by sexuality and gender. Indeed, if queer studies has recently engaged with renewed vigor the analytic categories of relations, bonds, and affects, this special issue specifies, historicizes, and analytically situates these bonds, relations, and affects in terms of the contradictions of the value-form: in terms of affective value, the value of labor, and the value of social relationships. In thus framing our issue, we take inspiration from such theorists as Wahneema Lubiano, who has noted how insistently the wage/labor ethos is gendered and how "without any specific contextualization, work is presented as its own absolute good, because work and ownership are what empower *men* to make decisions, to exercise freedom."[29] Following on a dazzling body of thought from Friedrich Engels (in *The Origin of the Family, Private Property, and the State*) to Luce Irigaray (e.g., in her essay "When the Goods Get Together"), Lubiano sees lodged within the production of value a spectrum of human relationality and social regulation not fully captured by the identity-labels of gender, sexuality, race, and kinship or family.[30]

Lubiano, like Spivak, proposes gender and sexuality as *internal*, necessary to producing both value and freedom. In her essay for this special issue, Carla Freccero uses the question of value as the occasion to take stock of the spectralization of queers: both in popular culture and in queer theory of the past twenty years. Rather than resist how culture dematerializes queerness, Freccero reclaims this abstraction as the ground for future historiographical work and posits a new theory of queer materiality. In an astounding queer constellation that ranges from an early modern treatise on the family to Louis Althusser, Slavoj Žižek, Jameson, and Irigaray, Freccero traverses the difficult divide between "subject" and "collectivity," exploring both contemporary and traditional sites where commodity exchange, sexual difference, and sexuality/desire converge.

Janet Jakobsen, too, asserts that sexual relations are part of, not prior or ancillary to, the relations of production, relying on the economist David Ruccio's work to understand the historical matrix of social and sexual relations. In an account that spans the inception of Protestant rationality to the contemporary conditions of what she terms the "secular" Protestantism in the United States, Jakobsen considers heteronormativity as a name for this matrix. That is, by understanding sex as a kind of fulcrum or nodal point among saliently interrelated but discontinuous vectors of social life (economic value, moral value, the predication of the subject, the formation of public policy), Jakobsen enables us to understand how fully heteronormativity has saturated the realm of late-capitalist production. Her strong reading of this historical matrix of social and sexual life usefully proliferates further questions. Some are corrective: to what extent does Marx naturalize "the family" as a restrictive model of social organization or follow hetero-reproductive logic, where queers are pathologized as non(re)productive? Some inquire into abstraction as such: can we press the value form into new service for thinking desire and sexuality? What routes, following these strands of feminist and queer theory (including the work of Gayle Rubin, Judith Butler, and others), allow for analyses of immaterial labor (or affective labor) that do not merely analogize them with material labor (or claim to supersede it)?

Grace Kyungwon Hong's essay, "Existentially Surplus," proposes "irrationality" as one rubric that helpfully propels this inquiry. Like the contributors we have been discussing, Hong is energized by a diverse lineage of thought, from Marx himself to queer of color critique. The latter, particularly Ferguson's *Aberrations in Black*, enables her to understand the production of surplus forms of life within capitalist social relations. Capitalism's death drive, or its irrationality, which is not external but endemic, rears its head in the specific politico-historical formation we call neoliberalism as disposability: following Zygmunt Bauman, Hong sees mass disposability, or the production of new categories of disposable people, as fundamental to the globalization of capital. Her ultimate question, then, has to do with the utility of the categories of race, gender, and sexuality in naming these vectors of valuation in the present moment. To be surplus, in other words, is to be raced, gendered, and sexualized, as she says, "in ways both old and new." We should not be surprised that Hong turns to Cherríe Moraga's body of work (across genres and decades), since Moraga's relentless and passionate voice has shaped crucial strains of feminist, queer, Chicana activism and art practice since the 1980s. What Hong finds in it for her project is the very dialectic of loss and utopia (or "making tribe") we cited earlier in this introduction, now crucially mediated through a discourse on death that is key, in Hong's understanding, to the condition of being surplus.

Lisa Marie Cacho echoes Hong's urgency in marking exclusion, particularly the insidious effects of the progressive political inheritance of affirming sexual and gender normativity in order to attribute social value to race and ethnicity. Her reading of Carla Trujillo's novel *What Night Brings* is not, however, an indictment of progressive traditions but instead a lively demonstration of what it means to read textual detail as social antagonism. In her attention to domestic and ritual elements of everyday life—including the loaded symbolism of a lowly egg, Cacho discovers in Trujillo's prose a shifting landscape of valuation, political alliance, and social struggle. The contradictions governing relations between poverty, patriarchy, heteronormativity, and violence become calibrated in Cacho's reading of the novel to offer insights into debates about immigration. Fixing her gaze on the novel's aspirational character, "Eddie-me," voiced through the longings/imaginings of the queer Marci, Cacho ultimately finds in the possibilities of queer gender (female masculinity, butch affect) the momentum for a preliminary recoding of the matrix of value.

In Meg Wesling's contribution, the question of value is front and center. "Queer Value" presses on the concept of value to mediate or "suture" the psychic and the material. Initially reconfiguring an idea of queer labor through a reading of a documentary about Cuban drag queens, *Mariposas en el Andamio* (*Butter-flies on the Scaffold*), Wesling proposes this reading as a way to understand "how we might articulate the labored economies of sexuality and gender more generally—that is, how the performance of gender and sexuality enabled, compelled, disciplined, and produced at any given historical moment constitutes a form of labor, accruing both material and affective value." *Mariposas* (a film about which one of us has written elsewhere) documents simultaneous historically specific transformations.[31] Indeed, what makes *Mariposas* an aspirational project worthy of our close attention, in Wesling's careful reading, is its attempt not to chart gendered and sexual "disidentifications" but to resignify normative gender and sexuality from the heart of revolutionary faggotry, a heart that is no less bound to the future of a local community than it is grounded in the flows of global exchange. Indeed, reading drag as a form of productive labor (and drawing on a lineage of distinguishing labor from work from Marx through Arendt), Wesling ultimately proposes a vision of gender as the self-conscious production of human work and therefore a deeply social understanding of the predication of the subject. This is, finally, a story about who we are and might be in relation to others and how we are or could be queer only in relation to material and social conjunctures. Back, then, to the future.

Notes

1. On the Dutch tulip bubble, see Fernand Braudel, *The Wheels of Commerce*, vol. 2 of *Civilization and Capitalism, 15th–18th Century*, trans. Sian Reynolds (Berkeley: University of California Press, 1992); and Anne Goldar, *Tulipmania: Money, Honor, and Knowledge in the Dutch Golden Age* (Chicago: University of Chicago Press, 2007).

2. The literature on finance and crisis is vast. See, for starters, Giovanni Arrighi, *The Long Twentieth Century: Money, Power, and the Origins of Our Times* (London: Verso, 1994); Gopal Balakrishnan, *Antagonistics: Capitalism and Power in an Age of War* (London: Verso, 2009); David Harvey, *The Limits to Capital* (London: Verso, 2007); Harvey, *The Enigma of Capital and the Crises of Capitalism* (New York: Oxford University Press, 2010); Anwar M. Shaikh and E. Ahmed Tonak, *Measuring the Wealth of Nations: The Political Economy of National Accounts* (Cambridge: Cambridge University Press, 1996); Gerard Dumenil and Dominique Levy, *The Crisis of Neoliberalism* (Cambridge, MA: Harvard University Press, 2011); Chris Harman, *Zombie Capitalism: Global Crisis and the Relevance of Marx* (New York: Haymarket Books, 2010).

3. The Panic of 1893 is treated in a great many works of history and receives particularly strong attention in Michael McGerr, *A Fierce Discontent: The Rise and Fall of the Progressive Movement in America* (New York: Oxford University Press, 2005); and in Lawrence Goodwyn, *The Populist Movement: A Short History of the Agrarian Revolt in America* (New York: Oxford University Press, 1978). It may also be worth noting that 1893 was the year the British created the Durand Line through India, demarcating Russian from British colonial interests in the region. On the Durand Line, see Vijay Prashad, *The Darker Nations: A People's History of the Third World* (New York: New Press, 2008).

4. Harvey, *Enigma of Capital*, 11.

5. "Neoliberal multiculturalism" is Jodi Melamed's term describing the ideology of race accompanying neoliberal political and economic policies. See Lisa Duggan, *The Twilight of Equality: Neoliberalism, Cultural Politics, and the Attack on Democracy* (Boston: Beacon, 2004); David Eng, *The Feeling of Kinship: Queer Liberalism and the Racialization of Intimacy* (Durham, NC: Duke University Press, 2010); Jodi Melamed, "The Spirit of Neoliberalism: From Racial Liberalism to Neoliberal Multiculturalism," *Social Text*, no. 89 (2006): 1–24; Jasbir Puar, *Terrorist Assemblages: Homonationalism in Queer Times* (Durham, NC: Duke University Press, 2007); Nikhil Pal Singh, *Black Is a Country: Race and the Unfinished Struggle for Democracy* (Cambridge: Oxford University Press, 2005).

6. Kevin Floyd, *The Reification of Desire: Toward a Queer Marxism* (Minneapolis: University of Minnesota Press, 2009); Miranda Joseph, *Against the Romance of Community* (Minneapolis: University of Minnesota Press, 2002); José Muñoz, *Cruising*

Utopia: The There and Then of Queer Theory (New York: New York University Press, 2009).

7. "The two processes—the accumulation of men and the accumulation of capital—cannot be separated; it would not have been possible to solve the problem of the accumulation of men without the growth of an apparatus of production capable of both sustaining them and using them; conversely, the techniques that made the cumulative multiplicity of men useful accelerated the accumulation of capital" (Michel Foucault, *Discipline and Punish: The Birth of the Prison* [New York: Vintage, 1995], 221). See also John D'Emilio, "Capitalism and Gay Identity," in *Powers of Desire: The Politics of Sexuality*, ed. Ann Snitow, Christine Stansell, and Sharon Thompson (New York: Monthly Review Press, 1983); and Gayle Rubin, "The Traffic in Women: Notes on the 'Political Economy' of Sex," in *Toward an Anthropology of Women*, ed. Rayna Reiter (New York: Monthly Review Press, 1975).

8. Roderick Ferguson, *Aberrations in Black: Toward a Queer of Color Critique* (Minneapolis: University of Minnesota Press, 2003); and Muñoz, *Cruising Utopia*.

9. Adorno, *Negative Dialectic* (London: Routledge, 1973), 115. To think in contradictions exposes the antagonisms that comprise social relations under capitalism because, as Alfred Sohn-Rethel has painstakingly argued, intellectual and manual labor are inextricable, and these antagonisms (between capital and labor, and between use and exchange value) embed themselves within the concept itself. See Alfred Sohn-Rethel, *Intellectual and Manual Labor: A Critique of Epistemology* (Atlantic Highlands: Humanities, 1977). See also Slavoj Žižek's engagement with Sohn-Rethel in *The Sublime Object of Ideology* (London: Verso, 1997).

10. A necessarily incomplete list of these movements would include the following organizations: AlQaws, Aswat, Critical Resistance, Queers Undermining Israeli Terrorism, Queers Undermining Israeli Apartheid, Queers for Economic Justice, Labor for Palestine, International Jewish Anti-Zionist Network, Gender Justice LA, No Human Being Is Illegal, Border Action Network, Left Turn.

11. On the structural nature of capitalist crises, see Arrighi, *Long Twentieth Century*; Balakrishnan, *Antagonistics*; Neil Smith, *Uneven Development: Nature, Capital, and the Production of Space* (Athens: University of Georgia Press, 2008).

12. Balakrishnan, *Antagonistics*, 102.

13. Gil Z. Hochberg, ed., "Queer Politics and the Question of Palestine/Israel," special issue, *GLQ* 16, no. 4 (2010); and Daniel Heath Justice, Mark Rifkin, and Bethany Schneider, eds., "Sexuality, Nationality, Indigeneity," special issue, GLQ 16, nos. 1–2 (2010).

14. Raymond Williams, The Country and the City (Oxford: Oxford University Press, 1975), 51.

15. Mike Davis, *Planet of Slums* (New York: Verso, 2006), 10.

16. Floyd explores this legacy at length in *The Reification of Desire*.

17. Fredric Jameson, *Marxism and Form: Twentieth-Century Dialectical Theories of Literature* (Princeton: Princeton University Press, 1971), 308.

18. Kenneth Surin, "The Future Anterior: C. L. R. James and Going Beyond a Boundary," in Grant Farred, ed. *Rethinking C. L. R. James* (Oxford: Blackwell, 1996), 192.

19. Schwartzenegger proposed cuts of up to $750 million to in-home supportive services (IHSS), which provides home care to seniors and people with disabilities, and proposed eliminating adult day health care provided through Medi-Cal. "Race to the Top" is President Obama's competition for federal funding for education reform, based upon measures of student and school performance. Diane Ravitch provides a careful indictment of that program's potential impact in her blog on the *Huffington Post*: www.huffingtonpost.com/diane-ravitch/obamas-race-to-the-top-wi_b_666598.html

20. Sara Ahmed, *The Promise of Happiness* (Durham, NC: Duke University Press, 2010); Lauren Berlant, *The Female Complaint: The Unfinished Business of Sentimentality in American Culture* (Durham, NC: Duke University Press, 2008); Ann Cvetkovich, *An Archive of Feelings: Trauma, Sexuality, and Lesbian Public Cultures* (Durham, NC: Duke University Press, 2003); Heather Love, *Feeling Backward: Loss and the Politics of Queer History* (Cambridge: Harvard University Press, 2009); Gayle Salamon, *Assuming a Body: Transgender and Rhetorics of Materiality* (New York: Columbia University Press, 2009).

21. Lauren Berlant, "Slow Death (Sovereignty, Obesity, Lateral Agency)," *Critical Inquiry* 33 (Summer 2007), 759.

22. Tavia Nyong'o, "School Daze" September 30, 2010, bullybloggers.wordpress.com/2010/09/30/school-daze/; Puar, this volume.

23. Gopal Balakrishnan, "Speculations on the Stationary State," *New Left Review* (2009), 14.

24. Elizabeth Freeman, ed., introduction to "Queer Temporalities," special issue, *GLQ* 13, nos. 2–3 (2007): 159; Molly McGarry, *Ghosts of Futures Past: Spiritualism and the Cultural Politics of Nineteenth-Century America* (Berkeley: University of California Press, 2008).

25. Puar, *Terrorist Assemblages*, xi.

26. Muñoz on Baraka: "If the condition of possibility for blackness is a certain radicalness in relation to capitalism's naturalizing temporal logic, the black radical tradition is engaged in a maneuver that helps elucidate queer futurity" (*Cruising Utopia*, 87). Puar on terrorist assemblages: "This unknowable monstrosity is not casual bystander or parasite; the nation assimilates the effusive discomfort of the unknowability of these bodies, thus affectively producing new normativities and exceptionalisms through the cataloguing of unknowables (Puar, xxiii). Thus "[O]pening up to the fantastical wonders of futurity, therefore, is the most powerful of political and critical strategies, whether it is through assemble or to something as yet unknown, perhaps even forever unknowable" (Puar, 222).

27. Muñoz, *Cruising Utopia*, 96.

28. Yan Hairong, "Positions without Identity: An Interview with Gayatri Chakravorty Spivak," *positions* 15, no. 2 (2007): 429.

29. Wahneema Lubiano, "But Compared to What? Reading Realism, Representation, and Essentialism in *School Daze*, *Do The Right Thing*, and the Spike Lee Discourse," in *Representing Blackness: Issues in Film and Video*, ed. Valerie Smith (New Brunswick: Rutgers University Press, 1997), 113.

30. Friedrich Engels, *The Origin of the Family, Private Property, and the State* (New York: Penguin, 2010), and Luce Irigaray, "When the Goods Get Together," in *This Sex Which Is Not One*, trans. Catherine Porter (Ithaca: Cornell University Press, 1985).

31. See Amy Villarejo, *Lesbian Rule: Cultural Criticism and the Value of Desire* (Durham, NC: Duke University Press, 2003).

PERVERSE JUSTICE

Janet R. Jakobsen

The date was February 15, 2003, and we were "united for peace and justice." It was a few short weeks before the U.S. invasion of Iraq, and more than 100,000 people were in New York City as part of the largest antiwar demonstration in the United States since the Vietnam era. This march, organized by the coalition of groups gathered together under the name United for Peace and Justice (UFPJ), was the culmination in the Northeastern United States of a number of actions that had begun as soon as it was apparent that the country's grief over the September 11 attacks in 2001 was going to be turned into legitimation for war, first in Afghanistan and then, with the most threadbare of connections to "terrorism," in Iraq.[1] Groups like Not in Our Name and New Yorkers Say No to War had formed early in the fall of 2001 and had been working steadily since then. If the February 2003 march was good evidence, they had also been working with growing effectiveness.

One thing that struck me at the time and that continues to concern me is that so much of this activity was carried out in the negative. It was incredibly important that those who had suffered most from the September 11 attacks on the World Trade Center stood up and said, as some of the victims' families did, "not in our name," just as New Yorkers said no to war. But the Bush administration, particularly in extending the war from Afghanistan to Iraq, had presented a powerful and seductive vision of what it was going to do that was positive in the world. Although it may seem impossible now to understand how this vision was thought to be in any way realistic, not only did the Bush administration advocate a "war on terrorism," one that was supposedly going to end terrorism, but the war in Iraq was going to lay the groundwork for peace to the Middle East and spread freedom and democracy in the region and in the world.[2] Theirs was a war not just *against* terrorism but *for* freedom and democracy.

Thus I was relieved that by the spring of 2003 queers, radicals, and many other groups that joined with UFPJ were for something, too, but what does it mean

GLQ 18:1
DOI 10.1215/10642684-1422125
© 2011 by Duke University Press

to be united for peace and justice? Here the question becomes much more difficult. If you went to the UFPJ website at that time, for example, you would have
found that to be for peace and justice meant being against the violation of the
sovereignty of Iraq through invasion and occupation.[3]

Perhaps the question of what it means to be for peace and justice is only the
preoccupation of someone trained in ethics, but I argue that this is also a broader
question, one important to queer theory, and one with serious consequences if our
answers remain vague. First, the vision that progressives have presented, when left
so indeterminate, is not compelling. For the Bush administration, specific things
were going to happen in their pursuit of freedom — the terrible reign of Saddam
Hussein would come to an end, democracy would be produced in Iraq and set an
example for the rest of the region, and other dictatorships would be put under pressure. All of this would provide the appropriate regional geography for the roadmap
to that ever-elusive peace between the state of Israel and the Palestinian people.
For progressives, the sovereignty of Hussein's dictatorship would be respected. If,
at the crucial moment when the war was engaged, you were not already politically
committed, if you did not already mistrust the Bush administration, which would
you choose?

Even now, after the Democratic administration of Barack Obama has offi-
cially ended combat operations in Iraq and US military operations have actually
expanded around the world, what is the progressive vision for contributing to a
better — more just and peaceful — world?

Freedom versus Justice

To answer the question of what it might mean to be *for* peace and justice, rather
than simply *against* the war or the invasion, it is useful first to understand the
term that was so pointedly left out of the title of United for Peace and Justice,
even as it was so frequently used by the Bush administration: freedom. The title
of United for Peace and Justice stands specifically as a counterpoint to the Bush
understanding of freedom. While I appreciate the strong critique of neoliberal
freedom implied by UFPJ's choice of title, I also worry about the implications of
choosing justice *instead of* freedom, rather than, for example, making a commitment to peace, justice, *and* freedom.

Freedom used to be a progressive term. As the historian Robin D. G. Kelley makes clear in his book *Freedom Dreams*, freedom was the organizing principle for movements dedicated to what we now term racial and economic justice
through the twentieth century in the United States and was, of course, the over-

arching term for the 1960s civil rights movements as well as women's liberation and gay liberation.[4] The predominance of freedom's allied term, *liberation*, itself came from a vision—sometimes not much more than a hope—of connection to worldwide anticolonial freedom movements. Now, however, progressives hardly go near the term *freedom*. This is partly due to the influence of a poststructuralist critique of the liberal implications of the term and partly due to the right-wing takeover of the term. This takeover has been so successful that "freedom" has come to mean only that form associated with neoliberal globalization, economic exploitation, and—since 2001—war.

As a result of this right-wing takeover, progressives have shied away from claiming freedom and have instead hewn much more closely to the path of justice. I think that this is a loss of progressive possibility. The division between freedom and justice tends to entrench a split between the movements or issues now associated with freedom (e.g., movements revolving around gender, sexuality, and sometimes race) and those associated with justice (e.g., movements revolving around economics, war, prison abolition, environmentalism, and sometimes race). This split is variously described and has, for example, been termed one between social and cultural politics, and less charitably between "real" and "irrelevant" (or frivolous) politics. And while, as I outline below, I have complete sympathy with the progressive critique of freedom in a neoliberal age, I also have real questions about how progressives embrace justice.[5]

First, justice is used to signal an affinity with the Left over against the Right, which in its most schematic sense is an affinity with Marxism over against capitalism (neoliberal or otherwise). However, Karl Marx did not necessarily promote the term *justice*. While there has been much debate over this question in Marxist circles, one current of thought argues that for Marx justice was not a meaningful term: there is no possibility of justice under capitalism and no need for justice with the achievement of communism.[6] The invocation of justice, then, will be hopelessly entangled with ideology. Insofar as justice is associated with liberal redistribution, its invocation can mislead us into believing that changes in the distribution of goods rather than changes in control of the means of production could bring about a just social order. In fact, contrary to the current progressive embrace of justice and distaste for freedom, some participants in these arguments maintained that Marx's texts demonstrate much more affinity with freedom than with justice.

Furthermore, there are pragmatic reasons to be concerned about the progressive embrace of justice, reasons related to, but not directly correlated with, the argument over interpretations of Marx. It has always been remarkable to me that justice, which currently signals left-wing affiliation, is also the term used by the state to describe the law, particularly the practice of incarceration: so-called criminal justice is hardly the stuff of radical politics. When I first started working on justice, a friend of mine who is a legal scholar immediately warned me that the power of the association between "justice" and the law was such that I could not escape implication in matters of the state. For my part, as an ethical theorist, there is good reason to think that the problem here is more than one of historical and institutional association. The form of justice based on the redistribution of goods as a means to undercut capitalism and the form of justice dedicated to the incarceration of those who are most often at the bottom of the capitalist hierarchy may seem diametrically opposed to each other. But it is also the case that criminal justice is itself a redistributive project. It deals not in redistributing goods but in redistributing pain. Insofar as it is supposed to bring "closure" to the victims of crime, it is because the pain that they suffer is now to be carried by the perpetrator.

In other words, I think it worthwhile to consider what we mean by justice, because whether we go with the activist invocation (like that of UFPJ), the institutional meanings (like those of the law), or the academic enterprise organized around the redistributive paradigm, the possibility is strong that *justice* is a term that does not necessarily describe a radical or even progressive project but is, rather (like freedom), a term deeply implicated in the current, neoliberal order of things.[7]

Queer theory may seem an unlikely place to turn for a substantively different sense of justice. Indeed, for some proponents of justice, sex is associated with personal freedom in ways that are deeply implicated in neoliberalism.[8] But through the rest of this essay, I hope to explore the question of whether sex, particularly sex understood through the lens of queer critique, has anything to offer that might help produce an idea of justice resistant to the machinations of neoliberalism. In raising this question, I argue not only that sex is not "merely cultural" but also that sex plays a pivotal role in constructing the policies that connect economic globalization and the ongoing wars that follow in the wake of those started by the Bush administration.[9] "Thinking sex" allows us to see connections not only between freedom and justice but also between justice and peace.[10]

The Problem of Freedom

Freedom was such a catchword for the Bush administration partly because in that single word a number of issues could be tied together and legitimated. The invocation of freedom articulated the administration's moral justification of (1) the "war on terrorism," (2) global capitalism, (3) the imperative to spread U.S.-style democracy, and (4) a conservative sexual ethic.

As I have argued elsewhere, the connections between the politics of sex and the Bush administration's politics of freedom are strong and politically powerful.[11] A sexual ethic grounded in the particular meaning of freedom used by the Bush administration provides necessary reassurance for claims to American moral exceptionalism.[12] Without the idea that the United States is a morally good nation, an idea confirmed by enforcing a national ethic of sexual conservatism, the distinction between the violence committed by US governmental forces in the name of "freedom" and that committed by those who, for example, violently resist American military activity throughout the world (including the postcombat US military activity in Iraq) would be harder to maintain. There are several reasons why sex can play such a powerfully symbolic role in support of American exceptionalism. One of the most important is that sex is not a separate sphere of moral goodness brought in to mask the greed and ambition of business and war; rather, sex is intimately tied to the ethics of capitalism and, ultimately, to war.

The tie between sex and capital can be traced back to incipient capitalism and the social transformations wrought by the Protestant Reformation in the sixteenth century. Much has been made, of course, of George W. Bush's Protestantism as a source for his political agenda, but as Ann Pellegrini and I have argued in *Secularisms*, the issue is not just the Protestantism of a particular US president but the Christian, and specifically Protestant, nature of US secularism and of US government in particular.[13] Thus, even though the occupant of the White House is no longer a Bush-style evangelical Christian, the Protestant roots of American sexual conservatism are still relevant. Moreover, the advent of neoliberal globalization has made the particular meaning of freedom that ties sex to capital once again ascendant. Terms like *freedom* and *liberty* have meant many things over the course of American history, but in the current moment the meaning articulated by the Protestant Reformers is especially salient.[14]

For the Reformers the meaning of freedom is first and foremost freedom from the Church, and the sign of this freedom, certainly for Martin Luther and John Calvin, is marriage over and against celibacy. Celibacy represented the moral ideal of the Church before the Reformation, and the Reformers' emphasis on marriage provides a counterpoint to this ideal. We do not always associate marriage with sexual freedom, but for the Reformers marriage represented not just freedom from the Church but a form of freedom that developed into what Michel Foucault has diagnosed as peculiarly modern: freedom that involves not wide-open libertinism but disciplined activity. And this type of disciplined activity,

activity that both regulated and produced freedom, is precisely how the Reformers understood marriage. As Calvin says, marriage makes one free: "[In comparison with celibacy] God prefers devoted care in ruling a household, where the devout householder, clear and free of all greed, ambition, and other lusts of the flesh, keeps before him the purpose of serving God in a definite calling."[15]

The crucial point that Calvin makes in this summary of his much longer critique of celibacy is not just that the discipline of marriage taken on by the devout householder makes that householder free—free from greed, ambition, and other lusts of the flesh—but also that this sexual ethic of marriage connects to Calvin's central economic morality: the importance of a calling.[16] For Calvin the calling connects an earthly vocation to the broader Christian duty to serve God in all things. Thus, the individual's economic vocation, including that of providing for his household, is part and parcel of God's will. The individual who fulfills his calling can know that his economic activity, including economic gain, is in the service of God. It is this idea of the calling that the sociologist Max Weber makes so much of in *The Protestant Ethic and the Spirit of Capitalism*, but Weber is utterly unconcerned with the fact that Calvin clearly ties the economic activity of the calling to the sexual activity of marriage. The structure of the household matters as much to Calvin as does the calling itself. The connection among the three—individual, household, and calling—means that, insofar as US politics is informed by this tradition, the autonomous individual is the basis for other forms of social relation, including families, communities, and the nation-state. Appeals to family and community are as likely to supplement and support individualism as to undercut it.[17] Perhaps, most importantly, the two fundamental terms, marriage and a calling, as bound together in the person of the devout householder, are definitive of a certain brand of Protestant freedom. In other words, for the Protestant Reformers (and for George W. Bush as well as many current policy makers in the US government), freedom has a sexuality, and it is not queer.

In placing sex at the center of a matrix that ties sexual arrangements to economic relations to government policy, I am invoking an expanded concept of heteronormativity, as developed by Lauren Berlant and Michael Warner and usefully glossed by Amy Villarejo, to describe not just a dominant set of sexual arrangements but the interwoven social relations that bring together the workings of gender, race, class, and nation.[18] Rather than simply invoke a long list of related categories, the conceptual power of "heteronormativity" becomes its ability to index their kaleidoscopic interrelation.[19] By understanding sexuality as situated in a dynamic matrix, it is possible to develop an analysis of sexuality as at once a relatively autonomous discourse and part and parcel of complex relations that made it possible, indeed morally imperative, for the United States to make war on the nation of Iraq and that help sustain US military action today.[20] The legitimating power for US military intervention of discourses that portray Muslims as sexually deviant—whether repressed and frustrated or polygamous and sexually excessive or both simultaneously—has been widely documented by both journalists and scholars.[21] Ideas about sexuality, imbricated in a matrix that includes ideas about nation, race, and religion, are all part of the prevailing conditions that allow for war.

In this essay, I am interested in exploring the contribution that Protestant secularism makes to this matrix. When I speak of the Protestant family, I mean not just the values of those who ascribe to a particular religion or even a (Protestant) secular worldview, but rather a world-making enterprise, one that has been particularly effective in the modern era and one that establishes boundaries between the heteronormative and the nonheteronormative, boundaries that are not just those of sexuality.[22] Through this project of distinguishing between those who are heteronormative and those who are not, Protestant secularism also draws any number of boundaries on the world at large, establishing a wide range of dominative and exploitative relations. In other words, Protestant heteronormativity mobilizes (without having to name) a politics that extends well beyond religion and sexuality to race, class, nation, war, and economics.

This Protestant normativity predicates the subject of modern freedom in the liberal political tradition: the autonomous individual who stands alone before God and acts on individual interests in the marketplace. The autonomous individual is not just any single human being but a particular way to understand and inhabit human being—a subjectivity—in which the individual understands himself to be free when he acts without influence from others.[23] Yet, as feminists (among others) have long argued, the autonomous individual does not exist autonomously but depends on the labor of those who enable his or her existence.[24] In the household that Calvin imagined for the individual with a calling, this would have been the labor of a wife, children, and servants. In the contemporary moment, this labor might be that of the service workers whose activity Saskia Sassen has documented as crucial to the development of neoliberal "globalization."[25] In both historical moments, the idea of autonomy obfuscates the dependency of the individual, as well as the potentially dominative and exploitative ways in which the individual's needs are met—whether within the household or through the market. The norms of autonomy need not dictate the lives of single human beings, who might be variously dependent on others and meet their needs in ways that are neither dominative nor exploitative, but to explore such possibilities it is necessary to move beyond the claim for autonomy as the basis for freedom.

The autonomous individual as the subject of freedom is also the subject of modern justice.[26] In other words, autonomy is not only the ideology of subjectivity under capitalism but the ascription of both value and citizenship to that subject under the law, including (or perhaps especially) the law of the sovereign nation. And this is where justice can be just as problematic as freedom. Justice does not necessarily get us out of the discourses that articulate modern subjectivity, political economy, and the nation-state. This same sense of autonomy, drawn from the liberal political tradition, undergirds the argument for sovereignty as the ground for international justice, the argument to which UFPJ appealed in making its case against the Iraq war. Just as the discourse of sexual freedom focuses on autonomous individuals, so also the discourse of national sovereignty is organized around the idea of autonomous nations.

Despite the assiduous avoidance of any idea of freedom in peace activism, the version of justice that provides a central principle for organizing is, in fact, based on modern freedom. UFPJ's choice to focus on sovereignty was undoubtedly a pragmatic one, allowing for an argument that made sense within the liberal theoretical framework that forms US public discourse. In liberal theory, national sovereignty can stand in for "peace and justice," because one major liberal meaning of justice is equality in freedom. To respect sovereignty is to respect justice, because it is to treat all nations as equal in their freedom to act autonomously within the space defined by their borders. It is also to produce peace, because to respect sovereignty, to refuse to violate the borders of another country, is to refuse to instigate a war. An appeal to sovereignty clearly states in generally accepted terms why it was wrong for the United States to start an unprovoked war with Iraq and why it is wrong to continue to occupy or otherwise maintain a military presence in that nation, in Afghanistan, or in any other nation. But the choice to focus on sovereignty does not establish any clear sense of what might actually make for justice in any of the areas of the world in which the United States is militarily active (or in the United States for that matter). We need not depend on a narrow vision of either freedom or justice, however. If sex was one of the keys to providing an integrated moral vision for economics and war in the US policy agenda, then sex can also provide the links for an alternative vision of justice.

Sexual Relations of Production

The productive aspects of what we term *conservative* sexual politics are a key to the connections between and among sexual politics, economics, and war. Sexual relations, when organized in terms of the Protestant ideal of marriage, are the materialization of the value of freedom.[27] In other words, sex within marriage is not just a symbol of capitalist discipline and values, it is not the realm of reproduction analogous to that of production, and it is not the functionalist site for discipline of the working classes. Sexual relations are part of the relations of production.

Let me explain what I mean by this claim. Sexual relations are part and parcel of the social relations that produce the possibility of labor and production within capitalism. And in the terms of the Protestant householder, sexual relations produce the autonomous individual not just literally but as a form of human subjectivity. Sex within the bounds of the Protestant ideal of marriage makes the individual the basic unit of social relations, rather than, for example, the community, the society, or any other possible configuration.

This argument is based on a particular understanding of the labor theory of value, one that acknowledges the importance of forms of subjectivity to the production of value. Heterodox economist David Ruccio has argued that movement away from the subjectivity of individualism is crucial to social movement away from the exploitation and domination of capitalist relations.[28] The question of alternative subjectivity is crucial to the "task of socialist transition," because "one of the conditions on which the existence of exchange relations is predicated is the social constitution of individuals capable of engaging in exchange." Ruccio continues, "In order for exchange to be successful—for example, to be perceived as equal exchange—a particular type of social identity and social agency must be created by sociohistorical forces whose outcome cannot be presumed at the outset."[29]

Sex constitutes the particular subject at the center of a matrix that produces not only the value of capital but also the moral value of freedom as synonymous with autonomy. Autonomous individuals understand themselves to be free. They fulfill their needs through wage labor, and they live in familial units that enable their existence in various ways: providing domestic labor, sharing wages, and/or accumulating capital. This matrix, regardless of the gender of its occupants, is heteronormativity. As a site for the embodiment of freedom, autonomy, and individuality, sex mediates between discontinuous but nonetheless interrelated vectors: economic value and moral values, the predication of the subject, and ultimately the formation of public policy.[30] In other words, the sexual relations of heteronormativity naturalize the realm of production: both the production of laborers and the organization of wage labor. Sex is not just a matter of "family values" but a matter of the particular organization of the production of value.

By connecting a particular subjectivity to economic and moral values, sex contributes to producing the value of freedom and the value of capital, and these

different forms of value drive both economic globalization and the "war on terrorism." In other words, the government policies of the last several decades that are
criticized as conservative are not just destructive—destructive of social possibilities and of human lives—they are also productive of the neoliberal order of things.

The production of neoliberalism is a matter for public policy because it
involves relations of production that are not simply or only "economic." As Ruccio points out with Serap Kayatekin, "The relations among and between the different spheres of economic and social life can be sketched in non-deterministic
ways. This allows us to argue both that subjectivities are constituted only partly
by economic processes and that cultural identities, in fact, are constitutive *of* economic processes themselves."[31] My argument, then, is not that the individual is
functionally necessary for capitalism or that capitalism has not also been able to
function in societies where the individual is not the primary social unit as it is in
the United States. Rather, it is precisely the imbrication of Protestant values and
the production of value that make sexual relations a central part of US policy both
domestically and internationally.

Sex in the form of the Protestant family is one way to make human beings
who value—morally as well as economically—participation in capitalism. Given
the undetermined relationship between the subjectivity of autonomous individuals
and the production of economic value in capitalism, we cannot simply read a given
subjectivity from the means of production, nor is this subjectivity the only one
that can work in and with capital. The indeterminacy of capitalist relations means
that other types of social relations, including other family formations, can also be
interrelated with capitalist production.[32] Part of the fight over global sexual politics is a fight *within capitalism* about which version of capitalist relations will pre-
dominate. The intensification of global investment in the individual is particularly
meaningful vis-à-vis neoliberalism's emphasis on privatization. But the indeterminacy of capital also means that capitalism may produce subjectivities that "challenge and seek to move beyond the 'objective dependency relations' characteristic
of the existing system of money and exchange."[33] It is this fact that grounds the
possibility for perverse justice.

Heteronormativity and the Economy

A further example helps show how sex works for neoliberal economics. In her
extensive study of gender policy in the World Bank, the political scientist Kate
Bedford has explored a set of development programs in Ecuador, organized and
funded by the Bank, their express purpose being to create heteronormative rela-

tions. The Bank funds projects that produce pamphlets on the benefits and value of companionate marriage and provides workshops in impoverished Ecuadorian communities on complementary gender relations. The Bank also funds small business loans, primarily to the women of these communities. The stated purpose of these loans is to empower the women in relation to local men, thus allowing for equitable marriages in the hope that women will have some access to economic resources and men will be drawn into household labor and child care. Bank documents include a strongly pathologizing discourse about alcohol abuse that implicates racial and class-based discourses directly in the production of heteronormativity. Because impoverished Ecuadorian men are generally understood to be dissolute, the idea is to give them an incentive to make commitments to the household and its labor. The hope is that such arrangements will enable women to enter the workforce, and child care (now to be done by men) will remain the private responsibility of the household.

The economic effectiveness of these programs for local development is unclear. The programs do not create an economic base for the local communities. They do not create sustainable incomes for the participants in the program. They do, however, attempt to create new gender and sexual relations through the combination of inducement and enforcement that is World Bank policy.[34]

One way to read these programs is as mistaken policies driven by an overly ideological institution willing to sacrifice effectiveness for ideology. But another reading is available if we take seriously that the World Bank wants to produce value. There is a distinction between producing value for the Bank and producing economic development in Ecuador. It may be that the policies fail in terms of "development" but that they are more successful in spreading the social relations and the values that undergird the global production of value. After all, the major criticism of the Bank is not that it is too driven by conservative sexual politics but that it is too driven by neoliberal economic policies. In other words, the efforts of this World Bank program may be directed in the end not toward local development per se but toward better integration of Ecuadorian communities into a privatized labor pattern, including privatizing household labor, that is part and parcel of neoliberal globalization.[35]

The idea that the World Bank's commitment to complementary gender roles is not simply an ineffective development program is borne out in the growing field of feminist economics. Feminists have done significant work to show that the matrix of social relations of which gender and sexuality are a part remains a central organizing principle in economic relations. They have made such claims over and against mainstream economics that persists in the view that the value-neutral nature of economic exchange ultimately makes gender, sexuality, race, or even nation irrelevant. Take, for example, the critique offered by Drucilla Barker and Susan Feiner in the conclusion to their book on feminist economics, *Liberating Economics: Feminist Perspectives on Families, Work, and Globalization*:

> Mainstream economists claim that their conceptual building blocks are objective, value-free, and scientific. We disagree. The fundamental categories of economic analysis are not neutral with respect to existing patterns of social subordination and power. The concepts of, for example, rationality and scarcity, maximization and equilibrium, commodities and exploitation, embody historically specific visions of normative masculinity, femininity, whiteness, and heterosexual orientation that are particular to the West. Indeed, the establishment of Anglo-European world dominance depended upon the creation of new patterns of social hierarchy and the intensification of old patterns of domination.[36]

This is a strong argument that goes to the heart of mainstream understandings of value-neutral economic exchange and profit-motivation. It suggests that social norms and values, including hierarchical and dominative norms, are central in constructing economic systems.

Having made this strong argument, Barker and Feiner then make a turn that seems to undercut part of the power of this opening: "The confluence of representations defines some work as women's and other work as men's. Such coding is largely, but not wholly, an effect of culture, discourse, and ideology." Now certainly, the caveat "but not wholly" opens some space for the intertwining of what they go on to distinguish as the "material" and the "cultural," but the overarching sense of the argument is that the reason that gender matters flows from the material persistence of undesirable jobs that become assigned to those who deviate from cultural norms. As they say, "Given the limitations of technology, there are always likely to be distasteful, monotonous, backbreaking jobs that need doing" (130) And then later, "Given the way that systems of representation (over)determine economic winners and losers, we can predict exactly who will end up with these jobs: women, people of color, and other culturally devalued groups" (131).

My argument is somewhat different. It is not the material parameters for the division of labor alone, nor the material limits of technology, that constitute some jobs as distasteful and monotonous and others as not, while cultural norms and values effectively assign those jobs to some groups and not others. Rather, cultural norms and values define some jobs as distasteful (an interesting choice of words in that it invokes the question of "taste"); they distinguish between some types of labor (e.g., thinking labor vs. manual labor); in making such divisions, they create some jobs as "monotonous" and others as interesting, and social norms and values make it possible to organize these divisions so that some jobs are back-breaking while others are not. Or perhaps, given the prevalence of back trouble across the economic spectrum, it is more accurate to say that some jobs break the back differently. (And some jobs provide health insurance to address such back trouble, while others do not.) But the very fact that we rarely think of office work as "backbreaking" shows the imbrication of values in organizing production. And, of course, one way that norms and values constitute jobs is in and through social categories such as gender and sexuality, race and nation.

Let us return for a moment to the World Bank's program for gender complementarity. Why choose heteronormativity as the way to promote economic improvement? What are the economic effects of such a program, not just in terms of development (something that Bedford's research shows has not necessarily been produced for the communities involved) but also in terms of the division of labor? The answer to these questions cannot simply be that cultural representations assign some jobs to women and others to men, because part of the point of the program is to get women into paid labor and to get men to do more household labor. While this program obviously enforces heteronormative household arrangements, there is a reversal here of some "traditional" roles (both in Ecuadorian society and in the United States where many of the officials promoting the program live and work). Why, then, develop a program that chooses a more progressive gender normativity rather than a more conservative one? The program does not just construct gender in a traditional way, but it does construct gender in a way that divides labor along the lines demanded by neoliberal privatization. It attempts simultaneously to increase workforce participation and to maintain domestic labor as a private matter. Rather than develop a child care program as a way to increase women's participation in paid labor, for example, the World Bank program aims to provide a privatized way to accomplish such labor by increasing men's willingness to take it on.

The choice of the World Bank to attempt to remake gender relations in Ecuador can be understood in light of the claim that Barker and Feiner make in the strong version of their critique: the spread of capitalism and economic dominance depends not on the value-neutral operations of the market but on "the creation of new patterns of social hierarchy" as well as "the intensification of old patterns of domination." In this sense, World Bank policies committed to heteronormativity are not sexually conservative. They seek to remake social relations so as to allow for "new patterns of social hierarchy" as well as "old patterns of domination" in the global economy.

The Justice of Perverse Relationships

If this is some of the work that heteronormativity does in today's world, what good can perversity do? After all, sex alone will not the revolution make. Certainly, a number of social theorists have pursued the question of how sex can contribute to a more general project of emancipation, from Herbert Marcuse's idea of sex and freedom to 1970s ideas of sexual liberation as the key to the end of exploitation to Antonio Negri's idea that taking back our leisure time could be crucially subversive of capital.[37] Given the regulatory nature of the Protestant ethic, and its dedication to marriage and family, all of these strategies are both powerful and appealing. None of them alone can be successful precisely because the Protestant ethic is both regulatory *and* constitutive of freedom. Here is where freedom falls short and justice is necessary. The question is not just how to free sex from the bonds of both family and capital but how to make relations that resist the logic of capital and in doing so open the door to alternative possibilities.

But if sex cannot undo global capital, it can be an important part of the project of resisting the construction of the world in the terms most suited to the prevailing economic system. In particular, sexual perversity can help create alternative economic units to that of the autonomous individual and the household. This possibility is particularly important in an era of neoliberal privatization, when the individual household is called on to carry ever-increasing burdens for producing social goods.

Perversion, in this sense, does not promise something that is utterly separate from capitalism. Perversions are themselves produced by the operation of capital. But, as Villarejo points out in her reading of Ferguson, normalizing discourses see these perversions as "symptom and nothing more", they "cannot read perversion as agency."[38] This type of queer theory recognizes capital as an agent of perversion but also raises the question of whether queer perversity can be an agent of economic justice. In taking this turn, queer theory is following the path laid out by its very name, the turning (perversion) of a term of derogation away from its intended effects.

As Miranda Joseph and David Rubin have argued, complicity with capital does not, in itself, signal a lack of moral value.[39] Rather, the pursuit of economic justice does not necessarily require continuing the search for what is purified of capital's touch. Queer theorists are often suspicious of such purity, because queer theory seeks to recognize the trace of the abject within that from which it is thought to be wholly other. To see capitalism's trace in our perversions does not undo the value of our actions but raises the possibility that those actions can be connected to others who also struggle in and against the domination and exploitation that the production of capital entails. Moreover, as several theorists have also suggested, the search for a purified outside or a future entirely free from capitalism entails ascribing to contemporary capitalist systems a totality and wholeness to which capital aspires but which it certainly has not achieved.[40] In other words, if we do not seek to delineate a pure (or purely perverse) realm from an impure capitalism, then new spaces open that might become sites for building justice.

Here Ruccio's work is extremely helpful, because if a particular form of human subjectivity is one condition that makes for a particular form of economic relations, then "changing the subject" is also a crucial part of the project of changing economic relations. One way to take up this struggle is to address both the social relations that produce the autonomous individual — including the sexual relations — and alternative formations of subjectivity.[41] For Ruccio these alternatives include the possibility of " 'decentered communities,' a form of social agency radically different from the individuality that is constituted in a society characterized by commodity exchange."[42] He does not presume that collective subjectivities must be either communal or coherent.[43]

The contribution made by queer theory and politics to this project is the possibility of turning the perversities induced by capitalism toward the project of producing alternative subjectivities, subjectivities that are neither communal nor coherent.[44] In the last chapter of *Love the Sin*, Ann Pellegrini and I argue that queer sex is a site for producing values.[45] Queer sex has this productive potential because it is a site for creating, enacting, and embodying different types of relationships. And these relationships form the basis for an alternative ethical vision. These relationships take various forms — from the army of ex-lovers of lesbian fame to the anonymity of public sex, to the buddy system developed in response to the AIDS crisis — but taken together they offer an alternative vision of relationship and of values that are neither communal, in the sense of coherent community values, nor individual in the sense of individual autonomy.

Instead, queer relations produce ethical values as the cultivation of relational possibilities, through norms that are sometimes strict — an army of ex-lovers is *never* supposed to fail, and in the midst of the AIDS crisis to fail one's buddy and not show up with the needed food or Gatorade for electrolytes or ride to the doctor could literally be a matter of life and death — and sometimes loose, perhaps the most loosely held being that of monogamy, as even proponents of monogamy are prone to nonmonogonous activity. At their best, these relational practices produce an alternative vision of sex and values. For example, while liberal freedom is grounded in the free choice of the individual whose only requirements are to respect the freedom of other such autonomous individuals, queer relations are grounded in activities that refuse the norms of the individual so that something else might be possible. It might, for example, be possible to be free and simultaneously not to be "autonomous" — not to have life organized only in the traditional relations of the family, for example, and not to be ultimately separate from other persons.[46]

This type of queer relationality has rarely been considered vis-à-vis the question of economic justice, yet what would it mean to take up queer relationality as part of a project for building the alternative subjectivities that might support proximate socialisms, anticapitalist coalitions post-Seattle, or other projects of economic justice? Perverse justice might open the door to programs that could address economic issues in a different framework. Elizabeth Freeman, for example, has argued that queer relations challenge the neoliberal logic of development, insisting "that various queer social practices, especially those involving enjoyable bodily sensations, produce form(s) of time consciousness, even historical consciousness, that can intervene upon the material damage done in the name of development" (59).[47]

Let us turn to an example to see how queer perversity might serve as a basis for economic justice. For example, is it possible that a queer approach to the AIDS crisis might also provide a vision of economic justice? How do we think of caring for those children orphaned by AIDS? Do we think of them only in terms of the "family"? In other words, are the choices for these children only adoption in families or institutionalization and care by the state? Are there alternative relational configurations for them and for those who care for them?

One intervention that queer theory suggests is that we look at relational configurations that are in the interstices between individual, family, community, nation/state, and the international. By rejecting the natural progression from individual to family to community to nation, we can see various possibilities for relationships that might allow us to address the ongoing effects of the AIDS crisis, including the economic effects. There are, for example, a wide range of grassroots organizations taking on the task of caring for children orphaned by AIDS.[48] Organizations like Health Global Access Project (Health GAP) are working to connect the need for prevention campaigns that distribute condoms to economic questions like those of debt relief and budget ceilings imposed by the International Monetary Fund that do not allow countries who receive IMF loans to adequately fund health care.[49] The Treatment Action Campaign in South Africa connected the distribution of condoms to questions of education, school access, and a "life skills" curriculum.[50] And as Richard Kim has noted, some AIDS organizations in the United States joined in this type of activism to connect sexual politics to questions of economic justice, a move that marks a major shift for queer-identified AIDS organizations like ACT UP.[51]

Gregg Bordowitz has suggested in relation to work that he has done with the Treatment Action Campaign in South Africa that transnational queer AIDS organizing is precisely the type of alternative subjectivity that could form the basis for new visions of economic justice. Bordowitz develops this idea from the concept of the multitude that Michael Hardt and Antonio Negri have proposed as the new subject of global movement for justice. The idea of a queer multitude is undoubtedly a perversion of Hardt and Negri's original conception, but Bordowitz makes the argument that, in fact, transnational AIDS organizing is the material base of such a multitudinous movement precisely because the fight against AIDS draws together an extensive range of issues from sexuality to economics to health care to education.[52] Perhaps most importantly, what conjoins those who participate in such a wide-ranging movement is not any single identity, family, community, or nation. In short, perverse relations (including those induced by HIV, a virus that does not respect the boundaries of identity) shift the configuration of both agency and movement.

The demand for relational justice grounded in a perverse multitude is quite different from the type of justice promoted by the US government and its "war on terrorism." Moreover, the Obama administration has continued to pursue policies that tie the national security apparatus to ideas about about religion and a Protestant subjectivity embodied through gender and sexuality. While ambivalent about whether it is pursuing a "war on terrorism" or some other form of global military endeavor (initially called "overseas contingency operations"), and despite bringing an official end to the war in Iraq, the Obama administration also continued the war in Afghanistan and expanded military interventions, most notably in Pakistan, Yemen, and Libya.[53]

Yet this administration's ties among Protestant familialism, economics, and national security are very close to home. Specifically, they can be found in the Office of Faith-Based and Neighborhood Partnerships. Obama has not only maintained the program that Bush established as the Office of Faith-based and Community Initiatives (itself an expansion of the Clinton-era "Charitable choice" in the 1996 "welfare reform" bill), he has expanded it in at least two directions.

The Obama administration's Office of Faith-based and Neighborhood Partnerships has been given the task of supporting both secular and religious community
groups, so as to "work on behalf of Americans committed to improving their communities no matter their religious or political beliefs."[54] The office has also been
given an expanded role. It will no longer be simply a funnel for monies to go to
community groups but will also have an advisory role on policy. Moreover, as the
initial charge to this office clearly articulates, this expansion into the administration's development of policy has a broad reach, including both domestic and
foreign policy issues:

> The Office's top priority will be making community groups an integral part
> of our economic recovery and poverty a burden fewer have to bear when
> recovery is complete.
>
> It will be one voice among several in the administration that will
> look at how we support women and children, address teenage pregnancy,
> and reduce the need for abortion.
>
> The Office will strive to support fathers who stand by their fami-
> lies, which involves working to get young men off the streets and into well-
> paying jobs, and encouraging responsible fatherhood.
>
> Finally, beyond American shores this Office will work with the
> National Security Council to foster interfaith dialogue with leaders and
> scholars around the world.[55]

The charge begins with the top priority of addressing economic recovery
and even directly naming poverty as a problem, but this agenda is followed by
two "key priorities" explicitly related to gender and sexuality: abortion reduction
and support for fathers "who stand by their families." Interestingly, the administration is hoping to bring men more directly into the question of gender and
sexuality by adding the explicit interpellation of "fathers" to the feminine (and
sometimes troublesomely feminist) politics of abortion. And in both cases —
support for "women and children" and support for (good) "fathers" — we see
Obama's approach of combining aspects of the policies advocated by what are
understood as the two "sides" of American politics into a new policy of "abortion
reduction" and "responsible fatherhood." While Americans cannot, nearly four
decades after *Roe v. Wade*, agree on the legality of abortion, the charge posits that
they should be able to agree that the world would be better if fewer women needed
to have abortions. Importantly, unlike the case of "responsible fatherhood," the
explicit means of reducing abortion is not mentioned, because there are radical

differences on method. Some advocate abortion reduction through universal sex education and readily available contraception, as well as economic possibilities for women so that their childbearing is not constrained by dire economic circumstances, while others advocate traditional family values, marriage promotion, and restrictions on the availability of abortion as a way to reduce the number of abortions performed each year. The key priority of responsible fatherhood, however, names the means of supporting fathers—getting them off the streets and into well-paying jobs—thus bringing together traditional liberal support for jobs programs with a more conservative support for the "traditional" two-parent family.[56]

Despite the sense that each policy brings together liberal and conservative elements, the overall effect of linking the two policies is to create a traditional vision of American gender roles, family structures, and their implications for policy. We have an explicit gendering in that different policy initiatives are directed toward women and men, and in its explicitness the policy is also traditional: women are tied to children, and while they need to be supported so that abortions are not necessary, they, unlike the fathers, apparently do not need well-paying jobs. (Gay, lesbian, or queer people are nowhere named.) In the space of this initial charge to the office, the move is relatively swift from a new recognition of the importance of community-based activists "no matter their political or religious beliefs" to traditional family values: a two-parent family of opposite genders, with the father working and the mother caring for children (although she may work, there is no mention of government support for this activity).

We have also moved very rapidly from economic recovery through the family to the somewhat startling naming of the National Security Council in the charge to an office focused on "neighborhood" partnerships. How is it that the domestic (in every sense of the word) gender normativity of the office is tied to what the administration here calls "the world beyond our shores"? The Obama administration's approach is undoubtedly different from that of the Bush administration. The turn globally toward interfaith dialogue instead of a "crusade" for freedom and the directive to take up dialogue with both "leaders" (presumably religious leaders) and "scholars" (perhaps thought of as secular?) marks the greater openness to the world that many commentators saw in Obama's 2009 speech in Cairo.[57] But the overall framework on which Obama draws maintains the Christian hegemony of the neoliberal world order. In particular, the dialogue model for interrelation across religious difference claims to be based in equality and openness but is actually framed by a Protestant understanding. The model of interfaith dialogue offers negotiation among different "faiths," a view of religion that mirrors the Protestant emphasis on belief as definitive of religion. If, however, practice or land is the basis for one's religion, then dialogue might not be the way to approach conflict. For interfaith dialogues the issue is talking through beliefs, rather than, for example, negotiating about land rights. As with the secular calendar, which is at once used across cultures and specifically Christian, these assumptions make the office's claim to be open to participation "no matter" what into a claim that is simultaneously universalist and specific.

Perhaps most disturbingly, this vision of an approach to the "world beyond our shores" that promises openness and delivers Christian universalism is part of the "Christian realist" model (drawn from Reinhold Niebuhr) that Obama expounded in his Nobel speech as a legitimation for his administration's initial expansion of the war in Afghanistan.[58] This approach is different from what Melani McAlister has termed the "benevolent supremacy" of the Cold War period (in which Niebuhr was writing), but it maintains the hegemonic presumptions of Christian realism. As such, it requires the same familial relations within the private sphere, as did Niebuhr's Christian realism. The concerns with gender and sexuality that are connected to the charge for interfaith dialogue make it apparent that Obama's approach takes up from Niebuhrian realism a split between the public and the private, the domestic and the foreign. This split is also an interrelation, hence the apparent ease of including both "domestic" and "foreign" concerns in the office. As the social ethicist and Niebuhr scholar Gary Dorrien points out, this split is also a way to understand what Niebuhr calls "moral man and immoral society" (which is also the title of Niebuhr's most famous book).[59] The split allows a strong emphasis on personal responsibility, on the importance of morality to human being, while realism also involves a recognition that social interaction will require moral compromise — hence the perennial immorality of society. What many mainstream commentators liked so much about Obama's Nobel speech is that he positioned himself and the United States as domestically moral — as humble, diplomatically open to others, and responsible. If in that responsibility we must become entangled in immorality, it is the best that we can do as human beings — such is reality. If peace becomes war — so be it — as long as we are personally (read here: sexually) responsible.

As with the Bush administration before it, the Obama administration has taken an approach that ties together economic justice (or at least economic recovery and concern about poverty) with Protestant familialism and national security. The purpose of perverse justice is to change the subject of economic recovery from the familially gendered "father" in need of a job to human beings living among social relations that are not split between private and public selves or between "fathers" and "others" (whether women or queers or nonprocreative men or "those beyond our shores").[60]

The turn to perverse justice may also provide a way to rethink the connections between economics and war, peace and justice. Making these connections requires a project of imagination, including moral imagination. As Marianne Hirsch has pointed out, the current moment is a good time to take up the exhortation of lifelong antiwar activist Grace Paley: "What we need right now is to imagine the real."[61] In contrast to the claims of Christian realism, Paley suggests that we can approach the real only through an act of imagination. For her, this imagination is crucially to imagine the lives of others. If, for example, we imagine the lives of those who are subjected to bombs or drone attacks or covert actions, whether in Afghanistan or Pakistan or Yemen or anywhere else the United States is militarily engaged, then perhaps it will be harder to think that war is peace. If we imagine people whose religious lives are not matters of faith, then perhaps dialogue will not suffice as a model for openness and equality. And if we imagine sexual possibilities that are confined neither by the split between public and private, nor by normative gender roles, then perhaps sexuality itself will become a space of openness rather than the moral collateral for a nation engaged in perpetual war. We could imagine a queer freedom alternative to the freedom of the autonomous individual (whether individual person or nation). We could also see peace as something more than the absence of war, as something fundamentally tied to justice, including economic justice. And we could imagine a justice distinct from the Protestant imperative to discipline and punish, one that embraces perversity in all its promise and possibility.

Notes

I am deeply indebted to a number of ongoing conversations in which I have been a fortunate participant over the past few years, including those with my Barnard colleagues Kate Bedford, Christine Cynn, Amanda Swarr, and Rebecca Young, and the New York University Center for Religion and Media working group "Sex, Secularisms, and Bodies Politic," organized by Ann Pellegrini, with Elizabeth Bernstein, Gregg Bordowitz, Elizabeth Castelli, Nicole DeBlosi, Lisa Duggan, Esther Kaplan, Richard Kim, Molly McGarry, and Kathleen Roberts Skerrett. I am also grateful to the directors of the Center for Religion and Media, Faye Ginsburg and Angela Zito, for inviting me to present an early version of these ideas.

1. www.unitedforpeace.org/article.php?list=type&type=27.
2. The country has apparently developed amnesia with regard to the persistence of those other things the United States had made war on in the second half of the twentieth century—the war on drugs or even the war on poverty.
3. This position, highlighting sovereignty, was formally codified as a UFPJ stance in

2004. See "UFPJ Position on Ending the War on Iraq," May 17, 2004, www.unitedfor
peace.org/article.php?list=type&type=70.

4. Robin D. G. Kelley, *Freedom Dreams: The Black Radical Imagination* (Boston: Beacon Press, 2003).

5. For a clear summary of this progressive critique, see David Harvey, *A Brief History of Neoliberalism* (New York: Oxford University Press, 2005).

6. For some of the parameters of these arguments, see Kai Nielsen, "Arguing about Justice: Marxist Immoralism and Marxist Moralism," *Philosophy and Public Affairs* 17, no. 3 (1988): 212–34; Allen W. Wood, "Justice and Class Interests," *Philosophica* 33 (1984): 9–32; Wood, "The Marxian Critique of Justice," *Philosophy and Public Affairs* 1, no. 3 (1972): 244–82; G. A. Cohen, "Freedom, Justice, and Capitalism" *New Left Review* I/126 (March/April 1981): 3-16; and George C. Brenkert, *Marx's Ethic of Freedom* (New York: Routledge and Kegan Paul, 1983).

7. See John Rawls, *A Theory of Justice* (Cambridge: Harvard University Press, 1971); Iris Marion Young, *Justice and the Politics of Difference* (Princeton: Princeton University Press, 1990); Young, *Global Challenges: War, Self-Determination, and Responsibility for Justice* (New York: Polity, 2006); and Nancy Fraser and Axel Honneth, *Redistribution or Recognition? A Political-Philosophical Exchange* (London: Verso, 2003).

8. See, e.g., Harvey, *Brief History of Neoliberalism*, 41.

9. See Judith Butler, "Merely Cultural," *Social Text*, nos. 52–53 (1997): 265–77; and Lisa Duggan, *The Twilight of Equality: Neoliberalism, Cultural Politics, and the Attack on Democracy* (Boston: Beacon, 2004).

10. Gayle Rubin, "Thinking Sex: Notes for a Radical Theory of the Politics of Sexuality," in *Pleasure and Danger: Exploring Female Sexuality*, ed. Carole S. Vance (1984; rpt. New York: Pandora, 1992), 267–319.

11. Janet R. Jakobsen, "Sex + Freedom = Sexual Regulation: Why?," *Social Text*, nos. 84–85 (2005): 285–308.

12. Janet R. Jakobsen, "Sex, Secularism, and the 'War on Terrorism': The Role of Sexuality in Multi-Issue Organizing," in *A Companion to Lesbian, Gay, Bisexual, Transgender, and Queer Studies*, ed. George E. Haggerty and Molly McGarry (Oxford: Blackwell, 2007), 17–37.

13. Janet R. Jakobsen and Ann Pellegrini, eds., *Secularisms* (Durham, NC: Duke University Press, 2008).

14. See Roderick A. Ferguson, "Of Normative Strivings: African American Studies and the Histories of Sexualities," and Chandan Reddy, "Asian Diasporas, Neoliberalism, and the Family: Reviewing the Case for Homosexual Asylum in the Context of Family Rights," in "What's Queer about Queer Studies Now?," ed. David L. Eng, Judith Halberstam, and José Esteban Muñoz, special issue, *Social Text*, nos. 84–85 (2005): 85–100, 101–120.

15. John Calvin, *Institutes of the Christian Religion*, ed. John T. McNeill, trans. Ford Lewis Battles (Philadelphia: Westminster Press, 1960) 1258, 4.12.4.

16. For a more extensive reading of both Luther and Calvin on this point, see Janet R. Jakobsen, "Freedom + Sexuality = Regulation: Why?," in "What's Queer about Queer Studies Now?," ed. David L. Eng, Judith Halberstam, and José Esteban Muñoz, special issue, *Social Text*, nos. 84–85 (2005): 285–308.

17. Miranda Joseph, *Against the Romance of Community* (Minneapolis: University of Minnesota Press, 2002).

18. On heteronormativity, see Lauren Berlant and Michael Warner, "Sex in Public," *Critical Inquiry* 24, no. 2 (Winter 1998): 547–66.

19. Amy Villarejo, "Tarrying with the Normative: Queer Theory and *Black History*," in "What's Queer about Queer Studies Now?," ed. David L. Eng, Judith Halberstam, and José Esteban Muñoz, special issue, *Social Text*, nos. 84–85 (2005): 69–84.

20. On relative autonomy, see Cornel West, "Marxist Theory and the Specificity of Afro-American Oppression," in *Marxism and the Interpretation of Culture*, ed. Cary Nelson and Lawrence Grossberg (Chicago: University of Chicago Press, 1983), 17–33.

21. Seymour Hersh reported on the military's dependence on Patai's scholarship in his articles on Abu Ghraib in the *New Yorker*. See Seymour M. Hersh, "The Gray Zone: How a Secret Pentagon Program Came to Abu Ghraib," *New Yorker*, May 24, 2004, www.newyorker.com/archive/2004/05/24/040524fa_fact. See also Jasbir K. Puar and Amit S. Rai, "Monster, Terrorist, Fag: The War on Terrorism and the Production of Docile Patriots," *Social Text*, no. 72 (2002: 117–48); and David Harrington Watt, *Anti-Fundamentalism: A Brief History.* (Ithaca: Cornell University Press, forthcoming).

22. Charles Taylor, "Sex and Christianity: How Has the Moral Landscape Changed?," *Commonweal: A Review of Religion, Politics, and Culture*, September 28, 2007, 12–18.

23. On the Protestant genealogy of autonomous individualism as the subject of liberalism, see J. B. Schneewind, *The Invention of Autonomy: A History of Modern Moral Philosophy* (New York: Cambridge University Press, 1998); on the predication of the subject, see Gayatri Chakravorty Spivak, "Scattered Speculations on the Question of Value," in *In Other Worlds: Essays in Cultural Politics* (New York: Methuen, 1987), 154–75. On the connection between the two, see Jakobsen, "Freedom + Sexuality."

24. See, e.g., Carole Pateman, *The Sexual Contract* (Stanford: Stanford University Press, 1988); Nancy Armstrong, *Desire and Domestic Fiction: A Political History of the Novel* (New York: Oxford University Press, 1987); Armstrong, *How Novels Think: The Limits of Individualism, 1719–1900* (New York: Columbia University Press, 2005); and Rey Chow, *The Protestant Ethic and the Spirit of Capitalism* (New York: Columbia University Press, 2002).

25. Saskia Sassen, *The Global City: New York, London, Tokyo* (Princeton: Princeton University Press, 2001). See also Sassen, "The Other Workers in the Advanced Corporate Economy," *Scholar and Feminist Online* 8, no. 1 (Fall 2009), www.barnard.edu/sfonline/work/sassen_01.htm.

26. It is the autonomous individual who is the subject of distributive justice, who enters the "original position" in John Rawls's famous philosophical theory of justice and who is alone responsible for his actions in a court of law *(Theory of Justice*, 1971).

27. Jakobsen, "Sex + Freedom."

28. On this point I have also been influenced (along with other theorists) by Gayatri Chakravorty Spivak's trenchant essay "Scattered Speculations on the Theory of Value." For my reading of Spivak, see Janet R. Jakobsen, "Can Homosexuals End Western Civilization as We Know It?: Family Values in a Global Economy," in *Queer Globalizations: Citizenship and the Afterlife of Colonialism*, ed. Arnaldo Cruz-Malavé and Martin Manalansan (New York: New York University Press, 2002), 49–70. See also Amy Villarejo, *Lesbian Rule: Cultural Criticism and the Value of Desire* (Durham, NC: Duke University Press, 2003), 28–35; and Joseph, *Against the Romance of Community*. For Ruccio's extensive arguments advocating a nondeterministic reading of Marx, see David F. Ruccio and Jack Amariglio, *Postmodern Moments in Modern Economics* (Princeton: Princeton University Press, 2003); and Stephen Cullenberg, Jack Amariglio, and David F. Ruccio, eds., *Postmodernism, Economics, and Knowledge* (New York: Routledge, 2001). See also the work of the journal *Rethinking Marxism: A Journal of Economics, Culture, and Society*, of which Ruccio has been the editor.

29. Ruccio, "Failure of Socialism, Future of Socialists?," *Rethinking Marxism* 5 (Summer 1992): 16. Ruccio argues that the great contribution of Marxian value theory is to question the presumption that either economic relations or the human beings who are the subject of those relations are naturally produced. For Ruccio, historically indeterminate production of the individual as the subject of capitalist exchange does not just occur within the confines of the economy, nor can it be read deterministically directly from a particular economic form. As he says, "The constitution of individual subjects as a form of social agency — including economic rationality, equality, private property, and so on — is produced in large part outside the economy, as a result of political and cultural processes" (16). My argument is related to Ruccio's but somewhat different in that I do not wish to simply separate the "inside" and "outside" of the economy. My concern is how various social relations, including those not commonly named "economic," are discontinuous but nonetheless interrelated sites for producing the autonomous individual as the subject of capitalism. In particular, sexuality is a site at which the moral values that make individuality normative come together with the production of economic value in its relation to the autonomous individual as a form of human subjectivity.

30. As Jordana Rosenberg has suggested, when understood in dialectical terms, this mediation is "the force through which necessarily incompatible 'vectors' are bound together and made productive. What holds the dialectical tension between, say, 'economic value and moral values' together and what makes it function in the ways that

it does under capitalism, is—sex" (Jordana Rosenberg, pers. comm., September 20, 2010).

31. Kayatekin and Ruccio, "Global Fragments: Subjectivity and Class Politics in Discourses of Globalization," *Economy and Society* 27 (February 1998): 87.

32. For a summary and critique of work on various familial formations in relation to capitalism, see Miranda Joseph, "Family Affairs: The Discourse of Global/Localization," in *Queer Globalizations: Citizenship and the Afterlife of Colonialism*, ed. Arnaldo Cruz-Malavé and Martin Manalansan (New York: New York University Press, 2002), 71–99.

33. Ruccio, "Failure of Socialism, Future of Socialists?," 17.

34. Bedford notes as an example of a way to account for economic growth that "simply makes no sense" the fact that this program shifts the criteria for economic productivity away from the consumption of purchased alcohol that actually does contribute to economic growth and toward "unpaid" labor when done by men. Kate Bedford, *Developing Partnerships: Gender, Sexuality, and the Reformed World Bank* (Minneapolis: University of Minnesota Press, 2009), 22.

35. Chandan Reddy has argued that US immigration policy has similar effects in that it uses heteronormative policies like "family reunification" to intensify neoliberal privatization ("Asian Diasporas, Neoliberalism, and Family," 110).

36. Drucilla Barker and Susan F. Feiner, eds., *Liberating Economics: Feminist Perspectives on Families, Work, and Globalization* (Ann Arbor: University of Michigan Press, 2004), 128. Hereafter cited in the text.

37. Herbert Marcuse, *Eros and Civilization: A Philosophical Inquiry into Freud* (Boston: Beacon, 1955); and Antonio Negri, *The Politics of Subversion: A Manifesto for the Twenty-First Century* (Cambridge, UK: Polity, 2005).

38. Villarejo, "Tarrying," 74.

39. Miranda Joseph and David Rubin, "Promising Complicities: On the Sex, Race, and Globalization Project," in Haggerty and McGarry, *A Companion to Lesbian, Gay, Bisexual and Transgender Studies*, 2007.

40. See Paul Smith, *Millennial Dreams: Contemporary Culture and Capital in the North* (London: Verso, 1997); and J. K. Gibson-Graham, *The End of Capitalism (As We Knew It): A Feminist Critique of Political Economy* (Cambridge: Blackwell, 1996).

41. As Ruccio says, "One of the implications of this kind of class analysis is that there is no one-to-one correspondence between the existence of markets or planning and a particular (communal or other) class structure. A debate that focuses solely on a choice of the allocative mechanisms (or on a particular—private or public—form of property relations) may do little in the way of achieving one of the ostensible goals of socialist transition, namely, fostering communal relations. Of course, class cannot be considered the only (or most important) factor in determining the transition to an alternative, collective or communal society. Such a move would replicate the essen-

tialist status of allocative mechanisms and property relations in the traditional forces-and-relations view" ("Failure of Socialism, Future of Socialists?," 18).

42. Ruccio, "Failure of Socialism, Future of Socialists?," 19.

43. The idea that a coherent community is not the natural alternative to the capitalist individual is particularly important because, as Miranda Joseph has so convincingly shown in *Against the Romance of Community*, community is not the romantic antidote to capitalism but its affective supplement. But, of course, the "romance of community" criticized by Joseph is not the only possible alternative to autonomous individualism.

44. Ruccio argues that "the same society that creates the conditions for the formation of individual subjectivity that serves to reproduce the relations of commodity exchange may also give rise to other types of subjectivity—including collective subjectivity—which challenge and seek to move beyond the 'objective dependency relations' characteristic of the existing system of money and exchange" ("Failure of Socialism, Future of Socialists?," 17). Although LGBTQ life is often articulated in terms of "community," Ann Pellegrini and I suggest that this is not necessarily an accurate rendition (or, at least not of the Q part of the equation). Queer politics may be more like a collection of direct-action affinity groups, groups not unconnected to each other but not all moving toward a single purpose either.

45. Janet R. Jakobsen and Ann Pellegrini, *Love the Sin: Sexual Regulation and the Limits of Religious Tolerance* (New York: New York University Press, 2003).

46. Janet R. Jakobsen and Elizabeth Lapovsky Kennedy, "Sex and Freedom," in *Regulating Sex*, ed. Elizabeth Bernstein and Laurie Schaffner (New York: Routledge, 2004), 247–70.

47. Elizabeth Freeman, "Time Binds, or, Erotohistoriography" in "What's Queer about Queer Studies Now?," ed. David L. Eng, Judith Halberstam, and José Esteban Muñoz, special issue, *Social Text*, nos. 84–85 (2005): 57–68.

48. For a rundown of such grassroots efforts in several areas of the world, which range from social movement organizations to aspects of Christian mission, see the Alliance for Youth Achievement, www.allforyouth.org.

49. See www.healthgap.org.

50. See www.tac.org.za.

51. Richard Kim, "ACT UP Goes Global," *Nation*, July 9, 2001.

52. Mary Hawkesworth has criticized Hardt and Negri's proposal for its failure to recognize gender difference, and they certainly do not take up issues of sexuality (Michael Hardt and Antonio Negri, *Multitude: War and Democracy in the Age of Empire* [New York: Penguin, 2004]; Mary Hawkesworth, "The Gendered Ontology of *Multitude*," *Political Theory*, 34, no. 3 [June 2006]: 357–64).

53. Heather Maher, "The End of the U.S. War on Terror," Radio Free Europe/Radio Liberty, April 16, 2009 http://www.rferl.org/content/The_End_Of_The_US_War_On_Terror/1609936.html (accessed April 21, 2009).

54. White House Press Release, "Obama Announces Office of Faith-based and Neighborhood Partnerships," February 5, 2009, www.whitehouse.gov/the_press_office/Obama AnnouncesWhiteHouseOfficeofFaith-basedandNeighborhoodPartnerships/.

55. White House Press Release, "Obama Announces."

56. In his inaugural address Obama also tied this conservative emphasis on responsible fatherhood directed mainly toward the poor—those who might need to "get off the streets"—with a new accountability across the economic spectrum, calling on Wall Street executives to be similarly responsible in their approach to their working life.

57. Even traditionally progressive and, thus, skeptical sites like the *Guardian* and the *Nation* heard Obama's Cairo speech as "a world away" from the approach of the Bush administration (Jonathan Freedland, "Barack Obama in Cairo: The Speech No Other President Could Make," June 4, 2009, www.guardian.co.uk/world/2009/ jun/04/barack-obama-speech-islam-west). The editor of the *Nation*, Katrina vanden Heuvel, simply called the Cairo speech "magnificent" in her blog ("Obama: Reset and Refocus," June 23, 2009, www.thenation.com/blog/obama-refocus-and-reset). For a report that puts transnational interreligious relations definitively within the realm of national security, see "Engaging Religious Communities Abroad: A New Imperative for U.S. Foreign Policy," Report of the Taskforce on Religion and U.S. Foreign Policy, Scott Appleby and Richard Cizik, Cochairs, Thomas Wright, Project Director (Chicago: Chicago Council on Global Affairs, 2010). The press release for this report positions it as "the next step" after Obama's Cairo speech "in developing a strategy to engage religious communities of all faiths in addressing foreign policy challenges" (www.thechicagocouncil.org/taskforce_details.php?taskforce_id=10).

58. Christian Realism emphasizes the doctrine of original sin and the resulting impossibility of achieving moral ideals in the world of fallen human beings. The ethics associated with Christian Realism encourages people to strive for social justice while recognizing that compromise will always be required by the circumstances of an imperfect world. Niebuhr, who had once been a pacifist, elaborated this ethical orientation as the basis for a Cold War foreign policy that legitimated the use of US military power as the lesser evil in a morally corrupt world. See Reinhold Niebuhr, *Moral Man and Immoral Society* (New York: Scribner's, 1932); and Niebuhr, *The Irony of American History* (New York: Scribner's, 1952).

59. Gary Dorrien, *The Soul in Society: The Making and Renewal of Social Christianity* (Minneapolis: Fortress, 1995).

60. For more on how social relations might actually be reconfigured through norms of perverse justice, see Janet R. Jakobsen, "Queer Relations: A Reading of Martha Nussbaum on Same-Sex Marriage," *Columbia Journal of Gender and Law* 19 (2010): 133–78.

61. Marianne Hirsch, "'What We Need Right Now Is to Imagine the Real': Grace Paley Writing against War," *PMLA* 124 (2009): 1768–77.

IDEOLOGICAL FANTASIES

Carla Freccero

> The fundamental level of ideology . . . is not of an illusion masking
> the real state of things but that of an (unconscious) fantasy structuring
> our social reality itself.
> —Slavoj Žižek, *The Sublime Object of Ideology*

*A*s the words *ideological* and *fantasies* in the title suggest, this is an argument
for the continued importance of thinking Marxism and psychoanalysis together
in the conjunction of "queer"—insofar as it references sex, desire, and subjectivity—and "capital." Both, within a certain Western tradition, are preoccupied
with understanding how ideology—itself, in Marxist and post-Marxist domains
of thinking, belonging to the order of "fantasy"—fashions subjectivities, whether
they be collective (the concern of Marxism) or individual (the concern, traditionally, of psychoanalysis). By revisiting a textual scene in the genealogy of capitalism
where commodity fetishism—the locus of Slavoj Žižek's redefinition of ideological
fantasy—makes its appearance as a rhetorical construction, I hope to show how
ideology works phantasmically to "eternalize" or "universalize" historical contingency, even as the historicization of this fantasy (its relegation to the "origins" of
kinship and exchange) conceals the repeated return of the same in late capitalism.
Commodity fetishism is the name of one of the most explicit figural convergences
of psychoanalysis and Marxism, and its critical genealogy is haunted by spectral
appearances of gender, sexuality, and racialization. What I want to focus on is how
a particular—and multiply displaced—subjectivity inhabits the scene of commodity fetishism and how commodity fetishism structures and marks not only the
objects but also the subjects of exchange, creating "real abstractions" that have
not ceased to perform their ideological work.

GLQ 18:1
DOI 10.1215/10642684-1422134
© 2011 by Duke University Press

Louis Althusser's writings on psychoanalysis constitute one of the most interesting Western Marxist efforts to engage psychoanalysis and Marxism. For
Althusser—whose most famous intervention in post-Marxist thought examines
the ideological construction of the subject and the relation between ideology and
modes of production—the ability to coarticulate, if not mutually implicate, the
two analytics seems crucial in order to theorize the relation between subjectivity and social relations under capitalism.[1] In "On Marx and Freud" Althusser
explores the commonalities between what he calls "two unprecedented and totally
unforeseeable discoveries [that] completely upset the universe of cultural values of
the 'classical age,' that of the rise and settling into power of the bourgeoisie," the
work of Karl Marx ("historical materialism") and the work of Sigmund Freud ("the
unconscious").[2] Both theories are, in Althusser's minimalist definition, materialist, since Marx and Freud both rejected idealist notions of the primacy of consciousness and its privileged relation to knowledge. They both produce necessarily "conflictual" and "scissionist" sciences insofar as they target what bourgeois
ideology most seeks to conceal and what positivist objectivity (one of the classic
liberal definitions of "science") most denies, its partisanship in a certain understanding of reality, in other words, its ideological character.

For Althusser, what links Freud's theory most directly to Marx's is the calling into question of "man" as a subject unified by consciousness and the concomitant decentering of that autonomous unified subject: "the ideology of man
as a subject whose *unity* is ensured or crowned by consciousness is not just any
fragmentary ideology; it is quite simply *the philosophical form of bourgeois ideology* that has dominated history" (114).[3] Marx displaced the individual from the
self-determining center or source of social relations and economic processes by
specifying that "individuals must be considered as *supports* (*Träger*) of *functions*"
in capitalism—and not "*the* (originary) *subjects* (as ultimate causes) of the entire
economic or historical process" (118). In Althusser's reading, Marx "abandoned
the bourgeois ideological myth that thought the nature of society as a *unified* and
centered whole [the macrocosmic expansion of this notion of the autonomous subject of history] in order to think every social formation as a system of instances
without center" (121). Thus what both theories provide, in part, are ways to
think about the material fragmentation of the subject in modernity. Where they
diverge, according to Althusser, or where, perhaps, the problem of bridging the
gap between them arises is in Marx's focus on social relations and the absence of
something like a "theory of the psyche," on the one hand, and Freud's inability to
extend his analysis of the individual to social relations or society more generally,
on the other (118).

In an earlier essay, "On Freud and Lacan," Althusser elaborates on the possibilities for extending psychoanalysis to social relations, an extension that finds some of its more developed implications in the work of Fredric Jameson and Žižek and sheds light on what motivates his efforts to combine these theories in "Ideology and Ideological State Apparatuses."[4] Althusser's Lacan turns Freudian psychoanalysis into a science with an object: the unconscious and its effects, which include the process of becoming human. In Althusser's understanding, Lacan demonstrates that the transition from biological being to human existence is effected through the "Law of Culture" (the Symbolic or the Oedipus complex) and that the formal properties of this law are those of language.[5] This redescription— resembling Marx's redefinition of history in *The German Ideology* as the ordinary and daily ways humans, by transforming nature, produce life—allows Althusser to conduct a powerful and eloquent defense of psychoanalysis as a material history of how the species becomes human and survives.[6]

Jameson works through many of Althusser's arguments in exploring the implications of Lacan's linguistically (and imagistically) oriented theory for a way to understand where "subjectivity" and "collectivity" might find their points of analytic coincidence.[7] He suggests that Lacanian theory allows for reconceptualizing the relation between the psychoanalytic and the social such that the "individual" and "the collective" are no longer the binary terms of opposition; instead, the discontinuities of lived experience might be brought into relation within a single system (349). Jameson painstakingly details how it is that language, and the domain of the signifier more generally, is both social—intersubjective—and alienating, even as it also constitutes a subject as such. He argues that what Lacanian psychoanalysis can contribute to Marxism is a "materialistic philosophy of language," since "the chief defect of all hitherto existing materialism is that it has been conceived as a series of propositions about matter . . . rather than as a set of propositions about language" (389). For Jameson, the Imaginary's structuration of spatial relations among objects and the rivalrous aggressivity that is introduced, before the subject, in the alienating relation between self and other, when further abstracted into the Symbolic's registers of linguistic alienation (thus not only situating the ego "in a fictional direction" but also describing the "incommensurability of the subject with its narrative representations"[381]), provide the contours of what a Marxist theory of the subject in ideology, begun but incompletely formulated by Althusser, would be.

Jameson revises both Althusser's deployment of Lacanian theory and Lacan's theory itself most decisively in his *historical* materialist conceptualization of the Real. Like Althusser, who defends the materialism of psychoanalysis by not-

ing that it posits a material reality outside consciousness that consciousness cannot completely grasp, Jameson argues that Lacanian psychoanalysis affirms "the
persistence, behind our representations, of that indestructible nucleus of . . . the
Real" (387), though "behind" is not quite accurate, even in Jameson's characterization, since he points out that it is both "indistinguishable" from the other orders
and independent of them, whence the notion of an asymptotic relation to the Real
as a limit-term for what "resists symbolization absolutely" (388–89). This means
that psychoanalysis, like Marxism, retains a conception of the referent; that referent, though, for Jameson, is "History itself" (384). This is nevertheless a conception of history influenced by Lacan's Real insofar as it is what cannot be captured
by representation and whose narratives can only "approximate it in asymptotic
fashion" (388–89). Thus, for Jameson, history occupies that "traumatic kernel"
within representation that cannot itself be represented. It is, as he says elsewhere,
what hurts.[8]

Jameson concludes that what Marxism requires is a theory of the subject
and its relation to ideology beyond Althusser's Lacanian model. Lacan provides,
for Jameson, a way to analyze a subject's *structural* relation to historical processes
through language and thus a way to theorize "an ideology of the collective" (395).
This would enable the analysis of the "post-individualistic experience of the subject" through a decentering of consciousness that would, as Althusser argued,
"liquidate" bourgeois individualism's remaining ideological grip (382): "The ideological representation must rather be seen as that indispensable mapping fantasy
or narrative by which the individual subject invents a "lived" relationship with
collective systems which otherwise by definition exclude him insofar as he or she
is born into a pre-existent social form and its pre-existent language" (394).

Žižek elaborates on this "mapping fantasy or narrative" when he develops Lacan's remark that Marx invented the symptom by linking the structure and
processes of commodity fetishism to those of the symptom.[9] Rather than Jameson's formulation of ideology as something that a subject *invents* (and here Jameson's language continues to reproduce his Marxist existentialist formation, even
though he has already argued that ideology — that mapping fantasy — cannot be
the deliberative invention of a subject), Žižek draws attention to the structuring
and externalizing role of form in both Marx's and Freud's analyses. For Žižek,
working through the arguments of Alfred Sohn-Rethel, the double abstraction
of the commodity-form — its abstraction from use-value and its abstraction, as
money, from the concrete sensuous properties of the particular commodity itself —
produce, as "the social effectivity of the market" (17), the "real abstraction" that
gives rise to the form of abstract thought but is not itself that thought (19). The

form that consciousness takes therefore is already articulated externally, in the Symbolic order, and is, for Žižek, "one of the possible definitions of the unconscious" (19). If the abstraction of thought is a result of the abstraction at work effectively in the practice of market exchange, then ideology is not located in the subject but in "reality itself" (21). This is, for Žižek, Marx's definition of the symptom. When intersubjective relations become social relations between things, when the relations of domination and servitude between people — a fetishism of persons — become defetishized and transferred to the social relation between commodities as things of value, this gives rise to the (hysterical) symptom of capitalism (26). This social symptom is a fissure in an ideological field that is, at the same time, like the Derridean supplement, necessary to that field's constitution (21). The logic is, however, more strictly fetishistic in the psychoanalytic sense than in the sense of reification alone, for it operates according to the famous Mannonian characterization of disavowal as "I know very well, but nevertheless."[10] "Knowledge," then, is not what is really at issue for Žižek. He points out that subjects in capitalism know very well that "money is in reality just an embodiment, a condensation, a materialization of a network of social relations" (31), but argues that "in their social activity itself, in what they are *doing*, they are *acting* as if money, in its material reality, is the immediate embodiment of wealth as such. They are fetishists in practice, not in theory"(31). This is what Žižek calls the "ideological fantasy":

> What they do not know is that their social reality itself, their activity, is guided by an illusion, by a fetishistic inversion. What they overlook, what they misrecognize, is not the reality but the illusion which is structuring their reality, their real social activity. They know very well how things really are, but still they are doing it as if they did not know. The illusion is therefore double: it consists in overlooking the illusion which is structuring our real, effective relationship to reality. And this overlooked, unconscious illusion is what may be called the *ideological fantasy*. (33)

Whether or not this represents a difference from the Althusserian position (it could be argued that Althusser says as much, albeit in different language), it helps clarify the subjective/objective binary that seems so often to separate psychoanalytic conceptualizations of subjectivity and the question of collective ideology. For example, in Žižek's Lacanian reading of Marx's commodity fetishism, where relations between people take the form of social relations between things, the point is not that the commodity-exchangers believe in the relation among commodities as objects of equivalent exchange-value but that the commodities themselves "believe" (34–35). This is Marx's famous anthropomorphization of commodities whereby commodity-exchangers become "mere personifications" of the commodities that are entering into relation with each other: "The persons exist for one another merely as representatives of, and, therefore, as owners of, commodities. In the course of our investigation we shall find, in general, that the characters who appear on the economic stage are but the personifications of the economical relations that exist between them."[11] Belief, too, is externalized and materialized in effective social activity.

Žižek's translation into "reality" and history of the terms of psychoanalytic subjectivity, his argument that the subject is phantasmically structured by capitalism's processes, and Jameson's description of language's crucial structuring mediation whereby subjectivity can be understood, via Lacan, to be a social relation— riven by the unassimilable Real—suggest possible techniques for bringing the kind of psychoanalytic understanding of subjectivity Althusser argued for to bear on a Marxist theory of the subject in ideology.[12] They suggest ways to read symptomatically the ideological fantasies articulated within the domain of linguistic subjectivity and to designate, as "limit terms" (to use Jameson's expression), the Real of the subject's desire as the "traumatic kernel" that the ideological fantasy seeks to efface.[13]

For Jameson, that Real is history; for Žižek, ideology's most cunning procedure is to overhistoricize, and that "if over-rapid universalization produces a quasi-universal Image whose function is to make us blind to its historical, socio-symbolic determination, over-rapid historicization makes us blind to the real kernel which returns as the same through diverse historicizations/symbolizations" (50):

> Let us take one of the commonplaces of the Marxist-feminist criticism of psychoanalysis, the idea that its insistence on the crucial role of the Oedipus complex and the nuclear-family triangle transforms a historically conditioned form of patriarchal family into a feature of the universal human condition: is not this effort to historicize the family triangle precisely an attempt to elude the "hard kernel" which announces itself through the "patriarchal family" . . . ? (50)

Žižek produces a symptomatic example of overhistoricization in this passage. Marxist feminism, in his view, critiques psychoanalysis for its universalization of the historical patriarchal family into the Oedipus complex and the Freudian nuclear family triangle. He suggests that this is feminism's attempt to "elude the 'hard kernel,' the Real of the Law, the rock of castration" (50).[14] But from the structural perspective of the analysis of commodity fetishism in Marx, the relation of "patriarchy" to "the family"—which, historically speaking, must in some way inform "the rock of castration," even in psychoanalytic accounts—is not strictly speaking a matter of historical contingency in the sense Žižek means. His own analysis of the objectifying and externalizing into abstract thought of the practice of commodity exchange suggests this, as does, within the Marxist tradition itself, Friedrich Engels's treatise on the family.[15]

Feminists such as Gayle Rubin and Luce Irigaray, working in part through Claude Lévi-Strauss's anthropological argument that women were the first exchanged goods, articulate the abstractions—material and psychic—that arise from such a set of concrete "historical" conditions.[16] Irigaray's commentary on the first chapter of *Capital*, volume 1 for example, enables a reading of commodity fetishism as founding a fantasy of symbolic exchange on the contradiction between "things" and "people" congealed in that exchange.[17] She argues that commodity exchange in Marx takes its form from the exchange of women, which ultimately results in a symbolic edifice dividing subjects and objects along the lines of sexual difference. Thus ideologies of sexual difference enable commodity fetishism, and commodity exchange, in turn, structures, as a "real abstraction," conceptions of sexual difference.[18] In this work, and that of many Marxist feminists on the relation between the "traffic in women" and capital, what may be said to constitute the blindness of "over-rapid historicization" is not the effort to understand how sexual difference and capitalism interact historically but the supersessionary narrative that often accompanies the discussion of origins (which came first, patriarchy or capitalism?) and the cause-effect relation between the two. Jameson's effort to reconcile diachrony with synchronous symbolic arrangements is instructive here, for although he argues that patriarchy is archaic, he insists on its structural coexistence with both early and late forms of capitalism:

> The analysis of the ideology of form . . . should reveal the formal persistence of . . . archaic structures of alienation—and the sign systems specific to them—beneath the overlay of all the more recent and historically original types of alienation—such as political domination and commodity reification—which have become the dominants of that most complex of all cultural revolutions, late capitalism, in which all the earlier modes of production in one way or another structurally coexist. The affirmation of radical feminism, therefore, that to annul the patriarchal is the most radical

political act—insofar as it includes and subsumes more partial demands, such as the liberation from the commodity form—is thus perfectly consistent with an expanded Marxist framework, for which the transformation of our own dominant mode of production must be accompanied by an equally radical restructuration of all the more archaic modes of production with which it structurally coexists.[19]

Further, in Rubin's imagining of a prohibited (or foreclosed) sexual desire preceding the sexual difference on which Lévi-Strauss builds his theory of the incest prohibition and its setting in motion of the first exchange-economy, the question arises of a theory of desire that is not necessarily sutured exclusively to the sexual difference on which both Jameson and Žižek's psychoanalytic Marxism depends.[20] For Rubin, it is also a question of historical priority, but it is possible to understand all of these arguments as naming an ideological fantasy that realizes itself in a certain determinate, externalized form. That commodity fetishism might include not only a certain phantasmic relation to objects but also, through the foreclosure or prohibition Rubin notes with regard to economies of exchange, to the subjects of exchange, suggests ways that queer desires may be said to animate the scene of capital.

To locate a figure for commodity fetishism, where sexual difference, sexuality/desire, and commodity-exchange converge, I turn to an early modern Italian treatise on the family, Leon Battista Alberti's *Della Famiglia*, a work that documents—as family portrait—a merchant-capitalist corporation based in kinship.[21] Composed as a fictional dialogue by one of the greatest Renaissance humanists of his day in the domain of visual and architectural theory, *Della Famiglia* explicitly stages discursive/ideological conflict among the (masculine) subjects of this family corporation. On this level, it illustrates Jameson's argument about the relation between cultural texts and ideology, that "the production of aesthetic or narrative form is . . . an ideological act . . . with the function of inventing imaginary or formal 'solutions' to unresolvable social contradictions."[22] Here these contradictions center directly on kinship as the organizing structure for emergent capitalism.

Della Famiglia is divided into four books: the first on generations (elders and children), the second on the wife ("De re uxoria"), the third on household management ("Economicus"), and the fourth on friendship ("De Amicitia"). In the prologue to the third book, the narrator explains that while the second book focused on young men and the criteria for selecting a wife, the third now deals with how to be a proper paterfamilias and the principles of good management

(154). It is, as the narrator also notes, an "imitation" of Xenophon's *Oeconomicus*, and it is precisely in the differences between these texts that the specificity of the early modern subject of capitalism—in contrast with ancient Greece—emerges.[23] Elsewhere I have argued that this chapter negotiates the divide between public and private, responding to the tension—occasioned partly by the political exile of the Albertis from Florence—between the values of a virilizing and public civic humanism modeled on ancient Greece and Rome and those, viewed as effeminizing in their private and domestic concerns, of mercantile endeavor.[24] This struggle between opposed values takes the form of a contradictory and symptomatic division of household labor by sex that plays itself out in the figure of the woman or wife.[25] Much could be said here about class struggle as a relation between the sexes, especially given the difference between Xenophon's context—where there is a slave economy and where gender inequality is divinely ordained—and Alberti's, where both incipient capitalism and Christianity collude to produce "freely" exploited (female) labor, but what emerges as the aporetic—and thus symptomatic—contradiction in book 3 is rather the relation between the commodity form and corporeality, the extent to which commodity fetishism is bound up with embodiment, sexuality, and gender.

For Isomachos, who is in dialogue with Socrates about the wife as household manager, the point is to distinguish the wife from the slaves through the question of ownership. Just as in the polis, "'the citizens do not believe that it is sufficient to pass good laws, but they also choose guardians of the laws who, acting in their capacity of supervisors, praise the law-abiding and punish the law-breakers,'" so too the wife is designated "guardian of the household laws" (9.14–15.159) for the sovereign citizen that is her husband. It is in this context that a diatribe against the wearing of cosmetics occurs. In the *Oeconomicus* it is a question of false advertising: Isomachos compares the wife's adornment to lying about his own possessions, if he were, for example, to claim that he has more property—and display counterfeit goods to prove it—than he does. In a dilation of the argument that points to the ambivalence in the discourse on cosmetics, he asserts to his wife that

> "just as the gods have made horses most attractive to horses, cattle to cattle, and sheep to sheep, so human beings consider the human body most attractive when it is unadorned. These tricks might perhaps succeed in deceiving strangers without being detected, but those who spend their whole lives together are bound to be found out if they try to deceive each other." (10.7–8.161)

In another comparison designed to prove his point, he likens his wife's cosmetic enhancement to his own:

> "Should I seem more deserving of your love as a partner in intercourse if I tried to offer my body to you after taking care that it was strong and vigorous and therefore glowing with a genuinely healthy complexion? Or if I presented myself to you smeared with red lead and wearing flesh-colored eye make-up and had intercourse with you like that, deceiving you and offering you red lead to see and touch instead of my own skin?" (10.5–6.161)

In a culture where homosexuality is one of the erotic options, and where feminine gendering of the male body through such enhancements degrades that body but is not unknown to attract men, the comparison offers up both the male and the female body as objects of desire.[26] In encounters between strangers, the text asserts, bodily "disguise," regardless of gender, attracts, but in the course of "use," the "deception" of the allure exposes itself.

In *Della Famiglia*, the diatribe against cosmetics — which takes up far more space than in the *Oeconomicus* and brings into intimate relation the human body, commodification, exchange-value, gender, and sexuality — points toward a social contradiction with regard to the wife's status:

> There was a saint in the room, a very lovely statue of silver, whose head and hands alone were of purest ivory. . . . "My dear wife," I said to her, "suppose you besmirched the face of this image in the morning with chalk and calcium and other ointments. . . . Tell me, after many days of this, if you wanted to sell it, all polished and painted, how much money do you think you would get for it? More than if you had never begun painting it?" "Much less," she replied. "That's right," said I, "for the buyer of the image does not buy it for a coating of paint which can be put on or off but because he appreciates the excellence of the statue and the skill of the artist. You would have lost your labor, then, as well as the cost of those ointments." (214)

The scene maps out nicely the convergence of fetish understood in the anthropological sense (a sacred object, usually figurative, in which a certain magical power inheres) and commodity fetishism, where the exchange-value of a commodity — the product, as the passage acknowledges, of labor — is seen to inhere in the commodity itself, to belong to it.[27] It also enacts a *mise en abîme* of commodification as a doubly gendered logic, targeting both the subject and the object of exchange, for while the labor of the "artist" produces a thing of value, the labor of the woman devalues it, even as her labor of "self-commodification," the narrator asserts, devalues the worth of her own body by "de-naturing" it:

> "But if those poultices could have that effect on ivory . . . you can be sure, my dear wife, that they can do your own brow and cheeks still greater harm. For your skin is tender and delicate if you don't smear anything on it, and if you do it will soon grow rough and flabby. . . . No, you will not be more beautiful with that stuff, only dirty, and in the long run you will ruin your skin." (214)

The aporetic structure of the argument—an encomium of the natural whose paradigmatic illustration is not a woman but a statue—strives to resolve by negating the recognition that the woman's body, which is supposed to be "natural," of use-value only, can be—is, in fact—a commodity with value that participates in a logic of exchange, and that the subject of such exchanges can also be the woman herself. In the passage that immediately follows this one, Giannozzo (the narrator) continues to impress his lesson on his wife by singling out a living example of (self-)commodification:

> "Besides, to make sure she did believe me, I asked her about a neighbor of mine, a woman who had few teeth left in her mouth, and those appeared tarnished with rust. Her eyes were sunken and always inflamed, the rest of her face withered and ashen. All her flesh looked decomposed and disgusting. Her silvery hair was the only thing about her that one might regard without displeasure. So I asked my wife whether she wished she were blond and looked like her?" (215)

On the one hand, an idealized image of an ivory and silver statue, the product of an artist's labor; on the other, a demonized image of a "hag" with chalky skin and silver or blond hair, the product of (failed) self-commodification. Yet even here one element of the image escapes the argument and acknowledges the possibility that the woman's self-commodification may in fact produce value and result in successful "exchange," for Giannozzo admits that the woman's hair—echoing, in its reference to silver as the currency of exchange, the precious metal that makes up the statue's material—does indeed attract. The paradigm of the self-commodifying woman is, of course, the prostitute, where use-value and exchange-value coexist, and it is thus perhaps no accident that the detail referred to is the blond hair, the legally required sign of a woman's status as purchasable from ancient Rome through early modern Italy. The sermon on cosmetics in fact concludes with the concern — also articulated, but without respect to gender, in Xenophon — that the self-commodification that cosmetics represents is about attracting strangers or outsiders.[28]

Several things have happened to the Xenophon subtext: the bodies have multiplied beyond those of the couple, and they are strangely, even contradictorily, hybrid, pointing to what Jameson identifies as the aporia or antinomy designating the place of ideology, "a logical scandal or double bind, the unthinkable and the conceptually paradoxical, that which cannot be unknotted by the operation of pure thought, and which must therefore generate a whole . . . narrative apparatus — the text itself — to square its circles" (82–83). A splitting occurs, like the split Irigaray argues produces, in capitalism, three bodies for "woman": the wife/mother (use-value; private property), the daughter (commodity/exchange-value), and the whore (use-value and exchange-value).[29] Cosmetics are no longer a matter of sexual attraction but a question of exchange-value: the woman's body has become — at least presumptively — commodified as an object of exchange. The body has also become a thing — it has been reified into the sacralized body of a statue. The text, by virtue of the comparison (saintly statue to female body), transforms a social relation into a relation between the commodity and its world of exchange. Like the "immaterial corporality" Žižek identifies as constituting the sublime body of money — its durable, immutable character as material abstraction — the human (woman's) body has become a sublime object, composed of precious metal and hard ivory.[30]

All the ingredients of Irigaray's analysis thus find their figuration here, lending confirmation to her argument about the isomorphism between capitalism and the traffic in women. The narrative transforms the relation between husband and wife — the center of the *oikos* — into a relation between producer-exchanger and commodity: the wife is a "perfect mother for [the] household," partly through her "nature" but mostly through the labor the husband expends in her "instruction" (208). That commodity, however, is haunted by Pygmalion's dilemma, figured by the binary images of the idealized, immobile ivory and silver statue and the excessively mobile white-skinned silvery-haired female neighbor.[31] If the ideological fantasy consists in acting "as if" commodities embody value and have worth, it is a fantasy that masks a desire to transform those commodities into proxy subjects who will "believe" for their exchangers and the uneasy recognition that these commodities may indeed have a subjectivity and an agency of their own.[32]

So far I have described the disavowed transformation of the body of the wife into a commodity and the accompanying contradictions that transformation produces: an acknowledgment of the commodity's abstract exchange-value and, simultaneously, the desire to "produce" the wife as something "natural," accompanied by the recognition that the commodity in question has a subjectivity, capable of extracting a value from its body that escapes the control of its producer-exchanger. But what has happened to the masculine subject in this process, he whose body (and value) is so prominently displayed in Xenophon's version of this queer economic arrangement of subjects and goods? In Alberti's text, the body of the husband has disappeared. How—and why—does this phallic economy *dis*embody its (masculine) subjects of exchange?

Jean-Joseph Goux's "archeology of phallocentrism" has linked the Lacanian phallus to money through the abstraction of body into form; he argues that a mythic or archaic renunciatory logic inhabits the access to phallic power whereby the initiation into (masculine) subjectivity is effected through a "cutting off" or detachment from corporeality.[33] For Goux, like Lacan, "there is no value or sense without a preliminary loss of something else, never identical, that tends to compensate for, to replace, to sublate" (44), although he will argue that Western philosophy effaces the loss in an idealizing valorization of the compensatory abstraction. That loss, and its compensation in symbolic/abstract power and value, is what his argument traces in a Lévi-Straussian genealogy of phallocracy as initiating symbolic economies of exchange (of goods, and signs) through the "originary" exchange of women:

> *Man is the giver, woman is the gift. Man is the exchanger, women is the exchanged.* Such is the principle of this archi-economy which is the basis for all economies (*oikos*: the household). The position of the exchanging subject, in opposition to the objects of the exchange (which are themselves people), marks a place, a function, which is not that of the "subject" whose aporias transcendental philosophy explores, but which may involve the essence of the subject's symbolic site. . . . Here we approach the originally sexed archi-exchange from which the exchange in general, including the economic one, can be conceived. (65)

For Goux, if men are in the position of agents of exchange in archaic kinship arrangements, while women act as objects of this exchange, then "it would be archaically, as a *male* subject, and in a close relationship to the phallic simulacrum, that the subject would constitute itself" (64), suggesting thus that the place of the subject in the Symbolic is archeologically marked—that is, in its originarily economic/ideological constitution — as masculine. For Goux, this process is effected through a double renunciation mandated, as he says, by the "generational constraints of sexual dimorphism" (65): a man must give up or "negate" his attachment to the mother while preserving a desire for the feminine (a negation of a negation). But this exchange-economy is further abstracted, becoming virtual; the incest prohibition the negation formalizes rests, as Lévi-Strauss remarks, on a "fiduciary guarantee" rather than a one-to-one exchange, such that "the masculine agent must consent to a sacrifice to which his returns . . . correspond only virtually and abstractly. The two terms of the transaction [renunciation of the mother and the acquisition of another woman] are completely dissociated and there is never in fact any socially recognizable reciprocity" (67).[34] The archi-economy of exchange becomes therefore a "real abstraction": "What remains is subjection to a universal law, a symbolic order which is the same for all, and to which the subject must submit. This symbolic order arises from the interiorization of certain demands which are no longer experienced as social demands, and above all not as the demands of a social *exchange*" (67).[35]

This abstract subjection (a renunciatory sacrifice) installs the regime of the phallus — a "monastic, celibate attestation of the detachment of 'matter' and 'nature' which guarantees integrity, identity, unity" (68) — as pure mediation, finding its counterpart in the regime that installs money as the general equivalent and renders exchange-value autonomous through money's "sublime body."[36] Thus, like Irigaray, Goux links the "problem" of the real abstraction of the exchange of women both to Lacan's Symbolic and to Marx's discussion of money as the general equivalent, conjoining them in a "symbolic economy."[37]

Goux's "mythic" genealogy goes a long way toward defining the psychoanalytic subject and the subject of ideology as an originarily masculine one constituted within an economy of exchange centered on sexual difference. Thus he is able, "anthropologically" as it were, to bring together sexual difference and commodity-exchange into a single system and to address the "real abstraction" deriving from the peculiar transformation of human goods into commodities that Irigaray and other Marxist feminists have so thoroughly critiqued.[38] For Goux, this sacrifice, this renunciation, refers back to incestuous heterosexuality, the male subject's originary attachment to the mother (and the sister). But the castigation involved in the abstraction from matter to ideality, the disappearance of the penis and the emergence of the phallus, testifies to a self-sacrifice that is made insufficiently apparent by the terminological distinctions of kinship positions (son, mother, sister). As Irigaray notes, the sacrifice may be articulated somewhat differently: "There is a price to pay for being the agents of exchange: male subjects have to give up the possibility of serving as commodities themselves."[39]

Alberti's text, in its proximity to and distance from Xenophon, suggests then another component of the abstraction into phallic mediation, for what is lost is the male body itself as an object of desire. What is abstracted, sublated into the body of the statue/woman, is the corporeality of the masculine subject, so that "he" disappears even as he becomes the agent of exchange. Indeed, in its displacement of the (male) body and its imagistic excess, the text confirms Jameson's speculation about the libidinal investment in commodities effected by the Imaginary's visual and objectal structuring: "The affective valorization of these objects ultimately derives from the primacy of the human *imago* in the mirror stage; and it is clear that the very investment in an object world will depend in one way or another on the possibility of symbolic association or identification of an inanimate thing with the libidinal priority of the human body."[40] Thus this scene of commodity fetishism in Alberti's text is itself fetishistic: the statue — "sacred," monumentalized, rigidified — memorializes the lost body of the subject; it is the repository of that loss, its "value."

Fetishism is, of course, the sign of a desire; for Freud, it is the desire to restore the missing maternal penis, in an oscillatory movement of disavowal, where the subject both knows and chooses to deny the absence the fetish replaces.[41] Although for Freud fetishism acts as a defense against the "horror" of castration for the male subject and the recognition that women are themselves "lacking it," Alberti's text suggests a rather different scenario, one that Freud points to but does not pursue:

> The penis is no longer the same as it once was. Something else has taken its place, has been appointed its successor, so to speak, and now absorbs all the interest which formerly belonged to the penis. But this interest undergoes yet another very strong reinforcement, because the horror of castration sets up a sort of permanent memorial to itself by creating this substitute. . . . One can now see what the fetish achieves and how it is enabled to persist. It remains a token of triumph over the threat of castration and a safeguard against it; it also saves the fetishist from being a homosexual by endowing women with the attribute that makes them acceptable as sexual objects.[42]

The intertextual transformation that results in a valuable statue of a saint as the becoming-commodity of an objectified body may very well memorialize castration, but it does so as a sacrifice of corporeality, a castigation of matter resulting in the erection of an ideal "image" in its place, as the movement from the bloody red ointment and "flesh colored" cosmetics on Isomachos's body to the pristine metal and ivory white of Giannozzo's statue suggests.[43] The sacrifice that abstracts matter, sublating it into the sublime body of value in the image of the phallus, "saves" the subject, as it were, from "homosexuality," or rather from the libidinal investment in its own body as an object of desire, one that is available for (self-)commodification (and thus for consumption) and that is also, like the "real" woman — a monstrous contrary of the statue — subject to decay. Indeed, the figure of the "hag," while serving as evidence that female self-commodification fails to install value in the commodity, exposes the sublimity of value to the "use" of corporeal embodiment, articulating the "knowledge" ("I know very well . . .") that occupies the other pole of the oscillatory movement of fetishism, even as its accompanying ambivalence continues to be expressed in the fetish of the silver hair.

The disavowal or "split knowledge" of this text (a knowledge that is not the subject's) consists then in the fantasy according to which a transmuted corporeality inhabits the commodity as value (this in compensation for a loss of the body as object of consumption or use-value) and the uneasy and intermittent recognition — figured by the aporetic commodity-woman, who oscillates between subject and object, exchanger and exchanged, subjectivity and corporeality — that the body of the commodity is really two bodies, one of which is consumed in use. The name of this split, these figures tell us — or rather point to as the place of the impossible Real — is sexual difference, a "real abstraction" whose form is (symptomatically) fetishistic.

Leo Bersani has argued that what may constitute the distinctiveness of male homoerotic subjectivity is the desire to be consumed in a self-shattering jouissance; "self-shattering," he writes, "is intrinsic to the homo-ness in homosexuality."[44] He muses that homosexual desire may be what permits the possibility of a reciprocity that resists the annihilative effacement of the other. "Can a masochistic surrender," he asks, "operate as effective (even powerful) resistance to coercive designs?"[45] If the masculine subject of ideology in this scene of commodity fetishism's investment in sexual difference may be understood to be, in some sense, constitutive in its renunciation of corporeality and its sublation into value in the body of the commodity, then it might be argued that it is also, and constitutively so, straight in its symptomatic avoidance of the embodiment that would make it vulnerable to consumption and use.[46] For Irigaray, of course, the subjectivity of the commodity is precisely what would permit a different symbolic and economic regime to obtain, one not based on the social reality of abstract exchange-value, and in "When the Goods Get Together" she imagines a lesbian utopia that does not split exchangers from exchanged, subjects from objects.[47] She also writes that in this homosocial symbolic system, where the agents of exchange are marked as masculine and the goods exchanged are marked as feminine, masculine homosexuality is proscribed because it disrupts this exchange relation.[48] "Furthermore," she writes, "Once the penis itself becomes merely a means to pleasure, pleasure among men, the phallus loses its power," since it is precisely the absence of that corporeality, its sublation, that the phallus represents.[49]

The fetishistic illusion—social reality—that governs capitalist exchange does not dissolve for being analyzed, abstracted recursively as it is into multiple symbolic domains. That commodity fetishism is intimately bound up with sexual difference, desire, and the disavowal of the subject's corporeality, its status as desiring and desired object, is a way to name a symptom of that social reality articulated in the ideological fantasy figured in and exposed by Alberti's text. This fantasy, and the abstraction into form that sexually marked commodity fetishism effects, appear as universal and eternal in the abstract symbolic systems to which they give rise, yet they are historical and historically contingent, dependent upon a convergence of modes of production with kinship systems. At the same time, the historicization of relations of exchange, their location in the "archaic" kinship systems that anthropology studies, may work to obscure the return of the same— heteronormative phallocracy—in capitalism, early and late, and in the symbolic and philosophical systems into which it is abstracted.

Notes

1. Louis Althusser, "Ideology and Ideological State Apparatuses (Notes toward an Investigation)," in *Lenin and Philosophy, and Other Essays by Louis Althusser*, ed. and trans. Ben Brewster (New York: Monthly Review Press, 1971).

2. Louis Althusser, *Writings on Psychoanalysis: Freud and Lacan*, ed. Olivier Corpet and François Matheron, trans. Jeffrey Mehlamn (New York: Columbia University Press, 1996), 106. Hereafter cited in the text.

3. "Since Marx, we have known that the human subject, the economic, political, or philosophical ego, is not the 'center' of history—we have even known . . . that history has no 'center' but possesses a structure that has a necessary 'center' solely in ideological misprision. Freud in turn reveals to us that the real subject, the individual in his singular essence, does not have the form of a self centered in an 'ego,' 'consciousness,' or 'existence'—be it the existence of the for-itself, the body proper, or 'behavior'—that the human subject is decentered, constituted by a structure that, too, has a 'center' solely in the imaginary misprision of the 'ego,' that is, in the ideological formations in

which it 'recognizes' itself" (Louis Althusser, "On Freud and Lacan," in *Writings on Psychoanalysis*, 31).

4. Althusser, "On Freud and Lacan," 13–32.

5. Althusser, "On Freud and Lacan," 25. "What is the *object* of psychoanalysis? It is that *with which* analytic technique has to deal . . . the 'effects,' prolonged in the surviving adult, of the extraordinary adventure that, from birth to the liquidation of the Oedipus complex, transforms a small animal engendered by a man and a woman into a little human child" (22).

6. "Since we are dealing with the Germans, who do not postulate anything, we must begin by stating the first premise of all human existence, and therefore of all history, the premise namely that men must be in a position to live in order to be able to 'make history.' But life involves before everything else eating and drinking, a habitation, clothing and many other things. The first historical act is thus the production of the means to satisfy these needs, the production of material life itself. And indeed this is an historical act, a fundamental condition of all history, which to-day, as thousands of years ago, must daily and hourly be fulfilled merely in order to sustain human life" (Karl Marx and Friedrich Engels, *The German Ideology, parts I and II*, ed. R. Pascal [New York: International Publishers, 1967], 16). Althusser writes: "Psychoanalysis . . . is concerned with a different struggle, in the sole war without memoirs or memorials, which humanity pretends never to have fought, the one it thinks it has always won in advance, quite simply because its very existence is a function of having survived it, of living and giving birth to itself as culture within human culture. This is a war that, at every instant, is waged in each of its offspring, who, projected, deformed, rejected, each for himself, in solitude and against death, have to undertake the long forced march that turns mammalian larvae into human children, that is, *subjects*" ("On Freud and Lacan," 23).

7. Fredric Jameson, "Imaginary and Symbolic in Lacan: Marxism, Psychoanalytic Criticism, and the Problem of the Subject." *Yale French Studies* 55–56 (1977): 338–95.

8. "History is what hurts, it is what refuses desire and sets inexorable limits to individual as well as collective praxis" (Fredric Jameson, *The Political Unconscious: Narrative as a Socially Symbolic Act* [Ithaca: Cornell University Press, 1981]), 102. See also "History . . . is not a text, for it is fundamentally non-narrative and nonrepresentational; what can be added, however, is the proviso that history is inaccessible to us except in textual form, or in other words, that it can be approached only by way of prior (re)textualization" (82).

9. Slavoj Žižek, *The Sublime Object of Ideology* (London: Verso, 1989), 11–53. Hereafter cited in the text.

10. Octave Mannoni, "'Je sais bien, mais quand meme . . . ,'" in *Clefs pour l'imaginaire d'une autre scène* (Paris: Seuil, 1969), 9–33. See also Carla Freccero, "Fetishism," in *New Dictionary of the History of Ideas*, vol. 2, ed. Maryanne Cline Horowitz (Detroit: Scribner's, 2005): 826–28.

11. Karl Marx, *Capital*, vol. 1, ed. Frederick Engels, trans. S. Moore and E. Aveling (1967; rpt. New York: International Publishers, 1992), 89.

12. Jameson writes, "We must understand the Lacanian notion of the Symbolic Order as an attempt to create mediations between libidinal analysis and the linguistic categories, to provide, in other words, a transcoding scheme which allows us to speak of both within a common conceptual framework" ("Imaginary and Symbolic," 359).

13. Paraphrasing Lacan, Žižek writes that "'Reality' is a fantasy-construction which enables us to mask the Real of our desire," reality being understood as "an 'illusion' which structures our effective, real social relations and thereby masks some insupportable, real, impossible kernel. . . . The function of ideology is not to offer us a point of escape from our reality but to offer us the social reality itself as escape from some traumatic, real kernel" (*Sublime Object of Ideology*, 45).

14. This is a moment where Žižek opts for a rather parodically ahistorical psychoanalytic framework over a Marxist one and where he adopts a distinctly non-Freudian view of psychic formations that are devoid of historicity.

15. Friedrich Engels, *The Origin of the Family, Private Property, and the State* (Harmondsworth, UK: Penguin Books, 1985).

16. Claude Lévi-Strauss, *The Elementary Structures of Kinship*, ed. Rodney Needham, trans. James Harle Bell and John Richard von Sturmer (Boston: Beacon, 1969); Gayle Rubin, "The Traffic in Women: Notes on the 'Political Economy' of Sex," in *Toward an Anthropology of Women*, ed. Rayna Reiter (New York: Monthly Review Press, 1975): 157–210; Luce Irigaray, *This Sex Which Is Not One*, trans. Catherine Porter (1977; rpt. Ithaca: Cornell University Press, 1985).

17. See "Women on the Market" and "Commodities among Themselves," in Irigaray, *This Sex*, 170–97.

18. Irigaray does not fully explore these implications of her argument, preferring to remark instead that her analysis of women as commodities may be analogical, but that "women are like commodities" may in effect be the analogy that gave rise to Marx's theory of commodities in the first place: "Will it be objected that this interpretation is analogical by nature? I accept the question, on condition that it be addressed also, and in the first place, to Marx's analysis of commodities. Did not Aristotle, a 'great thinker' according to Marx, determine the relation of form to matter by analogy with the relation between masculine and feminine? Returning to the question of the difference between the sexes would amount instead, then, to going back through analogism" (*This Sex*, 174n3).

19. Jameson, *The Political Unconscious*, 100.

20. Rubin argues that in order for a heterosexual incest taboo to pertain there must be a prior taboo against homosexuality. She writes, "The incest taboo presupposes a prior, less articulate taboo on homosexuality. A prohibition against *some* heterosexual unions assumes a taboo against non-heterosexual unions" ("Traffic in Women," 180). See also "Sexual Traffic," interview with Judith Butler, in *differences: A Journal of*

Feminist Cultural Studies 6, nos. 2–3 (1994): 62–99. Butler explores this notion as well, positing a melancholia of gender in heterosexual psychic formations whereby foreclosed (because prohibited) same-sex objects of attachment are incorporated as (heterosexual) gender identifications. See Judith Butler, *Gender Trouble: Feminism and the Subversion of Identity* (1990; rpt. New York: Routledge, 2000); Butler, *The Psychic Life of Power: Theories in Subjection* (Stanford: Stanford University Press, 1997); and Butler, *Antigone's Claim: Kinship between Life and Death* (New York: Columbia University Press, 2000).

21. Renée Neu Watkins, ed. and trans., *The Family in Renaissance Florence: A Translation of I Libri della Famiglia by Leon Battista Alberti* (Columbia: University of South Carolina Press, 1969). Hereafter cited in the text. See also Guido Guarino, ed. and trans., *The Albertis of Florence: Leon Battista Alberti's Della Famiglia* (Lewisburg, PA: Bucknell University Press, 1971).

22. Jameson, *The Political Unconscious*, 79.

23. Xenophon, *Oeconomicus: A Social and Historical Commentary*, trans. Sarah Pomeroy (Oxford: Clarendon, 1994). Hereafter cited in the body of the text, by book, chapter, line. The existence of a specific subtext for Alberti's treatise permits a reading of what Jameson calls *"the ideology of form,"* that is, "the symbolic messages transmitted to us by the coexistence of various sign systems which are themselves traces or anticipations of modes of production" (*Political Unconscious*, 76). The departures from Xenophon's subtext enable an identification of the specificity of the ideological fantasy and its symptoms in Alberti's work.

24. See Carla Freccero, "Economy, Woman, and Renaissance Discourse," in *Refiguring Woman: Perspectives on Gender and the Italian Renaissance*, ed. Marilyn Migiel and Juliana Schiesari (Ithaca: Cornell University Press, 1991), 192–208.

25. See Freccero, "Economy, Woman, and Renaissance Discourse," 199–201, esp. n. 19.

26. David Halperin identifies the *kinaidos*, or passive effeminate male, as a gender category in ancient Greece, identified by his makeup, dress, and bodily style. See David Halperin, *One Hundred Years of Homosexuality and Other Essays on Greek Love* (New York: Routledge, 1990); see also Halperin, *How to Do the History of Homosexuality* (Chicago: University of Chicago Press, 2002).

27. For a historical and anthropological account of the convergence between the fetish and commodity fetishism, see William Pietz, "The Problem of the Fetish II: The Origin of the Fetish," *Res* 13 (1987): 23–45.

28. "'As for outsiders, if you love me, think how could any of them matter more to you than your own husband. Remember, my dear wife, that a girl who tries harder to please outsiders than the one she should be pleasing shows that she loves her husband less than she does strangers'" (Alberti, *Della Famiglia*, 215).

29. Irigaray, *This Sex*, 185–86.

30. Žižek remarks, concerning this aspect of money: "This immaterial corporality of the 'body within the body' gives us a precise definition of the sublime object . . . the indestructible 'body-within-the-body' exempted from the effects of wear and tear is always sustained by the guarantee of some symbolic authority" (*Sublime Object of Ideology*, 18–19).

31. In the Greek myth, Pygmalion finds the women of the world too corrupt and therefore creates a statue of a woman made out of ivory; the statue is so beautiful that he falls in love with it. He prays to Aphrodite, and the statue comes alive. On the one hand, then, Pygmalion does not like women; on the other, he falls in love with the one he himself creates and wants her to be alive. See Ovid, *Metamorphoses*, trans. Rolfe Humphries (1955; rpt. Bloomington: Indiana University Press, 1983), bk. 10, 241–43.

32. Žižek comments, "in the Lacanian perspective ideology . . . designates *a totality set on effacing the traces of its own impossibility*" (*Sublime Object of Ideology*, 49).

33 Jean-Joseph Goux, "The Phallus: Masculine Identity and the 'Exchange of Women,'" *differences: A Journal of Feminist Cultural Studies* 4, no. 1 (1992): 40–75. Hereafter cited in the text.

34. "Sometimes . . . it [exchange] rests on a wider fiduciary guarantee, viz., the theoretical freedom to claim any woman of the group, in return for the renunciation of certain designated women in the family circle, a freedom ensured by the extension of a prohibition, similar to that affecting each man in particular, to all men in general" (Lévi-Strauss, *Elementary Structures of Kinship*, 478–79).

35. This is what, for Žižek, constitutes the surplus enjoyment of the Law: "Althusser speaks only of the process of ideological interpellation through which the symbolic machine of ideology is 'internalized' into the ideological experience of Meaning and Truth: but . . . this 'internalization,' by structural necessity, never fully succeeds, . . . there is a residue, a leftover, a stain of traumatic irrationality and senselessness sticking to it, and . . . *this leftover, far from hindering the full submission of the subject to the ideological command, is the very condition of it*: it is precisely this non-integrated surplus of senseless traumatism which confers on the Law its unconditional authority: in other words, which—in so far as it escapes ideological sense—sustains what we might call the ideological *jouis-sense*, enjoyment-in-sense (enjoy-meant), proper to ideology" (*Sublime Object of Ideology*, 43–44).

36. Žižek, *Sublime Object of Ideology*, 18.

37. See also Jean-Joseph Goux, *Symbolic Economies: After Marx and Freud*, trans. Jennifer Gage (Ithaca: Cornell University Press, 1990).

38. In "Imaginary and Symbolic in Lacan," Jameson seems to separate out the objects "proper to" psychoanalysis and Marxism: "To say that both psychoanalysis and Marxism are materialisms is simply to assert that each reveals an area in which human consciousness is not 'master in its own house': only the areas decentered by each are the quite different ones of sexuality and of the class dynamics of social history" (385),

though in *The Political Unconscious* he seems more willing to understand the relation between the two, much the way Goux, Irigaray, and Rubin argue their intimate
connection.

39. Irigaray, *This Sex*, 193.

40. Jameson, "Imaginary and Symbolic in Lacan," 355. This is yet another way that
    Alberti's text enacts the Pygmalion fantasy, by transforming the subject's artistry into
    a statue that then becomes animate through the subject's desire.

41. Sigmund Freud, "Fetishism (1927)," in *Sexuality and the Psychology of Love*, ed.
    Philip Rieff (New York: Collier, 1963), 204–9. See also Jean Laplanche and Jean-
    Bertrand Pontalis, *The Language of Psycho-Analysis*, trans. Donald Nicholson-Smith
    (New York: Norton, 1973); Mannoni, "'Je sais bien"; and Freccero, "*Fetishism*."

42. Freud, "Fetishism," 206.

43. The work of such feminist psychoanalytic theorists as Elizabeth Grosz, Judith Butler,
    and Teresa de Lauretis has made possible the extension of notions of fetishism to
    scenarios beyond Freud's and suggests that the fetish — in Freud, a "substitute" for
    the missing maternal phallus — can be the material sign of any body part or, indeed,
    a whole body, or a metonym of the body; as de Lauretis, expanding on Sara Kofman's
    observation that the fetish does not substitute for a "real" lack, points out, the fetish
    is the material sign of a desiring fantasy. These theorists, in reworking fetishism for
    lesbian desire, enable a different way to conceptualize masculine fetishism as well.
    See Judith Butler, *Bodies That Matter: On the Discursive Limits of "Sex"* (New York:
    Routledge, 1993); Teresa de Lauretis, *The Practice of Love: Lesbian Sexuality and
    Perverse Desire* (Bloomington: Indiana University Press, 1994); and Elizabeth Grosz,
    "Lesbian Fetishism?" *differences: A Journal of Feminist Cultural Studies* 3, no. 2
    (1991): 39–54. Interestingly, the colors of Xenophon's and Alberti's images, taken
    together, are themselves fetishistic; in medieval romance and elsewhere, the combina-
    tion of red and white is a sign of the (absent) beloved. I am suggesting, rather, that the
    body that is sublated and disappears into exchange value is the body of the subject of
    exchange.

44. Leo Bersani, *Homos* (Cambridge: Harvard University Press, 1995), 101. See also Ber-
    sani, "Is the Rectum a Grave?," *October* 43 (1987): 197–222.

45. Bersani, *Homos*, 99.

46. Bersani's reading of Monique Wittig's *Straight Mind* helpfully illustrates how a par-
    ticular practice can be seen to generate a "real abstraction" in terms compatible with
    this argument. Bersani argues that male heterosexuality can be seen as "a traumatic
    privileging of difference" that results in a "hierarchical attribution of value" (39–40).
    "The straight mind," he writes, "might be thought of as a sublimation of this privileg-
    ing of difference": "The straight mind thinks alone; as the history of philosophy dem-
    onstrates, the thinking of distinctions (that is, philosophical thought) performatively
    establishes the distinctiveness, and the distinction, of the thinker. Distinctiveness

and distinction: the philosophical performance can't help conferring value on itself, for that value is the very sign of its distinctiveness and its defense against an 'outside' dominated by the assumption that the world, the real, can be an object of thought, can be described, measured, known" (*Homos*, 40). See also Monique Wittig, *The Straight Mind and Other Essays* (Boston: Beacon, 1992).

47. "When the Goods Get Together" is an alternate translation of the chapter "Commodities amont Themselves" in Irigaray, *This Sex*, 192–97.

48. Goux makes the point that the position of the subject, in opposition to the object of exchange in this archi-economy, marks "a place, a function" that is not identical with the subject itself but is, rather, "the essence of the subject's symbolic site" ("Phallus," 65). So whereas one might read Irigaray's argument here as gender essentialist, one can also understand "masculine" as the designated term for a position or a site, along the lines Goux suggests.

49. Irigaray, "When the Goods Get Together," 193.

"IF I TURN INTO A BOY, I DON'T THINK I WANT HUEVOS"

Reassessing Racial Masculinities in *What Night Brings*

Lisa Marie Cacho

Dad loved paydays, and after a beer or two, he play-wrestled with me and Corin, then tickled us till we screamed. But the problem was you never knew what would make him mad. One minute he was laughing and playing. Next thing you know, bam! He's lashing across our legs with a doubled belt. I don't even remember what started it.

"Qué chinga! Son-na-va-biche! Marci, I—am—*sick*—and—*tired*—of—*you*—and *Corin*—and your—*pinche*—mierda!"

He liked to yell at us while he hit us.

"I've—*told*—you—time—and—*again* not to do this!"

—Carla Mari Trujillo, *What Night Brings*

*M*arci Cruz is the eleven-year-old queer Chicana/Mexican American protagonist of Carla Trujillo's novel *What Night Brings* (2003).[1] The domestic violence in Marci's home is a "time and *again*" recurring scene that escalates in intensity as the novel progresses, always provoked by only "this." "This" is Marci's queer female masculinity, her gender nonconformity and sexual nonnormativity; "this" is the noncompliant, defiant behavior of her sister, Corin. "This" is both children refusing "time and *again*" to be the good girls they are being raised to be. As Marci indicates, she and Corin are not protected by the economic security Eddie's paycheck should bring. When economic *stability* frames how child abuse is narrated, it complicates reading the violent insistence of patriarchal authority in working-class families of color as an unfortunate, but understandable, consequence of racism and exploitation.

GLQ 18:1
DOI 10.1215/10642684-1422143
© 2011 by Duke University Press

Delinking domestic violence from racialized poverty destabilizes the impulse to depathologize the Chicano patriarch, the Chicana/o family, and Chicana/o culture that aligns *What Night Brings* with critiques of Chicano cultural nationalism, many of which have illustrated that pathologizing nonnormative sexualities and gender deviances has been central to the defense and valorization of the Chicana/o family.[2] This essay considers whether the converse also applies: in what ways might the revaluation of queer bodies and female desire rely on the criminalization of the Chicano patriarch or, more generally, masculinities of color? By utilizing a queer of color analysis, I examine the Cruz family's Easter Sunday to illustrate how Trujillo's novel pathologizes the Chicano father figure and his need for remasculation in part to valorize Chicana female masculinity and its "queer" kin, recalcitrant Chicana femininity.[3] Then, to complicate the revaluation of queerness, femaleness, and nonnormativity as dependent on positioning the Chicano patriarch as the devalued other, I read a tangential moment in the novel that offers a different way to frame relationally devalued Chicana/o masculinities. From these readings, we can gather together alternative frameworks for understanding the violences of capitalist economies, which rely on normalizing heteropatriarchy, enabling us to complicate narratives that rationalize familial violence in cultures of color by overentangling emasculation with abuse and exploitation. I conclude by applying this analytic to a contemporary example: the narrative that positions undocumented immigrants in negative relation to criminalized men of color, often intentionally deployed during the immigrant rights marches of 2006. Political tensions around rights, norms, and social value are crucial for maintaining and concealing the workings of neoliberal capitalism. Thus, we must consider critically how practices of revaluation may unwittingly depend on an/other's criminalization. I argue that a queer of color analysis needs not only to challenge value hierarchies but to do so in ways that actively and purposely unsettle the state-sanctioned logic of social value as the precondition for political empowerment.

The Emaooulation Trap

Roderick Ferguson explains that the gender and sexual diversity within communities of color is partly produced by the needs of capital: "Nonwhite populations were racialized such that gender and sexual transgressions were not incidental to the production of nonwhite labor, but constitutive of it."[4] Capital requires that racial/ethnic groups transgress the ideals of gender (such as women of color working outside the home or across national borders) and the norms of sexuality (such as intimate relations formed outside marriage and reproduction). The US state names such transgressions "deviant" and "un-American" because these identities, relationships, and practices diverge from US ideals of domesticity and respectability, which in turn legitimates race-based legislation and regulations, such as residential segregation, exclusionary immigration laws, or Americanization programs.[5]

For men of color, insecurely underemployed, it is all but impossible to form and comfortably maintain nuclear families. Hence, in some ways, the surplus workforce is literally emasculated.[6] Working-class men of color's income instability necessitates and engenders nonnormative living arrangements, domestic responsibilities, and employment patterns that ensure their families' day-to-day survival is possible without them, normalizing emasculation.[7] As Gloria Anzaldúa writes, "Today's macho has doubts about his ability to feed and protect his family. His 'machismo' is an adaptation to oppression and poverty and low self-esteem."[8] Because restoring normative and socially valued manhood requires restoring gender privilege and sexual power in a socioeconomic system that denies him both, he is left with few remasculating options that would not reaffirm racialized discourses of social and sexual deviancy.

In this context, emasculation functions like a trap for men of color in the working classes. As Marci says, "[Eddie's] always talking about [huevos] like they're what make him special. I don't get it. If I change into a boy, I don't think I want huevos. Why would I want to go walking around with an Achilles heel right in the middle of my crotch?" (158). Because there are so few spaces outside the home for men of color to exercise male privilege over others, emasculating experiences are normalized for men of color; in fact, if men of color exercise male privilege — that is, gender dominance and sexual power — they are constructed as dangerous and deviant. Thus emasculation acts like a "trap" set specifically to ensnare men of color into the criminal justice system via the lure of criminalized activities within illegal economies. To lessen the risk of incarceration, violent remasculating practices often target multiply devalued and usually impoverished persons of color — namely, women, children, queers, and other disempowered men — whose overlapping and intersecting devaluations render them victims of violence but not victims of "crimes."[9]

The Easter Effect

Marci's refusal to perform conventional femininity and respectable domesticity often underlies or prefigures her father's violent outbursts, which are partly provoked by his desire for a household with heteropatriarchal hierarchies: "When Easter came we got new clothes so we could dress up for church. This meant going to J.C. Penny's to find our dresses, with my dad pulling out his charge card to pay. I got a hat, gloves, anklet socks, and patent leather shoes. Mom made me buy them. I don't know what she was thinking. I told her I wanted to wear pants with a Nehru jacket, but she told me she'd die first" (81). Marci's musings expose how family, church, and consumption all rely on the stable categories of sex and gender that her female masculinity threatens to unravel. This is the "Christmas effect" at Easter time, a time "when all the institutions are speaking with one voice."[10] For Eve Sedgwick, the Christmas effect is depressing because "they all — religion, state, capital, ideology, domesticity, the discourses of power and legitimacy — line up with each other so neatly."[11]

Because the one voice of Easter says the same thing, people are already primed to receive its messages, providing working-class Catholic families of color access to readily recognizable signs of respectability. The legibility of Easter (as the "Easter effect") affords families opportunities to counter racial and cultural stereotypes that pathologize nonheteronormative racial formations. In the novel, the Easter effect neatly rests the burden of Easter's propaganda at the patent leather–adorned feet of young girls. These girls' bodies and behaviors are supposed to display their family's normative moral values, sexual propriety, religious devotion, classed aspirations, and cultural respectability. Brand-new Easter outfits for little girls conveniently showcased at church neatly capture all these while also concealing the diverse sexual identities in the home. Because "female morality . . . is one of the few sites where economically and politically dominated groups can construct the dominant group as other and themselves as superior," as Yen Le Espiritu argues, women's sexuality — especially young unmarried daughters' — must be strictly regulated, which has "the effect of reinforcing masculinist and patriarchal power in the name of a greater ideal of national and ethnic self-respect."[12] Patriarchal power claims Easter's one speaking voice. When everything lines up neatly to discipline Marci's and Corin's bodies and behaviors, their father claims the right to explain (and not explain) why this is so: "This day is special, so you two stay in your clothes" (82).

Easter Huevos

Marci and Corin stay in their church clothes while they eat their Easter candy and peel their hard-boiled Easter eggs. In this scene Easter eggs are complexly symbolic. Like their Easter outfits, Easter eggs represent the exchange value of Eddie's labor, but they are also symbolic of his masculine privilege and patriarchal authority (as "huevos"). At the same time, the eggs can stand in for the unpaid labor of social reproduction in the home (as ovum). And in the margins that also frame the scene, the "two chocolate eggs the size of footballs" given to the girls from their presumably gay but also married Uncle Tommy detach human survival from biological reproduction (but not from sex) and reaffix it to pleasure. As Elizabeth Freeman argues, "Queers survive through the ability to invent or seize pleasurable relations between bodies."[13] The ensuing struggle over eating Easter eggs represents these competing systems of value and value practices in the home, exposing the cracks and fissures of the Easter effect, engendered from silencing competing and contradictory values, needs, and epistemologies to speak in one voice and draw neat lines. Although eruptions can take multiple forms and responses, such as co-optation, compromise, and coexistence, in the novel a seemingly banal rupture initiates a violent response.

Corin is playing with her food, eating only the heads of her marshmallow chicks and only the yolks of her Easter eggs. Because she is "so happy with her chocolate egg and Peeps," she is not paying attention to her parents' semicircuitous conversation with each other about Uncle Tommy's queer behaviors with their Catholic priest (83). Eddie is talking derisively about Uncle Tommy and his "special mass" while Marci keeps asking him, "what does jotito mean?" (83). His brother's and daughter's nonheteronormative masculinities are on his mind as among the multiple threats to the presumed social value of his manhood and his family's respectable domesticity, but his violence finds its focus on Corin halfeating her Easter eggs. He tells her, "Mira, in this house, nothing gets wasted. Everything costs me money and it's money I have to bust my ass for. You peel an egg, you eat it. The whole thing. Not just the parts you like" (84). Eating anything less suggests that Corin disrespects and devalues him — all but telling Eddie, he worked for nothing — or worse, telling him that his hard-earned labor bought self-indulgent pleasures for insolent, ungrateful children. Corin says, "But, Dad, I hate the white part. Marci eats it for me anyway" (84). He undoes his belt: "SLAM! The belt came across her mouth. . . . 'Don't forget *I'm* the one in charge,' he said pointing to himself. . . . 'Eat it, goddammit!' He picked up the egg and tried to cram it into Corin's mouth" (85–86). The mouth is important, symbolically and sensually. In analyzing the fragmentation of the Chicana lesbian body in Cherríe Moraga's writing, Yvonne Yarbro-Bejarano writes that "the mouth plays a crucial role in Moraga's sexual/textual project, fusing two taboo activities, female speaking and lesbian sexuality."[14] Eddie shoves huevos down Corin's throat, at once silencing her and forcing her mouth to be receptive to symbols of male sexuality and power — "the dirty egg white was smeared all over her face" (86). Even when the violence subsides and mutates into an apology, Eddie still claims her voice and his right to her forgiveness: "Now tell your daddy you love him" (88). Feeling emasculated, Eddie generates remasculating opportunities.

Corin is not unaware that everything costs Eddie money; she peels her eggs, eats the yolks, and leaves the white parts for Marci. For Marci and Corin, the nutritional value of Easter eggs has nothing to do with all the fun activities that the eggs enable once a year. The girls are literally deconstructing and reconstructing sacred symbols of reproduction and having too much fun while doing so — reflective of Freeman's contention that "making other queers is a social matter."[15] Marci reaches across the table to take her share, saying, "She doesn't like the white part, so I eat it. . . . I like it, so nothing gets wasted" (84). Eddie stops her hand and then slaps it away because for him, the fact that Marci makes sure nothing is wasted does not cancel out Corin's act of wasting. Eddie refuses to see eating as a social matter, intentionally divorcing Corin's wasting from Marci's salvaging because for Eddie eating is reduced to each family member's survival. Food as nutrition and eating as survival define him as the breadwinner, his job as necessary, his labor as essential, and his position in the family as central. For Eddie, pleasure is foreclosed because he imagines having fun not through meaningful relationships but without them: "I work my goddamn ass off day in and day out putting up with all kinds of bullshit just to be here for you guys, give you a little house to live in, and food to eat. . . . I could go away and live an easier life. Have fun. But I don't. I don't. And you know why? Because of *you*. You! Not me. *You*!" (88). Together, the sisters transform the act of eating from something you do to stay alive to something that can make you feel alive, so that eating, survival, and pleasure are inseparable and coconstitutive. In this way, the home, akin to Gayatri Gopinath's analyses, is not only a site of regulation, violence, repression, and discipline. The home, and the kitchen in particular, is the place where "female desire and pleasure [can be] configur[ed] as an infinitely productive and transformative activity that generates and is generated by the literal and metaphoric production and consumption of food."[16] Something as simple as eating can become a "transformative activity" when it destabilizes the heteronormative and patriarchal imperatives of the home and the nuclear family it houses.

Although domestic violence is about reestablishing patriarchal authority, it is not only a displaced response to emasculating work experiences. In this case, abuse is a response to family members' attempts to alter the home and the relations within it by disarticulating paid and unpaid labor from the pleasures it makes possible. I read this disarticulation as an experience of (but not necessarily a practice of) economic emasculation. Being invested in the economic meanings attached to food (as nutrition, sustenance, survival) betrays an investment in the social value assigned to gendered labor through those meanings (as breadwinner, head of household, sole provider), so that the notion that one's labor provides "a little house to live in, and food to eat" literally reads the breadwinner as essential and central to a family's survival. Revaluing and redefining the purpose of food compromises the economic provider's assumed power over his family and somewhat decenters his role within it. Hence, Eddie experiences the girls' pleasure in eating Easter eggs as emasculating because the products of his hard-earned labor are enthusiastically exchanged for female desire and queer pleasures.

Abandonment

If we read Eddie as a trope for the violence of Chicano cultural nationalism when it was/is invested in heterosexism and patriarchy—aggressively subjugating queer and heterosexual Chicanas and Chicanos—then it makes sense that his devaluation is necessary, especially if Trujillo's purpose is to revalue Chicana/o queerness and Chicana feminism as represented by the two daughters. As Lindon Barrett writes, "For value 'negativity is a *resource*,' an essential resource. The negative, the expended, the excessive invariably form the ground of possibilities for value."[17] Heteropatriarchal expressions and practices of Chicano cultural nationalism constitute the "negative resource" that renders legible the social and cultural value of Chicana/o queerness, femininity, and feminism. At the end of the novel, Eddie beats their mother; he hits her across the mouth, too, and keeps hitting her, over and over. Corin grabs his rifle and shoots him. To quote Rodríguez, "shooting the patriarch" symbolizes "the now-common move in Chicano/a and other ethnic studies scholarship to heavy-handedly render cultural nationalism the enemy that inherently generates sexism and homophobia."[18]

In *Urban Triage* James Kyung-Jin Lee offers a different, but related, way to read unforgiveable characters, the younger generations that leave them, and the places they leave behind. As he suggests, literature works in the age of multiculturalism to "teach us how to abandon people."[19] If we read *What Night Brings* as also a coming-of-age narrative that teaches us how to literally leave behind and move beyond the violences of poor and working-class racial/ethnic neighborhoods, then we need to deal with Eddie as also representative of criminalized poor men of color, many of whom, like Eddie, fall for the emasculation trap of racial masculinity. Eddie looks a lot like a stereotype. He epitomizes dominant portrayals of Mexican "machismo," which in American English refers simultaneously to overly aggressive male behaviors, excessive and outdated patriarchal beliefs, and the bodies of Chicano/Latino men. Unfortunately, for men like Eddie, stereotyped figures are easy to abandon because we speak about them as disciplining fictions. Stereotypes, however, are not empty categories that can be disavowed without consequence because they reference the real bodies of individuals of color. For instance, abandoning stereotypical men like Eddie was key to resolving the overaccumulation of surplus labor in the 1970s in California through what Ruth Wilson Gilmore calls the "prison fix."[20] Indeed, what Dylan Rodríguez refers to as the ever-increasing "prison regime" recruits all of us and teaches each and every one of us to abandon men like Eddie.[21] We may need to abandon Eddie, but we also need to figure out alternatives that do not include automatically handing him over to the prison regime.[22]

Perhaps the sad fact of so many locked-away lives is partly why critiquing minority cultural nationalisms' less-than-equal treatment of those who are female, queer, or criminalized is sometimes greeted with ambivalence, nervousness, and defensiveness. The impetus to represent heteropatriarchal relationships and gendered "traditions" as culturally normative not only enables unhealthy addictions to heterosexual privilege but also attempts to decriminalize and depathologize the family of color.[23] As R. Rodríguez notes, heteropatriarchal relationships within communities of color become revalued as naturalized "facts" of cultural traditions while deviations from normative gender and sexual roles become evidence for the devaluing, pathological, and castrating effects of racialized exploitation.[24] The criminalization of Chicano men has been (and continues to be) central to rendering Chicana/o families "deviant," and thus defending the Chicano patriarch has been historically inseparable from and integral to defending the Chicana/o family and disputing dominant critiques of Chicana/o culture.[25] Although queers of all colors have been primarily excluded from mainstream idealizations of family, LGBTQ persons of color are also subjected to the material and psychological violences engendered by the pathologization of families of color. How might queer critiques of cultural nationalism not only reimagine and reinvent the Chicana/o family and its criminalized father figure but also do so in ways that defend both from state violence and abandonment? This is especially important because, as I have been arguing, for revaluing practices to be legible to the American mainstream, they must be relational, so it is important to be mindful of how different persons can become an/other's unintentional "negative resource" even *within* communities and subcultures.[26] On the other hand, if social value is legible only relationally, how can we rethink revaluation's dependence on devaluation?

"Eddie-me"

According to the political theorist Massimo De Angelis, such revaluing and devaluing cycles are products of capital's modes of measurement. De Angelis argues that in today's capitalism the repetitive "busyness" of our lives places actions and social practices under constant scrutiny and never ending re-evaluation "and in thus doing so are *measured*."[27] He believes that this "mode of measurement," which is disciplinary and interiorized, is the "main enemy" of social justice struggles.[28] As such, when capital's value practices are used to measure and influence struggles for social justice (e.g., should we invest our time in this issue? is this protest worth doing?), the "values that have not meshed" (such as racialized respectability vs. racialized queerness) become "points of conflict" and are interpreted as incompatible, so that "one value is outside the other," reinforcing "false polarities" with "false alternatives."[29]

In the novel, a peripheral moment directs us toward how we might begin to deconstruct false polarities that narrate values and political investments as points of conflict, as outside and in "natural" or inherent opposition to one another. While not offering a solution to the problem of relational value practices, the following passage problematizes the assumptions behind the question I posed in the beginning of this essay (does the Chicano patriarch need to be pathologized to valorize queer Chicanas/os?); it does so by literally reimagining Marci and Eddie as potentially one and the same.

> I woke up in the middle of the night after dreaming that I'd turned into a man but through the whole dream I only saw the back of me, never my face. I was happy I was a man because Raquel was in the dream and she was looking at me like she wanted me. This felt good until my face showed and when it did, it was Eddie! I had turned into Eddie! . . . I wish I could have been Superman in my dream, or someone besides Eddie. I would have even been George Reeves with his flat-butt and ham-head, anything besides Eddie. It made me mad that Raquel wanted the Eddie-me. I wish she would have wanted the me-me. (192)

In her dreams Marci detangles her gender identity and her sexual desires from gender norms and sexual conventions, yet she cannot help but reassemble herself into "Eddie-me." She dreams she is both herself and her father, that the boy she sometimes wants to become will grow up to be Eddie, revealing how racialized female masculinities are restrained by the racial male masculinities that already "symbolically align" Marci with her father.[30] Marci's nonnormative masculinity may take on different forms as she grows up, but white masculinity will not be one of them, not even a parody, and not even subconsciously. Her dreams betray that her fears and fantasies are too linked to be distinct, too interdependent to be disconnected: "Eddie-me."

Marci does not dream she is just any boy. Dreaming she is Eddie precludes a romanticized reading of gender nonconformity as inherently radical or transformative. Rather, the passage emphasizes that she still inherits the ways in which Chicano male masculinities signify unproductive and "excessive" masculine impulses that need to be incarcerated by the prison-industrial complex, deported by the border control, contained by US legislation, or disciplined by the US military. Chicana female masculinity might be able to reconfigure Chicana/o masculinities as not needing male born bodies and as detached from sex and sexuality, but Chicana female masculinity may not be able to resignify Chicana/o masculinity as not macho, not sexually deviant, not criminal, and not nonnormative; it might not be able to detach its unsympathetic stigmas from the devalued bodies of color to which Chicano masculinity refers. In other words, she might be able to rework the meanings of the sign and its signifiers, but she cannot erase its incarcerated referent.

At the same time, this reading does not trivialize the importance of reworking racialized masculinity. Reworking racialized masculinity is no small matter. As Jack Halberstam writes, "If we shift the flow of power and influence, we can easily imagine a plethora of new masculinities that do not simply feed back into the static loop that makes maleness plus power into the formula for abuse but that re-create masculinity on the model of female masculinity."[31] When reading racialized male masculinity's influence over and on female masculinity, we might read Eddie-me as representative of the racial limits Marci confronts in reconfiguring masculinity as well as the violent potential within Marci to abuse her loved ones. But when we shift the flow of power and influence from Marci to Eddie, then Eddie-me also needs to be interpreted as Eddie without huevos. When Marci recreates Chicana/o masculinity through the desire for castration ("I'll have to ask God not to include [huevos] when he changes me"), she disarms the emasculation trap of racial masculinity—which in and of itself becomes most legible as a trap when the maleness of racial masculinity is destabilized through a queer of color critique. Hence, Eddie-me is also the potential within Eddie to be something else, a possible answer to Anzaldúa's call that "we need a new masculinity and the new man needs a movement."[32]

As an example of what José Esteban Muñoz terms disidentification,

Eddie-me interrupts the violent racialized, gendered, and sexualized cycles of devaluation and revaluation, interrupting the "static loop" as a capitalist mode of measurement. Muñoz explains that disidentification goes a step beyond decoding privileged messages and meanings by "recycling and rethinking" the codes themselves, such as using deconstructed eggs, huevos, and chocolate footballs "as raw material for representing a disempowered politics or positionality that has been rendered unthinkable."[33] By suturing these relationally defined and devalued "opposites," the social value claims that make each special are canceled out, reworked, and made intelligible. Eddie-me represents the unthinkable position of a politics of racial masculinity premised on willful emasculation and its *pleasures*, of the potential to politicize, in Joon Oluchi Lee's words, "the joys of the castrated boy."[34]

Empowerment and Impotence

I would like to end this essay by applying the methods of analysis explored in reading the novel to examine how these reading practices are relevant beyond the novel and its moment to interrogate how another common, contemporary, and related narrative of racialized economic emasculation might be unpacked and reframed through a queer of color analysis. Mainstream media utilized the 2006 marches for immigrant rights to invoke the narrative of racial emasculation as a way to undermine social activism and naturalize capitalist value practices by figuring impoverished US citizen men of color as in direct competition with undocumented Latina/o immigrants for decent wages and job opportunities. Effective arguments both for and against immigrant rights centered on the nuclear family of color, differing primarily in regard to the role they assigned to men of color—as either the family's main support or its most salient threat. We face a similar limit when we apply a queer of color critique to the tactical use of "family" and "criminality" in contemporary, popular narratives for and against undocumented immigrant rights.

When the demand for immigrant rights is juxtaposed against the high unemployment rates of US citizens of color, it risks romanticizing men of color as the sole and ideal financial provider, which represents the demand for decent wages not only as a privilege of citizenship but also as a gendered entitlement, a family necessity, and the young man of color's due inheritance. For instance, in a *New York Times* article after the 2006 May Day marches, Ronald Walters, director of the African-American Leadership Institute at the University of Maryland, was quoted as saying that "he feels torn [over supporting undocumented immigrants' rights] himself because of his concerns about the competition between immigrants and low-skilled black men for jobs."[35] Judging these waged workers as privileged or undeserving, that is, seeing state abandonment as "worse than" (rather than integral to) capital exploitation, naturalizes (and even unwittingly advocates for) gendered, intranational, and international wage differentials, which are necessary for competing capitals to accumulate surplus value.[36]

On the other hand, common images of criminalized men of color also worked to marshal support for undocumented immigrants' right to rights by posing a much different relationship of men of color to the immigrant family in the effort to disassociate illegality from criminality. For instance, the activist Elvira Arellano's claims to social value were partly dependent on normalizing already devalued and differently racialized and gendered categories: "I am not a criminal. I have nothing to be ashamed of. We are workers, mothers, human beings. We should be able to be proud of who we are."[37] Arellano has to claim legible value and discredit her criminalization by naming and shaming "criminals" as mutually exclusive with "workers, mothers, human beings." But her image as mother produces a disturbing, uncomfortable disconnect with her label as a "criminal alien" *only if* a sympathetic public equates those other legally vulnerable (and just as problematic) categories of "the criminal" and "the terrorist" with its own racist imaginings of men of color. This is not to fault Arellano, Walters, and other activists (but perhaps the reporters who cite them) for deploying family as a political tactic; rather, I gesture toward these interrelated narratives to highlight the difficulties of claiming social value for legally and economically vulnerable groups.

Arguably the immigrant rights movement's appeal to normative understandings of "family" was not the primary source of its power or inspiration. The entitlement to rights without legitimate (i.e., legal) claim to them was the movement's most motivating and most threatening attribute. In other words, *how* claims to "family" were mobilized might have been just as important as the claims themselves. Although undocumented immigrants sought rights and recognition, they did so through "disidentification," by reorganizing commonsense concepts, such as personhood, criminality, citizenship, and family, to make intelligible an unthinkable political position, rightless and empowered, a position that displaced the possession of political power (i.e., legal recognition) as a prerequisite to personhood. Because undocumented immigrants cannot even lay legitimate claim to the right to protest for rights, they must draw on other frameworks of social value to highlight the law's illegitimacy. In this example, disidentification deploys the family as a normative value concept to make the unthinkable legible. This legibility, however, rests on the stability of family traditionally defined and problematically protected.

    Decentering the state as sole authority over legitimate power and personhood requires being willing to expose our respective Achilles' heels, not just what makes us vulnerable to state violence but also what makes us susceptible to the state's seductions, to its promises for legal recognition. In this way, the affective power of the immigrant rights movement might have less in common with the family it cites than with the nuclear family's queer kin. Disidentifying with "legality" and "legal recognition" has the potential to rework and rethink those violent seductions that disenfranchise queers of color, undocumented immigrants, criminalized men of color, and victims of violence-but-not-crimes. To disidentify with legality demands alternative, even unthinkable, value practices, such as privileging emasculation over valorization, prioritizing pleasure between bodies over biologically reproducing them, striving for struggle rather than securing victory, and arming, rather than protecting, the unprotected.

Notes

1. Carla Trujillo, *What Night Brings* (Willimantic, CT: Curbstone, 2003), 11–12.
2. See, e.g., the works in these anthologies: Carla Mari Trujillo, ed., *Chicana Lesbians: The Girls Our Mothers Warned Us About* (Berkeley: Third Woman, 1991); Alma M. García, ed., *Chicana Feminist Thought: The Basic Historical Writings* (New York: Routledge, 1997); Cherríe Moraga and Gloria Anzaldúa, eds., *This Bridge Called My Back: Writings by Radical Women of Color* (Watertown, MA: Persephone, 1981). See also the single-author text, which speaks specifically on "the family" in Chicana/o cultural politics by Richard T. Rodríguez, *Next of Kin: The Family in Chicano/a Cultural Politics* (Durham, NC: Duke University Press, 2009).
3. I am referencing Rodríguez: "By extending the family beyond private, domestic space in order to situate it in the public sphere, we see how queers shift the terms of kinship that enable queer models of cultural citizenship" (*Next of Kin*, 18).
4. Roderick A. Ferguson, *Aberrations in Black: Toward a Queer of Color Critique* (Minneapolis: University of Minnesota Press, 2004), 13.
5. Ferguson, *Aberrations*, 11–18.
6. Ruth Wilson Gilmore, *Golden Gulag: Prisons, Surplus, Crisis, and Opposition in Globalizing California* (Berkeley: University of California Press, 2007), 70–84.
7. Ferguson, *Aberrations*, 11–18.
8. Gloria Anzaldúa, *Borderlands/La Frontera: The New Mestiza* (San Francisco: Aunt Lute Books, 1987), 105.
9. What I am calling the "emasculation trap" is inspired by but not the same as Beth

Richie's concept of "gender entrapment." See Beth Richie, *Compelled to Crime: The Gender Entrapment of Battered Black Women* (New York: Routledge, 1996).

10. Eve Kosofsky Sedgwick, *Tendencies* (Durham, NC: Duke University Press, 1993), 5.

11. Sedgwick, *Tendencies*, 6.

12. Yen Le Espiritu, *Home Bound: Filipino American Lives across Cultures, Communities, and Countries* (Berkeley: University of California Press, 2003), 160, 158.

13. Elizabeth Freeman, "Time Binds, or, Erotohistoriography," in "What's Queer about Queer Studies Now?," ed. David L. Eng, Judith Halberstam, and José Esteban Muñoz, special issue, *Social Text*, nos. 84–85 (2005): 58.

14. Yvonne Yarbro-Bejarano, "Deconstructing the Lesbian Body: Cherríe Moraga's Loving in the War Years," in Trujillo, *Chicana Lesbians*, 145.

15. Freeman, "Time Binds," 60.

16. Gayatri Gopinath, *Impossible Desires: Queer Diasporas and South Asian Public Cultures* (Durham, NC: Duke University Press, 2005), 147.

17. Lindon Barrett, *Blackness and Value: Seeing Double* (Cambridge: Cambridge University Press, 1999), 19, 21.

18. Rodríguez, *Next of Kin*, 7.

19. James Kyung-Jin Lee, *Urban Triage: Race and the Fictions of Multiculturalism* (Minneapolis: University of Minnesota Press, 2004), xxviii.

20. Gilmore, *Golden Gulag*, 87–127.

21. Dylan Rodríguez, *Forced Passages: Imprisoned Radical Intellectuals and the U.S. Prison Regime* (Minneapolis: University of Minnesota Press, 2006).

22. On women of color and domestic violence, see Natalie J. Sokoloff and Ida Dupont, *Domestic Violence at the Margins: Readings on Race, Class, Gender, and Culture*, ed. Natalie J. Sokoloff and Christina Pratt (New Brunswick: Rutgers University Press, 2005); INCITE! Women of Color Against Violence, *The Color of Violence: The Incite! Anthology* (Cambridge: South End, 2006).

23. Emma Pérez, "Sexuality and Discourse: Notes from a Chicana Survivor," in Trujillo, *Chicana Lesbians*, 159–84.

24. Rodríguez, *Next of Kin*, 41; Ferguson, *Aberrations*, 112–16.

25. See Rodríguez, *Next of Kin*, especially chapter 1, "Reappraising the Archive," 19–54. See also Leti Volpp, "Feminism versus Multiculturalism," *Columbia Law Review* 101, no. 5 (2001): 1181–218.

26. Barrett, *Blackness*, 21.

27. Massimo De Angelis, *The Beginning of History: Value Struggles and Global Capital* (London: Pluto, 2007), 3.

28. De Angelis, *Beginning of History*, 3.

29. De Angelis, *Beginning of History*, 192, 10–11.

30. Ferguson, *Aberrations*, 87.

31. Judith Halberstam, *Female Masculinity* (Durham, NC: Duke University Press, 1998), 276.

32. Anzaldúa, *Borderlands*, 106.

33. José Esteban Muñoz, *Disidentifications: Queers of Color and the Performance of Politics* (Minneapolis: University of Minnesota Press, 1999), 31.

34. Joon Oluchi Lee, "The Joy of the Castrated Boy," *Social Text*, nos. 84–85 (2005): 35–56.

35. Rachel L. Swarns, "Growing Unease for Some Blacks on Immigration," *New York Times*, May 4, 2006.

36. Massimiliano Tomba, "Differentials of Surplus-Value in the Contemporary Forms of Exploitation," *Commoner*, no. 12 (Summer 2007): 23–37.

37. Diana Terry, "The New Sanctuary Movement," *Hispanic* 20, no. 8 (2007): 43, 45.

EXISTENTIALLY SURPLUS

Women of Color Feminism and the New Crises of Capitalism

Grace Kyungwon Hong

$\mathcal{W}$hat does "crisis" look like under contemporary capitalism? This is a particularly vexing question because contemporary capitalism's signal characteristic is the *incorporation* of the formations that constitute crisis in an earlier moment. In this essay, I examine the shift from an earlier manifestation of capitalism in the United States in the late nineteenth and early twentieth centuries organized around production to one organized around speculation, in order to describe how racialized, gendered, and sexualized difference operate in the contemporary moment.

The previous era of capitalism was organized around the production of difference through surplus labor. In the industrial period of the late nineteenth and early twentieth centuries in the United States, the contradictions of capitalism were sublated through a particular nexus of gendered and sexualized racialization that emerged by exploiting *labor*. As Lisa Lowe observes, the US nation-state required a homogeneous citizenry while US industrial capital required a heterogeneous workforce, differentiated by categories of race that were articulated through gender and sexual nonnormativity.[1] This contradiction was managed by creating a citizenry defined around whiteness and masculinity, subtended by the production of racialized and nonnormatively gendered and sexualized workers who provided the labor force. This differentiated labor force was excluded from citizenship, thereby allowing the nation-state to define itself as homogeneous. Lowe situates the Asian immigrant as the paradigmatic figure for this worker alienated from citizenship.

Extending Lowe's argument, Roderick Ferguson identifies *surplus labor* as producing the very forms of racialized, gendered, and sexualized difference that capital requires but cannot entirely manage. Following Karl Marx, Ferguson observes that these differences are necessary to the production of surplus labor,

GLQ 18:1
DOI 10.1215/10642684-1422152
© 2011 by Duke University Press

the industrial reserve army, or the "relatively redundant working populations" who are superfluous during times of contraction but necessary in times of growth: "In the United States, racial groups who have a history of being excluded from the rights and privileges of citizenship (African Americans, Asian Americans, Native Americans, and Latinos, particularly) have made up the surplus populations upon which U.S. capital has depended."[2] These differences were "in large part, the outcome of capital's demand for labor," but because of the state's need for a homogeneous citizenry, "the state worked to regulate the gender and sexual nonnormativity of those racialized groups" (14), thus rendering the labor of these groups that much more vulnerable to devaluation and relegation to the category of surplus. However, although the production and regulation of nonnormativity allows capital to devalue this labor, these differentiated populations also provide "locations for possible critiques of state and capital" (15). As Lowe and Ferguson argue, these alienated subjects are vital to racial state and racial capital but are in excess of state and capital's capacity to explain or characterize them. Both Lowe and Ferguson situate culture — Asian American cultural production and the African American novel, respectively — as the site where these repressed contradictions of capital return.

Lowe's and Ferguson's emphasis on culture as the site of contradiction gestures to the importance of subjectivity to the operations of power. The contradictions of capital required a particular organization of subjectivity that privileged the possessive individual as the preeminent subject of the nation-state and that constituted these surplus populations as despised nonsubjects.[3] The nineteenth century saw the emergence of subjectivity as an internalized, individualized formation articulated through a sense of moral development and resolution to the social order. This incarnation of subjectivity can be called the propertied subject, or possessive individualism, as the political theorist C. B. MacPherson termed it.[4] While MacPherson observes that possessive individualism subtends Western Enlightenment political thought from Thomas Hobbes to John Locke, I have elsewhere argued that a particularly American version of this subject was instantiated through canonical American literature in the late nineteenth century, one that incorporated an exceptionalist narrative.[5] However, this American possessive individual was dependent upon the alienation of nonsubjects whose material contexts were the racial violence that emerged out of the contradictions between the racial state and racial capital. This nineteenth-century possessive individual, in other words, was organized around masculinity and whiteness. As such, those subjects whose material conditions precluded inhabitation of the propertied subject can be said to have been racialized and gendered through this exclusion from propertied subjecthood. I further argued that because women of color occupied this nexus of racialization and gendering, women of color feminism and the cultural production of women of color expressed the incoherence of this ostensibly universally available propertied subjecthood, that is, the cultural production of women of color demonstrated that the propertied subject was not universally inhabitable. Further, the cultures of women of color articulated alternative inhabitations of subjectivity that, while illegible to propertied subjectivity, allowed for new forms of collectivity and solidarity.[6]

In that earlier moment, the bars to possessive individualism marked by race, gender, and sexuality subjected populations to necropolitical violence, that is, vulnerability to a form of power fundamentally organized around the physical, social, and epistemological death of a population."[7] Propertylessness was not only an economic category (i.e., the condition of not owning particular things) but became a form of illegible and despised subjectivity (the inability to own) mapped onto race and gender.[8] As such, gendered racialization meant being categorically alienated from normative subjectivity, insofar as the contradiction between state and capital was resolved by constituting whiteness and masculinity as privileged categories. This was, in other words, an era of racial capitalism underwritten by an ideology of white supremacy, itself articulated through gender and sexual normativity.

World War II marked a turning point wherein the ideological alignments that legitimated this particular nexus of power began to crumble. The postwar era of racial capital is one marked by the emergence of a new deployment of difference that took its place alongside the old, what Howard Winant calls "racial dualism."[9] Jodi Melamed describes a postwar "sea change in racial epistemology and politics. . . . In contrast to white supremacy, the liberal race paradigm recognizes racial inequality as a problem, and it secures a liberal symbolic framework for race reform centered in abstract equality, market individualism, and inclusive civic nationalism. Antiracism becomes a nationally recognized social value and, for the first time, gets absorbed into U.S. governmentality."[10]

This shift was occasioned by the emergence of liberation movements in the mid-twentieth century that challenged the necropolitical formations of the earlier moment, formations articulated as both colonial violence and Jim Crow segregation. Liberation movements of the midcentury, including decolonization movements abroad and civil rights and black power movements (as well as corresponding movements in Chicana/o, Asian American, Native American communities) in the United States emerged to highlight the hypocrisies of US postwar ascendency as a global hegemon. Melamed observes:

> Politicizing the depth of Western and white supremacy, [anticolonial and
> antiracist movements] demonstrated that European powers and the United
> States claimed to be fighting an antiracist and antifascist war, while prac-
> ticing racism and fascism against people of color in the United States,
> Europe, and the colonies. . . . to define successfully the terms of global
> governance after World War II, U.S. bourgeoisie classes had to manage the
> racial contradictions that antiracist and anticolonial movements exposed.
> As racial liberalism provided the logic and idiom of such management, it
> became an essential organizing discourse and force for U.S. postwar soci-
> ety and global power. (4)

Racial capital transitioned from managing its crises entirely through white supremacy to also managing its crises through white liberalism, that is, through the
incorporation and affirmation of minoritized forms of difference. This meant normalizing racialized populations once positioned as entirely nonnormative. Asian
American racialization is a particularly stark example of this. Nayan Shah documents how the popular press, politicians, census enumerators, and public health
officials characterized San Francisco's Chinatown, home to Chinese "bachelor
societies," predominantly made up of male laborers because of immigration
restrictions on Chinese women, as "the preeminent site of urban sickness, vice,
crime, poverty, and depravity" in the late nineteenth and early twentieth centuries.[11] These early homosocial bachelor communities were represented as harbor-
ing perverse practices, including cross-race and same-sex intimacies occasioned
by opium usage, sodomy, prostitution, and the like. Yet by the 1940s, with the
establishment of more Chinese American nuclear families, Shah finds these same
sources working to articulate Chinese American communities as incorporable to
US society. This process was exacerbated in the wake of the Immigration and
Nationality Act of 1965, which incorporated a "professional preference" that
allowed for the migration of professionalized managerial and technical labor from
Asia in the context of a Cold War contest over scientific progress. At the same
time, as Chandan Reddy observes, through the "family preference" also enacted
through this law and a subsequent 1990 amendment to the immigration code that
requires the sponsoring family to guarantee that they and those they sponsor will
not apply for welfare benefits, US capital recruited low-waged, vulnerable labor
from Asia while shifting the social burden to the impoverished communities that
could least afford them.[12]

It is thus the postcolonial moment, the decolonizing moment, in the mid-
twentieth century, rather than the eighteenth century as in Michel Foucault's peri-

odization, that brings about the possibility of affirming and managing *minoritized* (racialized, sexualized, gendered) life. In the wake of the liberation movements of the mid-twentieth century, we have seen a new form of power that affirms racialized, gendered, and sexualized difference yet levies death and destruction to poor, racialized, sexually "deviant" populations. In this era, we see subjects with access to capital and citizenship in ways previously unimaginable. Aihwa Ong traces the emergence of a global Asian technological and professional class that utilizes citizenship "flexibly" and that is accorded forms of "pastoral" care whether or not these professionals are actually citizens of a particular nation.[13] M. Jacqui Alexander documents the creation of a class of elite global south nationalist bureaucrats that, in the wake of decolonization, facilitates the neocolonial extraction of wealth from the global south to the global north in such places as Trinidad and Tobago and the Bahamas.[14] Cathy Cohen describes how new categories of jobs in social welfare, policing, and government administration created an African American middle class in the post–civil rights era that served as a conduit for the violent disciplining of the African American poor.[15] Similarly, this era also sees the emergence of homonormative gay and lesbian identities that mark themselves as parents, tourists, homeowners, and taxpayers, and in so doing, exacerbate the conditions which lead to utter devaluation of poor, racialized, sexually and gender deviant populations.[16] This new form of (bio)power is marked by the rampant proliferation of carceral and deadly regimes *enabled by* the *limited* incorporation and affirmation of certain forms of racialized, gendered, and sexualized difference.[17]

Such differences still operate to mark the "surplus" of capital, but as surplus populations as well as surplus labor. As discussed earlier, industrial capitalism produced contradictions around surplus *labor* as racially, sexually, and gender differentiated. Contemporary capitalism, however, has shifted to center on speculative economies. If, as Marx observed, circulation of money as capital is an end in itself, we might see neoliberal capitalism, which has been unmoored from its already tenuous connection to production, as centrally a speculative enterprise. While published almost a decade before the global financial crisis of 2008, Jean Comaroff and John Comaroff's description of "a decidedly *neo*liberal economy whose ever more inscrutable speculations seem to call up fresh specters in their wake" seems particularly prescient right now.[18] They observe, "In the upshot, production appears to have been superseded, as the *fons et origo* of wealth, by less tangible ways of generating value: by control over such things as the provision of services, the means of communication, and above all, the flow of finance capital. In short, by the market and by speculation" (5). If there is one thing that the recent financial crisis reminds us, however, it is that "there is no such thing as capitalism sans production, that the neoliberal stress on consumption as the prime source of value is palpably problematic" (7).

Ferguson's formulation that surplus labor is both "superfluous and indispensible" is useful for understanding the contemporary production of surplus populations as *nonlaboring* subjects, that is, the populations that are surplus not to production but to speculation and circulation. If the fundamental characteristic of capitalism is circulation, rather than production, and if contemporary capitalism has increasingly been organized around finance capital acting in and of itself, rather than anchored by production, today's populations are not only surplus *labor* but are also merely surplus: existentially surplus. In other words, currently, certain populations are not necessary to capital as potential sources of labor, but instead are useful for their intrinsic lack of value. While labor exploitation is certainly still important, certain populations are not destined ever to be incorporated into capitalist production as labor. As David Korten observes, global capitalism "treats people as a source of inefficiency, ever more disposable."[19]

These conditions require a new definition of difference. While the nonnormativity indicated by race, gender, and sexuality still indexes the importance of surplus labor, it is also the marker of *purely surplus* populations, populations who are *existentially surplus*. Ruth Wilson Gilmore's analysis of the prison-industrial complex in California provides a clear and compelling example of the rise of surplus populations as a result of speculative capitalism's need to continually expand. Gilmore observes that the boom in prison building, and the corresponding 500 percent increase in the state prison population in California since 1982, was not related to crime rates. Instead, Gilmore traces how prisons were the solution for a nexus of capitalist needs: the need to invest an overaccumulation of speculative capital; the need to warehouse African Americans who once had been employed as blue-collar workers in defense and other industries that had since been relocated overseas; the need to shift state bureaucracies from Keynesian social welfare to another governing function; and the availability of rural land.[20] In this context, Gilmore notes, African American prison populations function within the prison-industrial complex not as *labor* but as raw material. Put differently, African American criminalization, which is legitimated through narratives of racialized, gendered, and sexualized deviance, is not only a way to relegate subjects to surplus labor pools but also a way to relegate to surplus existence. In the era of the primacy of speculative capital, being surplus means being extinguishable. To be "surplus" in this moment is to be valueless, unprotectable, vulnerable, and dead. It is to be racialized, gendered, and sexually nonnormative in ways simultaneously old and new.

As a part of the neoliberal response to these social movements, subjectification became organized as a choice, available to populations that were once categorically excluded from normative subjectivity. In the late twentieth and early twenty-first century, in the globalization/neoliberalism era, this subject still operates as a mechanism of power. Indeed, as Reddy observes, the post–World War II era is marked by the extension of the US state into practices of subjectivity. That is, *subjectivity*, rather than citizenship, became the site where the state attempted to impose itself as an institution of universality.[21]

However, in this later era, this subjectivity becomes instrumentalized. That is, while the notion of a moral subject is still crucial, this subject is not incorporated into a social order organized around notions of Western civilization and progressive, teleological historical development. Instead, one's ability to articulate oneself as a moral subject becomes a means of legibility within a structure of biopolitical regulation. Being a moral subject means having claims to protection from necropolitical violence, to having a claim to exist, and for one's existence to be protected. Not choosing to inhabit this moral subjectivity means relinquishing one's claims to protected life. In this era, race, gender, and sexuality as identity categories do not automatically situate one as alienated from moral subjectivity. This, however, does not imply the declining significance of race, gender, and sexuality but describes a new procedure for determining who is on the protected side of the life-death divide, and who is on the vulnerable side, a procedure that nominally extends protection to certain people of color, gays, and women but that creates in its wake even more brutal legacies of racialized, gendered, and sexualized death and devastation.

As mentioned earlier, many scholars have identified the emergence of homonormativity as perhaps the most exemplary manifestation of neoliberalism's incorporation of previously despised subject formation. As Reddy has argued, the emergence of homonormativity is central to the neoliberal turn. Neoliberal reorganization of the US state in the service of contemporary capitalist modes of production is anchored through "family" as "a regulative formation in the current governmentality" (107). Reddy observes that gay and lesbian claims to "family" status through the vocabulary of same-sex marriage resignifies the US state as the locus of legitimacy and freedom. At the same time, the US state deploys "family" for nonnational and noncitizen labor *not* as a way to secure these laboring populations' legitimacy or freedom but as the exact opposite: as a way to condition them for labor exploitation. Reddy notes that while immigration to the United States is largely spurred by the demand for low-wage, "unskilled" labor, the preference category through which most migrants enter the United States is through the "family reunification" category. In this way, gay and lesbian claims to "family rights" are an example of what Reddy terms "the political and economic disenfranchisement of the racialized noncitizen immigrant and the racialized citizen poor [that] is devised in the name of securitizing civil society for its entitled subject, the citizen-as-capitalist and its juridical clones" (105). In other words, family is a category of normativization for the citizen-as-capitalist, but *only* insofar as it is simultaneously a category of exploitation for the noncitizen immigrant and the racialized citizen poor. In this context, the racialized poor are rendered vulnerable so as to produce them as a form of surplus labor, but they are also abjected as backward, homophobic, and patriarchal as a way to render them as morally bankrupt and exclude them from a privileged liberal subjecthood: existentially surplus.

The proliferation of existential surplus means that contemporary capitalism rewrites our relationship to death at a basic and fundamental level, changing our experience and inhabitation of life and death. If power operates differently now, through the differential dispersal of life and death, then abjecting death or evacuating it of meaning legitimates this differential dispersal. That is, the very definition of the "good life," and thus the only possible goal or aim of politics, becomes narrowed to the protection of life, as the protection of life becomes the only way that subjects are marked as valuable. Yet, following Foucault, we can see how this narrow pursuit of the protection of life (for some) is precisely a way to exacerbate death (for many others).[22] In this context, it is precisely in the condition of being unprotected that we find alternative expressions of the political, of life and death. These alternative expressions are, in a sense, unrecognizable as politics, because the notion of the political has been so thoroughly captured by the pursuit of protection of life. This alternative episteme characterizes the state of living death, of surplus, as both about the lapse of meaning and the symbol of the unrepresentable (as typically death is understood), but also importantly about myriad, varied, excessive meanings for death. While *life* is the epitome of what "we cannot not want" in these stubborn refusals to let one's politics be entirely subsumed by the pursuit of the protection of one's own life, we find another, more precarious mode of being that takes seriously Cherríe Moraga's query: "But how many lives are lost each time we cling to privileges that make other people's lives more vulnerable to violence?"[23]

In this context, neither the affirmation nor abjection alone of certain privileged forms of subjectivity can constitute a crisis. On the one hand, in the wake of the liberation movements of the mid-twentieth century, the affirmation of previously degraded forms of subjectivity became a part of the apparatus of power. Ferguson writes, "In the U.S. context, Western Man suffered his greatest upset because of the race and gender-based movements of the sixties and seventies." In the wake of these movements, Ferguson observes, "These new tales of origins would mint another political entity and object of love, a new article called minority culture. Minorities would go from being members of empty-handed generations to people headstrong with histories and civilizations." Yet this was not the lessening of power, but a redeployment of it: "The arrival of this new object did not usher in a season of unbridled liberation but provided the building blocks for a new way to regulate."[24] Because the limited and narrow modes of affirmation of difference occasion exacerbated violence for abjected subjects, it does not follow that the entire abdication of affirmation and embrace of abjection constitutes a crisis for capitalism.[25]

In this context, Moraga stages a simultaneously affirming and abject relationship to valued and visible forms of subjectivity, and does so by staging her complex relationship to biological reproduction. Biological reproduction has become an immensely important site for marking which subjects are deserving and which are not. David Eng insightfully notes the centrality of parenting to contemporary norms of citizenship and social belonging in the United States. In an essay on transnational adoption, Eng writes:

> Anthropologist Ann Anagnost suggests that, for white, middle-class subjects in the era of late capitalism, the position of parent has become increasingly a measure of value, self-worth and "completion." Indeed, I would suggest that the possession of a child, whether biological or adopted, has today become the sign of guarantee not only for family but also for full and robust citizenship — for being a fully realized political, economic, and social subject in American life.[26]

The child becomes the apotheosis of citizenship, the figure that, as Lee Edelman puts it, "alone embodies the citizen as an ideal."[27] In this context, procreation — whether biologically or through adoption — becomes a way for previously despised gay and lesbian subjects to narrate themselves as deserving, moral, and responsible.

In this context, procreative temporalities constitute a horizon of legibility and representability for gay and lesbian parents. Yet this does not mean that all who procreate are extended this form of protected subjectivity. As Cathy Cohen observes in her foundational essay "Punks, Bulldaggers, and Welfare Queens," we cannot assume that there is a "uniform heteronormativity from which all heterosexuals benefit." She notes, for example, "the stigmatization and demonization of single mothers, teen mothers, and primarily, poor women of color dependent on state assistance."[28] Likewise, Moragadoes not inhabit "queer motherhood" easily. Instead of using motherhood as a way to claim normativity, she represents herself as tempting death even or especially at the very moment when she seems to be embracing incorporation and affirmation through reproduction. For Moraga, motherhood brings her closer to, not farther away from, the kinds of despised subjects who continually face devastation and death as a result of their abjected status: her friends dying of AIDS, her parents' generation who are dying away, their memories and histories fading with their deaths. Moraga engages death by marking the ways in which she is constantly in danger of annihilation by being *wrong* in her motherhood. Moraga writes herself into abjection as a mother not only by being a lesbian mother but also by foregrounding how motherhood makes her not radical enough, not butch enough, not nationalist enough, too nationalist, and so on. In this way, Moraga represents motherhood both as mode of legibility and as akin to the abjection faced by other nonnormative subjects.

As Sandra Soto has observed, perhaps no other Chicana feminist has so centrally articulated the dialectic of power and abjection as Moraga.[29] Moraga's most famous essay, "A Long Line of Vendidas," activates the process of embracing betrayal by taking on La Malinche as the figure through which to speak.[30] Yet as Soto notes, Moraga's entire body of work can be seen to "place a high premium on the public elaboration of private feelings of anxiety, guilt, and fear" (254). Yet the purpose of this writing is not, as in nationalist mobilizations of such affects, to overcome the losses that produced such feelings: "Moraga's lesson to her students is no self-help healing regimen, nor is it a call to put forth universal truths about the shared pain of being human. Rather . . . Moraga means to intertwine meaningful personal revelation with ethnonationalist desire . . . ; the more affective and visceral the experience or desire recounted, the more meaningful and tangible the political result" (255). In other words, rather than use loss as a way to justify a compensatory formation, whether as the patriarchal family or as the ethnonationalist community, Moraga finds her politics in the very location of loss and its attendant affects. This is not to claim, of course, that Moraga does not desire these compensatory mechanisms, as Soto notes: "There is a nagging sense that in relation to the poststructuralist orientation of queer theory, Moraga's occasional objectification of race, reification of binary oppositions, refusal to critique models of authenticity, and modernist-inflected conceptions of power and resistance can seem misguided, if not flat footed" (238). Yet Soto argues that because these tendencies in Moraga's work occur in the context of Moraga's constant sense of shame over her inadequacy as a racialized subject because of her ability to "pass" as white, her half-white parentage, her lack of Spanish linguistic ability, and her queerness, that Moraga's writing can never produce a sense of belonging within an ethnonationalist community or of attainment of a nuclear family ideal.

Moraga's *Last Generation* (1993), a collection of poetry and prose, and *Waiting in the Wings* (1997), a memoir of her experience of motherhood, are no exceptions to this tendency. Moraga's ruminations on the impossibility of banishing death in the process of bringing forth life are oblique meditations on the exacerbated vulnerability to death that the protection of life mandates. In doing so, Moraga situates queer Chicana subjectivity as providing the potential for articulating ways of being solidly situated in, but in excess of normative reprosexuality, generational temporality, and the forms of history that they imply. In contrast to a normative narration of history and generational reproduction, Moraga describes an epistemological formation that both privileges life and articulates the impossibility of preserving life:

> My family is beginning to feel its disintegration. Our Mexican grandmother of ninety-six years has been dead two years now and la familia's beginning to go. Ignoring this, it increases in number. I am the only one who doesn't ignore this because I am the only one not contributing to the population. My line of family stops with me. There will be no one calling me, *Mami, Mamá, Abuelita* . . .
>
> I am the last generation put on this planet to remember and record.
>
> No one ever said to me, you should be a writer some day. But I went ahead and did it anyway.[31]

For Moraga, being a Chicana lesbian writer means being able to record rather than "ignore" the disintegration of this particular version of family. Because Moraga is a lesbian and thus, in her view, unable to continue the family line through reproduction, she is given a kind of vision: the gift and burden of being unable to ignore a dying generation by turning her attention to the newly birthed, by celebrating the fact that the family "increases in number." This generation of her *tiós* and *tiás*, Moraga informs us in her introduction to the volume, will take a particular kind of culture with them: "lo mexicano will die with their passing" (2). In *Waiting in the Wings*, Moraga describes this generation as the "last real generation of the Mexican-American Moraga clan . . . none of us are as much family as they. And as my uncle's generation goes, the family goes with it in that profoundly Mexican sense."[32] Others can ignore this passing by counting children, Moraga says in *The*

Last Generation, "but I cannot accept it. I write" (2). In this way, Moraga articulates the importance of preserving what is lost through death, but not by producing "life" in the usual, reproductive ways.

Lisa Tatonetti argues that Moraga's association of lesbianism with loss in *The Last Generation* reproduces the notion of the Chicana lesbian as "traitor" to her Chicano nation. Tatonetti writes, "An observer rather than a participant, Moraga contributes to this perceived cultural disintegration by virtue of her same-sex desire: she equates lesbian sexuality with childlessness, which she represents as familial absence and cultural betrayal. The traditional Chicano portrayal of the lesbian as Malinche, a traitor to her race, is thus fulfilled."[33] In contrast, she reads Moraga's queer motherhood in *Waiting in the Wings* as a way to recuperate the Malinche figure not as traitor but as "the *savior* of Chicano culture" (240; emphasis in original). In contrast, I read Moraga's description of her childlessness less as a sign of "internalized homophobia" (240), as Tatonetti describes it, than as a way to see and remember what normative reprosexuality erases. Taking into consideration Soto's argument that Moraga *recuperates* the Malinche figure, we can read queer motherhood in *Waiting in the Wings* as an extension of, rather than a break from, the "traitorous" childlessness of *The Last Generation*.

In *The Last Generation*, Moraga imagines the possibilities that emerge out of childlessness, later writing in a poem called "I Was Not Supposed to Remember":

> I am a woman, childless
> and I teach my stories to other
> childless women and somehow
> the generations will propagate and prosper
> and remember pre-memory. (98)

Childlessness in this formulation is not, as Tatonetti argues, a moment where Moraga reproduces the misogyny of the Malinche tradition. Rather, childlessness becomes for Moraga a way to imagine other modes of producing culture and of creating community—creating a lineage that does not depend on the erasure of alternative pasts. The generations created by Moraga and her clan of "childless women" "somehow" queerly exist not by producing children but by teaching "stories." In doing so, these generations "remember pre-memory," or in other words, what is not supposed to be remembered, what normative hetero-reproduction would "ignore" and forget.

Tatonetti's analysis of Moraga as registering an "internalized homophobia" is exactly symptomatic of articulations of value that Moraga's centering of abjection seeks to evade. That is, Tatonetti's implication that Moraga's utilization of Malinche indexes her insufficiently radical queer politics delineates an unspoken but present criteria of what constitutes proper queer politics that, while condemning *heteronormative* criteria of value, manifests another set of criteria.

Moraga's use of "last" gestures to another kind of temporality than that of linear propagation, yet still situated within a generational temporality. Moraga posits *herself* as the "last generation." If she is the last generation who is "put on this planet to remember and to record," this last generation is, definitionally, *queer*. That is, her queerness makes her childless and thus able to see, remember, and write what the childbearing would ignore. Rather than the "last" signaling the end of a sequence—a series of generations that ends with her—the "last" instead marks a different inhabitation of time. That she is the last does not necessarily imply that there was anyone before her, because her queer way of creating generations is unexplainable ("somehow") and so cannot be understood within the mundane conceptions of biological generations. She is last because the work she does as her generation is to remember what cannot be folded into linear time: "pre-memory." She does so by both celebrating life and documenting death.

Moraga's impetus to preserve this pre-memory expands her preoccupation with her immediate blood family to cosmic proportions. Noting that she is completing the book in 1992, "500 years after the arrival of Cristóbal Colón," she situates the death of this generation of Chicanos as the culmination of centuries of death and destruction following the "violent collision between the European and the Indigenous, the birth of a *colon*ization that would give birth to me" (1–2; emphasis in original). The demise of this generation is the demise of this entire race that was created out of this violent collision. Moraga writes of "a sense of urgency that Chicanos are a disappearing tribe" that spurs her to write (2). In this way, Moraga does not celebrate or ignore the violences of death, loss, and abjection.

If Chicanos are a disappearing tribe, and this disappearance is the culmination of five centuries of colonialism, Moraga's project in this book is not only to document the end but also to imagine a new beginning. What it means for Moraga to revitalize this tribe is to reimagine it as queer. In her essay "Queer Aztlan: The Re-formation of Chicano Tribe," Moraga writes of the need for "a new Chicano movement" (154). She writes, "Chicana lesbians and gay men do not merely seek inclusion in the Chicano nation; we seek a nation strong enough to embrace a full range of racial diversities, human sexualities, and expressions of gender" (2). This is a dangerous line to tread and is again a manifestation of Moraga's refusal to be affirmed by any criteria or system of value. That is, Moraga is not unaware of and indeed is deeply critical of the "dangers of nationalism," its "tendency toward separatism" that can "run dangerously close to biological determinism and a kind of fascism," and in particular of Chicano nationalism and "its institutionalized heterosexism, its inbred machismo, and its lack of a cohesive national political strategy" (148–49). It is easy enough to dismiss minority nationalism altogether, in a moment when facile critiques of "identity politics" provide the vocabulary for this dismissal.[34]

Why, then, does Moraga take up nationalism in order to "queer" it? She writes, "I cling to the word 'nation' because without the specific naming of the nation, the nation will be lost (as when feminism is reduced to humanism, the woman is subsumed)." She urges us to "retain our radical naming, but expand it to meet a broader and wiser revolution" (150). Moraga describes this revolution as queer, indigenous, and feminist, and represents this new community as a means of "making culture, making tribe, to survive and flourish as members of the world community in the next millennium" (174). For Moraga, Queer Aztlán is a vision of a new set of possibilities: "As we are forced to struggle for our right to love free of disease and discrimination, 'Aztlan' as our imagined homeland begins to take on a renewed importance. Without the dream of a free world, a free world will not be realized" (164). This notion of a Queer Aztlán names and imagines a possibility that is impossible in the present. It is an example of what José Muñoz calls "queer utopia": "a structuring and educated mode of desiring that allows us to see and feel beyond the quagmire of the present. . . . an insistence on potentiality or concrete possibility for another world."[35] In invoking a millennial cosmology spurred into existence, but ultimately uncontained by, the violence of European colonization, Moraga invokes a different temporality, a temporality not subsumed to the "'dream world' of individualism, profit, and consumerism" but another trajectory (4). This queer, indigenous, and female cosmology is one in which life and death are not sequential but coincident. Queer Aztlán names the possibility of *coexistence* of two radically contradictory temporalities, one called "life" and the other "death." Thus, in embracing Queer Aztlan, Moraga is not unmindful of the dangers of nationalist politics. Indeed, it is the very contradiction inherent in "Queer" and "Aztlan" that produces the possibility of crisis and contradiction.

The potential dangers of such a politics becomes manifestly evident in this section, in particular in Moraga's curious lack of ambivalence around the category of the indigenous. Unlike lesbian, female, nationalist, mother, or Chicana, all of which Moraga subjects to intense scrutiny as a way to reveal the systems of valuation and devaluation in which they traffic, Moraga's representation of indigeneity is entirely affirmative. In situating indigeneity as an unqualified category through which she finds affirmation, Moraga not only departs from the trajectory of her work but also replicates the erasure of indigenous peoples that organize Mexican and US nationalisms. Norma Alarcón argues that Mexican mestizo nationalism and Chicano nationalism appropriate the image of the native woman, sanitizing her as a way to make her the foundation of a mestizo civilization or Chicano community.[36] In contrast, Alarcón observes that Chicana feminism's recuperation of "La Malinche" is a way to invoke the native woman *in her abjection* rather than in an affirmative mode, as with Mexican mestizo nationalism or Chicano nationalism. In a reversal of some of her earlier work, Moraga posits indigeneity in such uniformly valued terms in *The Last Generation*, rather than in the ambivalent terms with which she articulates other categories.

This is particularly striking in Moraga's discussion of motherhood. For what happens when this queer Chicana writer becomes a mother, as in *Waiting in the Wings*? Does her foray into motherhood mean that she, too, joins the ranks of those who celebrate the "increase" in the family by "ignoring" the dying, be it the generation of her parents or a generation of queer men? Quite the opposite: we find that *Waiting in the Wings* is nothing less than a sustained meditation on motherhood not as a guarantee of life and value but as vulnerable to death and devaluation. From the epigraph by Michel de Montaigne, which reminds us that "to practice death is to practice freedom," to the very end, Moraga's experience of bringing forth life is not a way to forestall death but a process haunted continually by the presence of death. Moraga's son, Rafael, is born three months premature, and his ability to survive is uncertain. Moraga writes of the overwhelming terror that Rafael's brushes with death inspire in her.

Yet the text's preoccupation with death is not merely attributable to any parent's universal terror at the possibility of losing a child but entirely determined by Moraga's queer Chicana subjectivity. Moraga's effort to create queer of color family means bringing Rafael into the world at the very moment when her queer family is dying of AIDS. Interlaced throughout the narrative of Moraga's pregnancy, Raphael's birth, and his struggle to survive in an infant ICU, and the changes Raphael's presence brings for Moraga's work as a writer and her relationship with her partner, Ella, are the stories of deaths: her friends Tede and Rodrigo and Ronnie, all activists and artists and men who remind her, as Moraga writes in *The Last Generation*, "how rare it is to be colored and queer and to live to speak about it" (177). Moraga finds out that her baby will be a boy just a few days before she learns that Tede has AIDS. In that moment before the advent of antiretrovirals, having AIDS is tantamount to a death sentence, and Moraga reflects: *"There is meaning in the fact that my fetus has formed itself into a male, a mean-*

ing I must excavate from the most buried places of myself, as well as from this city, this era of dying into which my baby will be born."[37] What does it mean to create a queer family, the text seems to ask, when one generation's birth is accompanied by another generation's premature death?

Yet it is not only queer family whose deaths must be reconciled to Raphael's life, but blood family as well: Moraga's *tió*, a part of the very generation whose imminent passing inspires Moraga's theorization of queer childlessness as an alternative way to tell history and mark time in *The Last Generation*, dies when Raphael is two—by then a healthy and prospering child. Moraga writes, "I try to write about the impossible, the ordinary beginning of one life and the passing of another. Watching a life enter and another exit within the same brief moment of my family's history" (118). The entire text, in this way, is the evidence of Moraga's attempt to inhabit motherhood and family differently, to produce children and create family not as an attempt to master death or to reconcile and thus erase the abjection and loss of death by positing family and children as the epitome of life. If, as Moraga observes in *The Last Generation*, normative biological reproduction and generational temporality is predicated on ignoring death, *Waiting in the Wings* is her attempt to do the "impossible"—which is craft a version of queer motherhood that recognizes the death that inheres in life and vice versa. For Moraga, queer family means "a relentlessly intimate acquaintance with death" (177), a kind of death-in-life.

As the book progresses, death's meaningfulness expands and widens, provoking Moraga to engage death rather than repel it. She experiences an epiphany of sorts about death in the hospital waiting room while Rafael undergoes a surgery to combat a potentially deadly intestinal infection. She writes, "In the midst of our prayer, I realize suddenly—so profoundly—that my tightest hold against death cannot keep Rafaelito here. . . . The holding itself is what Rafaelito does not need. He needs to be free to decide: to stay or to leave. . . . I only knew my clinging so tightly to my son's waning life could surely crush him and all the heart I had; and there would be no heart left to either mourn or raise a son."[38] At this moment, she decides to accept death and to understand death as a form of possibility. After this epiphany in the waiting room, although she still says she "*does not know how to write of death*" she also attests that Rafael's tenuous hold on life has "*introduced me to living with the knowledge of death*."[39] While she didn't "understand death" earlier, Moraga has access to death as "knowledge." This knowledge however, is a part of *living*.

Moraga's texts thus delineate her investment in finding a way to value life that does not at the same time abject death—a project perhaps better described as positing herself as both legible to and erased by multiple and sometimes contradicting systems of value. In these texts' refusal to entirely conform to, and also to entirely reject, these systems of value, we can identify a crisis in valuation and meaning that can be produced only out of contemporary conditions of existential surplus.

Notes

I thank the members of LOUD Collective, my writing group, for their generous and rigorous readings of this essay in an earlier draft form. My great appreciation goes to Chandan Reddy for his insights about the centrality of subjectivity to late nineteenth- and twentieth-century modalities of power. I thank the anonymous reviewers whose careful readings of this essay helped me immeasurably. Finally, I thank the editors of this special issue, Jordana Rosenberg and Amy Villarejo, whose rigor and brilliance in their own scholarship is matched only by the thoughtfulness and generosity with which they edit others'.

1. Lisa Lowe, "Immigration, Citizenship, Racialization: Asian American Critique," in *Immigrant Acts: On Asian American Cultural Politics* (Durham, NC: Duke University Press, 1996).
2. Karl Marx, quoted in Roderick Ferguson, *Aberrations in Black: Toward a Queer of Color Critique* (Minneapolis: University of Minnesota Press, 2004), 15. Hereafter cited in the text.
3. See Benedict Anderson, *Imagined Communities: Reflections on the Origin and Spread of Nationalism* (London: Verso, 1983).
4. C. B. MacPherson, *The Political Theory of Possessive Individualism* (Oxford: Clarendon, 1962).
5. See Grace Kyungwon Hong, "The Possessive Individual and Social Death: The Complex Bind of National Subjectivity," in *Ruptures of American Capital: Women of Color Feminism and the Cultures of Immigrant Labor* (Minneapolis: University of Minnesota Press, 2006).
6. See Grace Kyungwon Hong, "Histories of the Dispossessed: Property and Domesticity, Segregation and Internment," in *Ruptures of American Capital.*
7. Achille Mbembe, "Necropolitics," *Public Culture* 15, no. 1, (2003): 11–40.
8. Orlando Patterson's description in *Slavery and Social Death* that the enslaved person and, indeed, "all oppressed peoples" are rendered oppressed by a state of "generalized dishonor" is perhaps the most famous formulation of the centrality of subjectivity to enslavement. See Orlando Patterson, *Slavery and Social Death: A Comparative Study* (Cambridge: Harvard University Press, 1982), 12. Saidiya Hartman argues this state of generalized dishonor survived the transition from enslavement to "freedom,"

observing that such dishonor was assigned to freed African Americans under the structures of debt peonage through tropes of individual responsibility. See Saidiya Hartman, *Scenes of Subjection: Terror, Slavery, and Self-Making in 19th Century America* (New York: Oxford, 1997). Patricia Williams shows that this sense of blackness as dishonor permeates our social field as a notion of "black anti-will." See Patricia Williams, "On Being the Object of Property," in *The Alchemy of Race and Rights* (Cambridge: Harvard University Press, 1991).

9. Howard Winant, *The World Is a Ghetto: Race and Democracy since WWII* (New York: Basic Books, 2001), 8.

10. Jodi Melamed, "The Spirit of Neoliberalism: From Racial Liberalism to Neoliberal Multiculturalism," *Social Text*, no. 89 (2006): 1. Hereafter cited in the text.

11. Nayan Shah, *Contagious Divides: Epidemics and Race in San Francisco's Chinatown* (Berkeley: University of California Press, 2001), 1.

12. Chandan Reddy, "Asian Diasporas, Neoliberalism, and Family: Reviewing the Case for Homosexual Asylum in the Context of Family Rights," *Social Text*, nos. 84–85 (2005): 101–19.

13. Aihwa Ong, *Flexible Citizenship: The Cultural Politics of Transnationality* (Durham, NC: Duke University Press, 1999); Ong, *Neoliberalism as Exception: Mutations in Citizenship and Sovereignty* (Durham, NC: Duke University Press, 2006).

14. For an analysis of the role of global south black state managers, see M. Jacqui Alexander, "Not Just Any(Body) Can Be a Citizen: The Politics of Law, Postcoloniality, and Sexuality in Trinidad and Tobago and the Bahamas," *Feminist Review* 48 (1994): 5–23.

15. For a discussion of the role of the black middle class in the post–civil rights era, see Cathy Cohen, *The Boundaries of Blackness: AIDS and the Breakdown of Black Politics* (Chicago: University of Chicago Press, 1999). See also Michelle R. Boyd, *Jim Crow Nostalgia: Reconstructing Race in Bronzeville* (Minneapolis: University of Minnesota Press, 2008).

16. For useful critiques of homonormativity, see Reddy, "Asian Diasporas, Neoliberalism, and Family"; Lisa Duggan, *The Twilight of Equality? Neoliberalism, Cultural Politics, and the Attack on Democracy* (New York: Beacon, 2004); Martin Manalansan IV, "Race, Violence, and Neoliberal Spatial Politics in the Global City," *Social Text*, nos. 84–85 (2005): 141–55; José Muñoz, *Cruising Utopia: The Then and There of Queer Futurity* (New York: New York University Press, 2009); David Eng, *The Feeling of Kinship: Queer Liberalism and The Racialization of Intimacy* (Durham, NC: Duke University Press, 2010); Riccke Manansala and Dean Spade, "The Non-Profit Industrial Complex and Trans Resistance," *Sexuality Research and Social Policy* 5 (2008): 53–71.

17. See Angela Davis, *Are Prisons Obsolete?* (New York: Open Media, 2001); Julia Sudbury, ed., *Global Lockdown: Race, Gender, and the Prison-Industrial Complex* (New

York: Routledge, 2005); Cathy Schneider and Paul Amar, "The Rise of Crime, Disorder, and Authoritarian Policing: An Introductory Essay," *NACLA Report on the Americas* 37, no. 2 (2003): 12–16.

18. Jean Comaroff and John Comaroff, eds., *Millennial Capitalism and the Culture of Neoliberalism* (Durham, NC: Duke University Press, 2001), 2. Hereafter cited in the text.

19. David Korten, *When Corporations Rule the World* (East Hartford, CT: Kumarian Press, 1996), 13.

20. Ruth Wilson Gilmore, *Golden Gulag: Prisons, Surplus, Crisis, and Opposition in Globalizing California* (Berkeley: University of California Press, 2007).

21. See Chandan Reddy, "Freedom's Amendments," in *A Freedom with Violence* (Durham, NC: Duke University Press, 2011). Hereafter cited in the text.

22. Foucault writes, "This death that was based on the right of the sovereign is now manifested as simply the reverse of the right of the social body to ensure, maintain, or develop its life. . . . Wars . . . are waged on behalf of the existence of everyone; entire populations are mobilized for the purpose of wholesale slaughter in the name of life necessity: massacres have become vital" Foucault, *History of Sexuality*, vol. 1 (New York: Vintage, 1980), 137.

23. Gayatri Chakravorty Spivak, "Bonding in Difference," in Alfred Arteaga, ed. *An Other Tongue: Nation and Ethnicity in the Linguistic Borderlands.* (Durham, NC: Duke University Press, 1994), 161. Cherríe Moraga, *The Last Generation* (Boston: South End, 1997), 163–64.

24. Roderick Ferguson, *The Re-Order of Things* (Minneapolis: University of Minnesota Press, 2012).

25. Queer theory has produced much useful work that recuperates abjection. See, for example, Heather Love, *Feeling Backward: Loss and the Politics of Queer History* (Cambridge: Harvard University Press, 2007).

26. Eng, *Feeling of Kinship*, 101.

27. Lee Edelman, *No Future: Queer Theory and the Death Drive* (Durham, NC: Duke University Press, 2004), 11.

28. Cathy Cohen, "Punks, Bulldaggers, and Welfare Queens: The Radical Potential of Queer Politics?," *GLQ* 3 (1997): 453, 455.

29. Sandra K. Soto, "Cherrie Moraga's Going Brown: 'Reading Like a Queer,'" *GLQ* 11 (2005): 237–63. Hereafter cited in the text.

30. Cherríe Moraga, "A Long Line of Vendidas," in *Loving in the War Years* (Boston: South End, 1983).

31. Moraga, *Last Generation*, 9. Hereafter cited in the text.

32. Moraga, *Waiting in the Wings*, 119.

33. Lisa Tatonetti, "A Kind of Queer Balance: Cherríe Moraga's Aztlan," *MELUS* 29 (2004): 244. Hereafter cited in the text.

34. See, e.g., Wendy Brown's narration of "politicized identity" as simply Nietzschean ressentiment (*States of Injury: Power and Freedom in Late Modernity* [Princeton: Princeton University Press, 1995], 66–76).

35. Muñoz, *Cruising Utopia*, 1.

36. Norma Alarcón, "Chicana Feminism: In the Tracks of the 'Native' Woman," in *Between Woman and Nation: Nationalisms, Transnational Feminisms, and the State*, ed. Caren Kaplan, Norma Alarcón, and Minoo Moallem (Durham, NC: Duke University Press, 1999).

37. Moraga, *Waiting in the Wings*, 32; emphasis in original.

38. Moraga, *Waiting in the Wings*, 64.

37. Moraga, *Waiting in the Wings*, 64.

QUEER VALUE

Meg Wesling

This essay approaches the relation between Marxism and queer theory by considering the question of value. More specifically, I want to address how an interrogation of the concept of value can make room for a materialist reading of sexuality that goes beyond the identifiably LGBTQ to address the historical specificity of capital's investment in formations of sexuality. The production of sexual identity, through which unpredictable constellations of desire, knowledge, and practice become concretized into limited models of sexual identity, is bound up in the way capital produces subjects accommodated to its own needs.[1] Thus the question of value offers one important conceptual space for rethinking and contesting the regulatory mechanisms that enforce such concretizations.

In offering the phrase *queer value*, then, I do not mean simply to "queer" the notion of value by pointing to its indeterminacy, its instability, its refusal to remain fixed along the vectors of use or exchange. As important as such indeterminacy is to my discussion here, what I mean is for queer to recontextualize value as that concept which mediates between the material, the cultural, and the psychic. That is, "queer value" sutures together two domains too often understood to operate autonomously: the psychic realm of desire and the material realm of accumulation and exchange. In making this claim, I build on a significant archive of feminist scholarship that has interrogated the relations between cultural and economic value, pointing to the necessary interconnectedness of such concepts and foregrounding the material in critical evaluations of the cultural.[2] Queer value addresses what Gayatri Spivak has identified as the "necessary complicity" between the cultural and the economic that allows the feminist critic to register the effects of her investments in seemingly benign value-systems within uneven global distribution of resources and division of labor.[3] It is, to use the comparison Spivak offers, to see within the schemes of evaluation the domination of some values over others, the workings of exploitation. But more on this later.

GLQ 18:1
DOI 10.1215/10642684-1422161
© 2011 by Duke University Press

To get to an understanding of "queer value," this essay entertains the question of labor through a reading of the film *Mariposas en el Andamio* (*Butterflies on the Scaffold*) (dir. Margaret Gilpin and Luis Felipe Bernaza; 1996), a Cuban documentary about a community of drag performers (or *transformistas*) in La Güinera, a suburb of Havana. I focus on this example because it offers a compelling language for orienting us to the type of "work" we call queerness. This is not simply a film about how queers *work*. Rather, *Mariposas* engenders a way to think about the productive value of queer labor, pointing to how Karl Marx's account of value and labor might be refashioned by the productive capacity of queers to make explicit the value of their various forms of labor and to contest the alienation characteristic of the wage-labor system.

In particular, the film asks that we reconsider the production of gendered and sexualized subjects; *Mariposas* is profoundly engaged with the circulation and resignification of particular commodities, including music, clothing, and others, and thus inextricably linked to the global distribution of resources. Moreover, the film asks that we understand the production of gendered bodies and desiring subjects as a repetitive form of labor, and in this sense it engages readings of drag as performative so as to make the case for acknowledging such performances as ritualized, disciplined, and highly invested forms of labor. As such, the intervention the film makes is in no way limited to the lives and labors of queers. Rather, the film exemplifies how we might articulate the labored economies of sexuality and gender more generally — how the performance of gender and sexuality constitutes a form of labor, accruing both material and affective value.

In what follows, I suggest that we take seriously the notion of affect in relation to labor. "Affectively necessary labor" is Spivak's term, one that aims to mark the liminal space between the material and the social. As I explore in greater detail below, *affectively* necessary labor is usefully distinguished from *socially* necessary labor, or the minimal necessary labor needed for the worker to reproduce himself or herself. Affectively necessary labor introduces myriad forms of social activity that go beyond subsistence and reproduction — those activities that work toward the aims of the body's comfort, pleasure, and the satisfaction of desire — and that we would want to acknowledge as labor.[4] Thus the daily, repetitive performances through which bodies are socially legible as gendered (whether coded as queer or straight) make up a kind of affectively necessary labor; that is, the compulsory repetition of gender as performance might usefully be understood as a form of self-conscious labor that produces value, both material and social, even when (or precisely because) that performance is asserted to be natural. Following Louis Althusser, we might conclude that this labor is valuable precisely in the extent to which the gendered subject submits "freely" to the imperative of this continual labor, and regards the product of that labor — gender identity — not as an imposition from outside but as something that originates from within.[5] The most obvious example of the labor of gender is "women's work": the physical, strenuous labor of childbirth, child rearing, caring for the elderly, and the like, and the emotional work of maintaining the state of relationality, caretaking, and accommodation — this is a kind of compulsory gendered labor that accrues value for capitalism without monetary remuneration for the individual laborer. But what I hope to point to is that these examples are just the most obvious forms of the labor intrinsic in all gendered identities. It is the realm of affect that renders such performances to seem as though they are spontaneous, the reflection of the subject himself or herself rather than the internalized form of subjection that makes legible each individual as a social subject.[6]

Gender as Global Commodity

What kind of commodity is gender? Or, what happens to our understanding of the commodity when we think of gender as the outcome of compulsory labor? As Marx explains, labor produces not just commodities but the laborer as a commodity. To the extent that, under capital, the laborer does not own the products of his or her efforts, the laborer is alienated from his or her labor. This is what Marx calls the "estrangement" of the capitalist laborer, in which the product of the laborer's efforts becomes an object, with an "external existence" that appears as "something alien" to the laborer: "The product of labor is labor which has been congealed in an object, which has become material: it is the objectification of labor."[7] There is another sense of estrangement, however, in the very process of production as well as in its object. Because this labor is compulsory rather than chosen, the laborer finds that toil "does not affirm himself but denies himself."[8] This labor thus separates the worker from what Marx affirms as the "life-engendering" process of self-chosen work; capitalism alienates laborers by separating them from nature, from themselves, and from their "species-being," their essential connection to the collective humanity around them.

For Marx, the distinction between chosen and unchosen labor is crucial, and we might distinguish between alienating *labor* and self-actualizing *work*, to borrow Hannah Arendt's terms. The antinomy between work and labor is, for Arendt, a crucial marker of the subject's alienation under capital. Labor, for Arendt, is the compulsory, repetitive, and alienated effort that produces commodities to which the laboring subject has no connection. It is by necessity "slavish," involving repetitive tasks that the laborer cannot claim or are "unproductive" in the sense that they are ephemeral or immediately consumed. As she writes, "It is indeed the mark of all laboring that it leaves nothing behind, that the result of its effort is almost as quickly consumed as the effort is spent."[9] Work, on the other hand, is at least one step removed from alienated labor, in that it produces something that carries within it the mark of its relation to the worker. Here Arendt seeks to correct what she sees as a slippage in Marx between two distinct forms of production: labor and work. While Marx is most interested in the predication of laboring subjects by extracting surplus value, Arendt calls to our attention the important relation between workers and the object they produce. It is the object's capacity to endure, at least for a time, its own usage without being entirely consumed that marks the distinction between the activity of labor and that of work. This durability, Arendt argues, "makes them withstand, 'stand against' and endure, at least for a time, the voracious needs and wants of their living makers and users." In this capacity, "the things of the world have the function of stabilizing human life. . . . Men . . . can retrieve their sameness, that is, their identity, by being related to the same chair and the same table" (137). Laboring is the dull activity meant to sustain the living body, while work is what leaves a mark behind it, contributing to the objective world.

There is an additional distinction as well, however, which is that the capacity to work depends necessarily on one's freedom from labor. Here is where Arendt reads the class distinctions of modern society. While in slave societies slaves could not work, it was their *labor* that secured the master's freedom to work. This is a crucial distinction; as the autonomy of "free" subjects rests in their ability to leave a mark in the concrete world, this must mean that they are liberated from the mundane routine of labor. Significantly, it is the mark of modern society, for Arendt, that this distinction between labor and work is mystified, and that the subject constituted in the wage labor system, by extracting surplus value for labor, is offered as an alternative to alienated labor, not (socially meaningful) work but *play*. As she writes, "All serious activities, irrespective of their fruits, are called labor, and every activity which is not necessary either for the life of the individual or for the life process of society is subsumed under playfulness" (127). Within the structure of wage labor, the social imperative toward "making a living" overrides the objective value of work, dividing all human activity into (profit-oriented) labor and (non-profit-oriented) play.

What the "queer" brings to this discussion is a revision of the relation between work, labor, and play. One thinks here of the example of drag, which is the practice at the center of the film reading that follows. On the one hand, such a distinction seems to match at least one possible reading of drag performances, since the spirit of play is certainly present in each spectacle. Indeed, elements of play are everywhere evident in the rituals of camp, and the drag performances as *Mariposas* presents them are no exception to this logic. This play, however, might not be read as the antithesis of labor. It is, rather, a kind of work that uses play, in some instances, to establish its autonomy as work, to refuse the alienating or estranging effects of labor. As Matthew Tinkcom argues, the playfulness of camp allows for glimpses of a certain kind of work, the (queer) subject's intentionality invested in the object, and thus switches such an object to a different register of value—not purely exchange or use value but something else, the register of plea-sure.[10] Useful for us here is Tinkcom's emphasis on camp as an altered mode of *production*, drawing our gaze from the consumptive registers of the spectacle to offer a vision of camp as "the marks of queer labor that allow for visions of work to emerge."[11] To speak of camp, or drag, as a productive form of work begs the ques-tion of value. That is, the "work" of camp, which offers us insight into subjectivity produced through work, allows as well the chance to consider how drag's perfor-mances of gender might constitute forms of value, produced through the subject's perpetual labor. In other words, drag (as playful work) paradoxically reveals not just the social construction of gender but its status as labor, as the coercive or compulsory efforts that produce the gendered body which capital needs for its productive system.

Mariposas

Mariposas en el Andamio is the appealing work of American filmmaker Marga-ret Gilpin and Cuban filmmaker Luis Felipe Bernaza.[12] Completed in 1996, the film opened at the Havana Film Festival and circulated widely, to great acclaim, at various international film festivals, both queer and straight.[13] The narrative, as I mentioned above, tells the tale of the emergence of a drag community in La Güinera, a settlement outside Havana. While not the first film about gay life in Cuba—other films, like the aptly named documentary *Gay Cuba* (dir. Sonja deVries; 1995) and the feature film *Fresa y chocolate* (*Strawberry and Chocolate*) (dir. Tomas Gutierrez Alea; 1993), were much more widely circulated—*Mariposas* is unique in several ways. For one thing, its scope is small; the film focuses exclu-sively on La Güinera and the history of this community of queer men who live there, interviewing the performers, their families, their neighbors, friends, and other residents. More importantly, its focus is unique for this genre, as it seeks not simply to celebrate the endurance and creativity of gay Cubans in the postrevolutionary state but to work at revealing a more complex relationship between these subjects and the future of the revolutionary goals themselves. That is, the film works hard to detail how the drag community is an essential part of the success that the settlement has enjoyed and to suggest, none too subtly, that in the proliferation of sexual identities La Güinera, and Cuba more generally, comes to fulfill the revolution's transformative aims.

Mariposa's opening sequence links the *transformistas* to the regeneration of the community and, by extension, the nation. The first shot is a close-up of one of the performers in full drag, complete with makeup and blue feather boa. Backlit, surrounded by orchids, this *transformista* lounges, at ease with the camera's lingering gaze. We then move through a sequence of shots of the performers, all in various stages of preparation: applying foundation, slipping on high-heeled shoes, painting on lipstick, gazing in the mirror while myriad attendants gaze on. Meanwhile, a Cuban ballad accompanies the preparations with doleful lyrics: "Spring butterfly, golden soul, if you see her tell her to return to the gardens of my illusions; perhaps she'll never come back." Before cutting to the opening credits, this sequence ends by offering a vision of a butterfly transformed: one performer walks onto a lushly decorated stage, smiling triumphantly, and spreads her arms in a dramatic gesture of welcoming, as if with wings to take flight. She is followed by the film's dedication: "To the workers of the community of La Güinera, Havana, Cuba. To Fifi with love."

The first and last shots of the sequence, each featuring a *transformista* in glorious attire, offer a sort of affective gauge for viewers, as the camera is oriented to look on the performers kindly and with great delight. That is, the camera quickly establishes a relation of affection with the performers, inviting viewers to perceive themselves as part of the appreciative, intimate audience. Cutting back and forth between performances and preparations, the camera stages such distinctions to invite us into the intimacy of this community. When center stage for the camera as well as for the community assembled to watch, the performers seem triumphant, fully at home in their spectacle. The sequence of preparations thus seems to offer viewers a moment of intimacy, a behind-the-scenes glimpse of the transformation process. Setting up quickly what will be a steady pattern of movement between front and back stages, *Mariposas* situates viewers as part of the collective transformation, sharing, like the many friends who assist in the dressing rooms, in the communal efforts and pleasures of the performances.

Importantly, the dedication, "with love," articulates the affective style already indicated through the camerawork. Closely linked to the butterflies' process of transformation, the film does indeed hint, more and less explicitly, at the *transformistas'* place among the workers to whom the film announces its dedication. To reiterate this point, viewers next witness a series of interviews detailing the history of La Güinera and outlining its development as a socially progressive community. With great pride, the interviewees offer a history of community collaboration in building La Güinera, both structurally and ideologically. As viewers watch black-and-white footage from the early days of its settlement, the voice-over describes how La Güinera had been a "marginal area" whose overgrown land was cleared by squatters newly arrived from outlying areas. The spirit of revolutionary collaboration is ever-present in the telling of the tale, as viewers learn that these new residents established the new community through collective labor: "They said, 'we'll build your house today and mine tomorrow.' They bought rum and were ready! At night they began—the next day they moved in."

Rehearsing the revolutionary language of cooperative productivity, the sequence announces the story of La Güinera as a triumphant one. This is a tale of notable achievement, tracing the steady transformation of La Güinera into a vibrant community that, as viewers learn at the end of the film, was recognized for its cultural development with an award from the United Nations Environment Program in 1995. Before this finale is revealed, however, viewers have more to learn about the community, and they meet a variety of local figures, each intervening to contribute with pride to the telling of the tale. From the family doctor who boasts of the "high incidence of delinquency" now "eradicated" through education and training, to the construction workers who lead us on a short tour of first buildings they completed, the film offers a vision of collaboration toward a common goal, taking great pride in the community that has resulted from this effort.

It is toward the end of this sequence that Fifi appears, a woman introduced as the head of construction, who details with pride the sequence of building projects and number of completed apartments before continuing: "This met the needs of the neighborhood. We set out to build new houses and to build the new 'man' in our society." This is the first clue to the double registers of transformation the narrative wishes to link. As the chief of housing construction, Fifi voices the interconnectedness of the material and cultural production of this new community; new houses and new men both appear essential to the success story the documentary wants to tell.

Making this connection more explicit, Fifi soon addresses the camera to insist emphatically that there is "something I don't want to leave out, the drag queen performances in the construction workers' cafeteria." Then, during successive sequences of clips from various drag performances, she elaborates:

> At first I rebelled. I'm an older woman. I wasn't accustomed to running around with this class of people. . . . I said, "no, keep them away. I don't want to hear about people who run around with a double façade." . . . I wouldn't be doing my duty to society. I'm too old for this stuff. I've never been involved in these things.

Fifi recalls her own transformation, one enacted not across the visual markers of gender but through the conscious and psychic registers of social awareness and political consciousness. As viewers learn at various points in the film, Fifi became a domestic at age nine and has thus spent her life among workers such as those featured in the film. As if to reinforce the significance of the possibility afforded by her role in the collective work of La Güinera, she then tells the camera, "I couldn't enjoy much of my childhood. Now I've had the opportunity to work on the development of La Güinera and I feel like a new woman."

From the outset, then, *Mariposas* wants to chart the multiple strands that are interwoven to form the progressive social fabric of La Güinera. Mingling with Fifi's story of her own journey — her emergence as "a new woman" — and that of the community's development is the story of the drag shows and the workers' cabaret. As Armando, one performer, describes,

> We started seven years ago. We began at the bottom. Our costumes weren't like today's. We didn't have resources. We used sheets for fabric, no sequins, nothing. . . . I realized I'm proud of one thing. In the short time we worked . . . this was the headquarters, the cradle of cross-dressing in Havana. Hundreds of drag queens came through here who never thought they would do this work. I'm satisfied — our sacrifice paid off.

Running parallel to the story of La Güinera's success is an equally satisfied story of the drag queens and of their emergence as an important part of the community. La Güinera's evolution as an exemplary postrevolutionary site, the drag performers' emergence as part of the community's social fabric, and Fifi's own conversion tale are intertwined, the clips juxtaposed, fading into each other, to emphasize the mutual dependence of these transformations. This is an important feat, because it links the interviews of the drag performers to a larger dialogue, beyond that of community acceptance. Echoing an earlier interviewee's insistence that "we don't seek tolerance. Tolerance is a misguided notion. Tolerance is smug," the film suggests that the drag performers are not simply accepted as part of the new society; they are integral in building a new social formation. This seems to be the larger context for Fifi's assertion that they set out to "build new houses and to build the new man in our society." The drag performances become paradigmatic rituals that mark each of these transformations, heralding a new social possibility essential to the openness and collaboration behind her vision of the "new man." Such a move links drag to the social transformations of postrevolutionary Cuba, integrating the politics of sexual transgression to the aspirations of a utopian, anticapitalist revolutionary project.

Thus far, the film seems to be a very localized picture of a movement for social equality, articulated around affirming a queer politics of gender mobility and sexual identity. By establishing gender and sexuality as the currency through which viewers might evaluate the success of Cuba's revolutionary project, the film charts what must be understood as a quite particular vision of queer community building, inextricably linked to the specificities of postrevolutionary Cuba and its well-documented history of repression and exile in relation to homosexuality.[14] Certainly the film is meant to engage with such a history by offering a substantially different vision of the sexual politics of the revolution and of the "new man" in particular. At the same time, however, the film subtly expands its gaze outward, not only pointing to the broader material conditions in which the drag shows take place but linking such conditions to the international politics surrounding Cuba's financial and social climate. One early scene features Armando holding up a black, sequined robe, noting that, among the dyed goose feathers and sequins, he integrated "crinoline, tulle, and plastic, normally used for garbage bags. It's 'airy' and functional for a costume." What follows this scene is an elaborate explication of the material production of each *transformista*. One performer, while carefully applying eyelashes, laments that "although you won't believe it, I'll lose an eye at any moment. This is acetate. Real eyelash glue disappeared from our world." Her companion then adds, "Other drag queens use their own eyelashes or they make them out of horse or wig hair. . . . Since I can't buy them I make them out of . . . carbon paper from the office." Then a third performer, attaching fingernails, explains, "This is *baje*—glue. If it gets on my dress it'll ruin it. It's used to glue shoes and for many other things." Demonstrating an ingenuity in replacing the items beyond their reach, each performer highlights the material production of her transformation, thus pointing to the extensive and expensive labor that goes into each performance.

In scenes such as these, the film demands more of its audience, asking viewers to consider drag not simply as spectacle but as intricate, careful work. The camera lingers long and often on the *transformistas* as they prepare for their performances, and in its careful recording of such preparations, the film details the elaborate construction of gender. Neither the film nor the interviewees calibrate the success or failure of the performances according to their abilities to re-create with fidelity the seemingly natural markings of gender. Indeed, aside from one brief moment in which a construction worker recalls his first visit to the cabaret and notes that "I really thought [the performers] were women," the question of verisimilitude is entirely absent. Likewise, the film refuses to isolate any one *transformista* as the focus of its inquisitive gaze. Instead, viewers meet and revisit each *transformista* one by one, so that as the stories unfold, their sympathies rest not with any one person but with the community into which they are slowly becoming integrated.

Mariposas, then, provides a complex account of the collaborative work of drag and the material and social costs and rewards of such work. Even while the film borrows from the generic conventions common to filmic representations of drag, it refuses to participate in the potential reification of the *transformistas* as objects of fascination, nor does it remain content to simply enjoy the spectacles presented. In this sense, it shares something of the "ambivalent disobedience" that Judith Butler attributes to drag. For Butler, such rituals constitute "repetitions of hegemonic forms of power which fail to repeat loyally and, in that failure, open possibilities for resignifying the terms of violation against their violating aims."[15] I would add that *Mariposas* features such repetitions not so much as a failure as a refusal to "repeat loyally," and in this distinction we see a crucial reworking of the social meaning of drag. Put differently, *Mariposas* might be understood to take issue with the reading of drag as "disidentification," marking queer subjects' "failed interpellation within the dominant public sphere."[16] As Fifi's comments make clear, far from lamenting (or celebrating) queer subjects' distance from the normative as standards for how bodies signify, the film tries ambitiously to resignify the normative itself, as part of the rich possibility of this new social order.

The film, then, is less a vision of disidentification than a resignification of the identificatory possibilities of a postrevolutionary moment, with both local and global significance. The stories the performers tell, the day jobs they describe as necessary to support their community, and the resources they conjure to make the performances possible all emphasize an ingenuity and camaraderie in the face of economic difficulty. The earlier footage of the settlement and the history situates La Güinera within the economic crisis of the late 1980s and 1990s, in which the fall of the Berlin Wall marked a loss of aid from the Eastern European socialist bloc, exacerbated by the tightening of the US embargo, as enacted in 1992 through the "Cuban Democracy Act" (or, Torricelli Law), which imposed extraterritorial sanctions against third-party companies doing business with Cuba. The Helms-Burton Act, which extended the provisions of the Torricelli Law, was signed into law by President Bill Clinton in 1996, the year of the film's release. The film's seemingly local focus is thus inseparable from the larger context of Cuba's situation in the global economy, and the performers refuse any possible eclipsing of this global context.

Thus *Mariposas*, in an incredibly nuanced fashion, works at every turn to link the local politics of sexual desire and gender identity to an international politics of economic exchange. Though the United States is never mentioned, the effects of the embargo against Cuba mark the film. First, there is the disappearance of eyelash glue, fabrics, makeup—the very materials of gender's production. Later, in a particularly campy scene, one performer graciously accepts coins tossed onstage before exclaiming with mock exasperation, "I'm sick of this local money. Damn it, throw me a Washington," only to dramatically collapse in disbelief when presented with a dollar bill. Such moments place La Güinera within the global economy and the particular history of US-Cuba relations. This interconnectedness is nowhere more evident than in the transformation of American pop hits by Céline Dion and Bonnie Tyler into catchy Spanish ballads to accompany these drag performances, highlighting again how seemingly natural categories of gender are imbricated in the global circulation of commodities and engendered through networks of cultural exchange and appropriation that reach far beyond La Güinera's borders.

If the transnational exchange of goods and images sets the material conditions for producing the gender transitivity at the heart of the film, such exchanges are not to be read as the particular privilege of queerness. Rather, this vision of sexuality, of gender, and of queerness enacts a highly localized vision of community yet is no less implicated in the material conditions of globalization. This, then, is the film's second intervention: the insistence that the drag performers contribute a form of affectively necessary work, one inextricable from the material conditions of postrevolutionary Cuba and the ideological transformations of the members of the settlement community. In long, careful sequences detailing the preparation for the performances, the camera demands over and over again that viewers attend to the considerable care and effort that goes into producing each gendered performance. Moreover, in showing the tremendous collective effort behind this gender mobility, these scenes expose the nexus of *social* relations that go into producing the gendered body. The film's interrogation of the production of the gendered body thus invites viewers to consider the "naturalness" of gender as the outcome of a set of social relations whose product is then made to stand apart from those relations; to borrow Marx's terms, we could read the gendered body as "a mysterious thing" where "the social character of men's labor appears to them as an objective character stamped upon the product of that labor."[17] This suggests a vision that exceeds performativity as a model for understanding the relationship of drag to the "real," featuring drag not just as performance but also as socially necessary *work*. This point is made most clearly by Armando, a performer who asserts that "I'm proud of one thing . . . thousands come through here who never thought they'd do this kind of *work*," a comment followed later by the explanation, "I want a place for us, where we can work. . . . we need a gay organization." This narrative troubles the notion of drag as recognition of interior subjecthood, encouraging us to see how drag is the basis for an evolving community of workers. Armando's insistence that a gay organization is necessary speaks to the sense of collective effort behind the production of these gendered performances and, by extension, of gender itself. The camera's insistent focus on transformation refuses to naturalize the (re)production of these otherwise normative gender categories. Literally an exposé on the mode of gender production, the repetition of these scenes marks such performances as work, exposing the nexus of social relations that go into producing the gendered body.

The emphasis on the labor of gender and the productivity of the drag performers insists on a remapping of use value onto those bodies formerly seen as antithetical to the nation's reproductive needs. Such a reading of value — queer value, as it were — comes through in numerous scenes, not only from the performers themselves in their discussions of the "important cultural work" they perform but also in interviews with other members of the community. As a local congressman puts it, "They are what they are, but they're giving people something that others who aren't like them, don't give." Later, one construction worker reiterates: "They're the people who are giving this neighborhood a new level, a new character." These are scenes that elaborate on drag as social utility, as a form of productive work. To the extent that utility is *the* marker of value in the film, viewers are introduced to a language of community based not on individuality but on the use value of individuals to the social whole. When we think of drag simply as performance we situate it within a logic of exchange that levels the distinctions between the kinds of work that go into that production, abstracting the labor of gender and sexuality by reading drag as the providing of a service; the body's value rests only in spectacle. By highlighting gender as a process of production, the film resists the alienation effectuated by discourses that assert the innateness of gender identity while resisting as well the narrative of drag that locates its value as surface, pure spectacle.

Against the seeming playfulness of drag, then, and its familiar reading as campy spectacle, the film offers a vision of drag as socially valuable work, necessary for the future success of the social whole. This is nowhere clearer than in Fifi's closing comments: "I think this type of work should go on all over the country because of the respect, pride, and responsibility with which they work. . . . If the nation accepts these cultural workers, these workers for the society, as we did here in La Güinera, we'll be successful as a nation." This moment marks Fifi's final transformation from skeptic to passionate supporter, envisioning the drag queens as paradigmatic cultural workers for an evolving society. As careful readers (and viewers) will remember, the film is dedicated "to Fifi with love," and she is at its center, acting not just as spokesperson for the performers and community alike but serving as a touchstone for the audience whose sympathies the film works to elicit. Fifi's own journey in the film makes of her a different sort of butterfly, suggesting that drag is but one of the many transformations necessary for a harmonious, productive postrevolutionary society. At the same time, it is the drag performers who clearly lead the way with such a charge, pointing again to the important cultural work they perform.

To make the claim, as I did above, that the film resists the alienation complicit in the regulatory arrangements of gender is, of course, to make quite a critical leap. Clearly, the film works to call the constructedness of gender to viewers' attention, and, as I hope to have shown, it does so by paying particular attention to the socially useful work that is mystified when normative gender categories are made to appear seamlessly and effortlessly natural. I have argued that the film parts company with other drag documentaries by bringing to the performative nature of drag a consideration of gender as a labored production, one that constitutes an important kind of cultural work. I want to turn now to a more focused consideration of the kind of labor entailed in the production of gender and to think more broadly about how the film's narrative and formal aspects open up some possibilities for reconsidering the relation between Marxism and queer theory. To take seriously Fifi's closing gesture of considering the drag performances an important kind of cultural work is to shift evaluative registers, moving from one set of questions about the performative (Does the drag seem real? Are we convinced? Are we entertained?) to another set of concerns about the value that such work produces. Following the film's language, then, the questions we must ask are these: what sort of work is drag, and what kinds of value accrue to repeating this particular performative enactment?

These questions return us to the matter of the work-labor-play relation. While *Mariposas* features the playfulness of drag as camp, it allows for much more: a vision of gender as the self-conscious production of human work. To use Arendt's language, drag appears in the film as a new kind of *work*, one that refuses the alienation of *labor* by claiming self-referentiality through the commodity, by investing in and articulating the body as the site of that self-actualizing labor. That is, what we witness in the film is a decided refusal of the estrangement between process and product; instead, we see the production of the gendered body through a process in which the social relations between producers is meticulously acknowledged and reaffirmed at every stage.

It is certainly true that *Mariposas* highlights a specific community in a particular historical moment, and I would not want to be understood to be taking, from this particularized example, evidence of a grand potential for the undoing of the regulation of gender and sexuality. Rather, the claim I want to make is much more specific, about the vision the film offers, which is a narrative of drag as *work*—that is, the self-conscious predication of the subject who produces himself or herself in social relation to others. Here Fifi's comments about the *transformistas* as cultural workers points to their transformative effect on the community, their fully invested, self-conscious labor in relation to the spectacle they produce. It suggests that we might employ the categories of labor and work as sites for considering how different productions and performances of gender and sexuality are compelled, solicited, and enacted in relation to particular material and social conditions. It asks us, that is, to consider how the labor encompassed in the production and performance of gendered bodies is in no way peripheral to producing "normative" disciplined subjects and how such productions have material effects as well as cultural and psychic ones.

This brings us back to our titular question, for to invoke the category of labor is to start at the beginning of Marx's famously messy chain of value. This chain has been most compellingly opened up in Gayatri Spivak's "Scattered Speculations on the Question of Value," and it is Spivak's investigation of value, as a site in which the "necessary complicity" of the cultural and economic becomes most visible, that I want to build on here.[18] Spivak introduces the question of value to trouble its operation in a seemingly strict economic sense. The crux of the problem is the enigmatic meaning of value, which "escapes the onto-phenomenological question" ("what is it") in Marx's analysis of the money-form (155). Spivak wants to illuminate the discontinuities in this chain, moments of contradiction that trouble the smooth transition between elements in the chain and put the whole category of value into question. Most importantly, she looks to use value as one site of such a troubling, as use value is both "outside and inside the system of value-determinations," that is, as what indicates the using up, not circulation of a commodity: use value is "outside the circuit of exchange" (162), and thus it cannot be accounted for within the labor theory of value, as the accumulation of (surplus) value through the subject's capacity to labor and to create "a greater value than it costs itself" (154). In this sense, value can be defined only once use value is "banished" or subtracted from the equation; at the same time, exchange value is a sort of "superfluity or a parasite" of use value, dependent on that very subtraction, and thus use value finds itself reintroduced into the circuit of exchange.

By examining use value as what points to the "randomness" of value-determinations, Spivak works against what she calls a "romantic, anti-capitalist" tendency that would want to invest in use value the capacity to fix the notion of value outside the fickle, exploitative mechanics of exchange. Against such readings, where use value "seems to offer the most secure anchor of social 'value' in a vague way" (161), it is use value that puts the entire chain into crisis, illustrating how the impossibility of pinning down value in economic terms is matched by a similar open-endedness in the cultural. In other words, arguments that look to use value to establish the fixity of value-determinations in the cultural as an antidote for the uneven schematics of value in the economic miss the "irreducible complicity" between both registers of such value-determinations: "The consideration of the textuality of Value in Marx . . . shows us that the Value-form in the general sense and in the narrow . . . are irreducibly complicitous. It implies the vanity of dismissing considerations of the economic as 'reductionism'" (164).

It is this complicity between the cultural ("the general sense") and the economic ("the narrow") that I am trying to illuminate. To think of drag as work is to claim for it a kind of value that seems at first glance to be merely "cultural." Fifi's assertion that the *transformistas* perform a kind of important *cultural* work reaffirms such a distinction, leaving unasked (or unaskable) the question of the value such work produces.

As Spivak's example of canon-formation makes clear, however, such moments of cultural value-determination are never outside the economic machinations of value and, by extension, the presence of exploitation. Rather, the import of her argument is to read the economic into value-systems where it would seem to be absent, and to see that absence as a mystification that reinforces the very "epistemic violence" through which some subject-effects "are effaced or trained to efface themselves"; in other words, as she writes, drawing on Benjamin, "a 'culturalism' that disavows the economic in its global operations cannot get a grip on the concomitant production of barbarism" (168). To this end, Spivak argues, questions of cultural value are in no way exempt from the workings of exploitation. The point, then, is not to extricate the sexual from the economic, the psychic from the material. Nor is it to read sexual desire or identity as determined by capital, abandoning the psychic to the dominance of the material. Rather, as Spivak admonishes, "the best one can envisage is the persistent undoing of the opposition, taking into account the fact that, first, the complicity between cultural and economic value-systems is acted out in almost every decision we make; and secondly, that economic reductionism is, indeed, a very real danger" (166).

Let us return here to the question of gender. To think the production of gender as a form of labor (the repetitive, compulsory performance of the body to produce its own gendered "self" as an object that appears independent of that repetitive creation and "natural" in the world) is to begin to have a way to think about the costs of such labor and to question the forms of value it accrues. *Mariposas* does not reveal a set of unusual social relations produced on the site of the gendered body as much as reveal how gender is a product of a collective effort and is necessarily linked to material and political interests. In the film, these interests are linked to the negotiation over what constitutes the "new man" in postrevolutionary Cuba and what ideological contours that identity will take in relation to the reality of harsh economic conditions. Instead, more generally, we are asked to consider the value of different gender identities. While it is hard to put a definite number on that value, the continued difference in pay accorded to men and women, the gendered segregation of jobs, and the inflated numbers of women who live at or below the poverty line suggests in no uncertain terms that the daily execution of a convincing performance of masculinity is highly valued indeed.

To keep the concept of value at the forefront of our analysis of queerness is to recognize that queerness is a part of the establishment of hierarchies of value and that the practices and desires wrapped up in the category of sexuality constitute forms of affectively necessary labor, not just ensuring the workers' reproduction but also producing and preserving the space within capitalism for such desire and reorienting our understanding of sexuality as crucially but unevenly linked to capital. What the queer notion of value offers, then, is a way to stage the ambiguities of this complicity between cultural and the economic, and to keep this complicity constantly in mind. That is, I do not mean to "queer" value but to suggest that queer labor — that is, the affectively necessary work of queer desire — both demands and enables a vision of the indeterminacy of value. As importantly, however, the value (both cultural and economic) of the queer opens up ways to think about the labor of sexuality and gender identity beyond what is recognizably queer. How, for example, might we think about the heteronormative or the queer identities constituted in relation to the productive conditions of the global sex trade, or the trafficking in undocumented labor, or even the new circuits of international adoption? How might we begin to account for the everyday labor of gender that is compulsory for each particular regime of production, whether in maquiladora work, international tourist sites, or domestic child-care centers?

To return to the politics of the film, I would add that the validation of drag as socially valuable work is not an uncomplicated one. The notion of socially useful work would seem, in some ways, to participate in the postrevolutionary logic that draws too drastic a distinction between valuable work and nonvaluable or frivolous labor, and I want to resist the moral coding that often intersects with that distinction. Moreover, the embrace of queer spectacle and gay and lesbian rights has become a suspicious marker of the state's own investment in a display of modernization; to the extent that the extension of rights and recognition to gay, lesbian, and queer subjects has been part of the advancement of a neoliberal political agenda across the globe, we have good reason to be suspicious of such campaigns. That said, what is unique about *Mariposas* is its linking of such rights to the collective good of the postrevolutionary state — not in individualist or market terms but as part of the ideological work of nation building. These workers provide a labor that the film marks as necessary and value-laden work, rather than simply celebrate it as spectacle. (That is, obviously it is spectacle, but it is not only that.)

As I hope to have shown, the question of value reminds us of the imbricatedness of sexual desire and gender identity with material practices of production, accumulation, and exploitation, and helps us resist the temptation to see queerness as necessarily resistant to or outside such practices. On the contrary, it is by wishing to make queer desire do the work of extricating us from capital's exploitative capacity that we miss the opportunity to explore such possibilities as they arise.

Notes

1. See John D'Emilio, "Capitalism and Gay Identity," in *The Lesbian and Gay Studies Reader*, ed. Henry Abelove, Michèle Aina Barale, and David M. Halperin (New York: Routledge, 1993), 467–76. See also Rosemary Hennessey, *Profit and Pleasure: Sexual Identities in Late Capitalism* (Routledge: New York, 2000).
2. Among the more important of these is Judith Butler's "Merely Cultural" and Nancy Fraser's response, "'Heterosexism, Misrecognition, and Capitalism': A Response to Judith Butler," both from *Social Text*, nos. 52–53 (1997), 265–277; 279–289. Important recent contributions to this conversation include Lisa Duggan, *The Twilight*

of Equality? Neoliberalism, Cultural Politics, and the Attack on Democracy (Boston: Beacon, 2003); and Kevin Floyd, *The Reification of Desire: Toward a Queer Marxism* (Minneapolis: University of Minnesota Press, 2009).

3. Gayatri Chakravorty Spivak, "Scattered Speculations on the Question of Value," in *In Other Worlds: Essays in Cultural Politics* (New York: Routledge, 1988), 154–75.

4. See also Antonio Negri and Michael Hardt, "Value and Affect," *boundary 2* 26, no. 2 (1999): 77–88.

5. Louis Althusser, "Ideology and Ideological State Apparatuses" in *Lenin and Philosophy and Other Essays* (New York: Monthly Review Press, 1971), 182.

6. In her discussion of Spivak, Amy Villarejo introduces the concept of affective value to recognize that "affect and desire are not banished from considerations of economy, nor are they relegated to the sphere of women's work or considerations of reproduction" (*Lesbian Rule: Cultural Criticism and the Value of Desire* [Durham, NC: Duke University Press, 2003], 35.) Such concepts understand sexuality and capitalism as distinct registers, necessarily interconnected. I am greatly indebted to Villarejo's discussion of value and her reading of *Mariposas*, which has helped me clarify my own thinking of the film and its approaches to questions of work and labor. While Villarejo's discussion of value is more comprehensive than my own, what I hope to have added to this ongoing conversation is a consideration of the production of normativity through the compulsory labor of gender.

7. Karl Marx, "Economic and Philosophic Manuscripts of 1844," in the *Marx-Engels Reader*, ed. Robert C. Tucker (New York: Norton, 1978), 71.

8. Marx, " Economic and Philosophic Manuscripts," 74.

9. Hannah Arendt, *The Human Condition* (Chicago: University of Chicago Press, 1958), 87. Hereafter cited in the text.

10. Matthew Tinkcom, *Working Like a Homosexual: Camp, Capital, Cinema* (Durham, NC: Duke University Press, 2002).

11. Tinkcom, *Working Like a Homosexual*, 13.

12. The film is in Spanish, with English subtitles. All quotes included here are from the film's subtitles.

13. Margaret Gilpin, pers. comm., July 2006.

14. This history has been at the center of most academic discussions of sexuality in Cuba, making *Mariposas* all the more unique as a cultural text. See, e.g., Emilio Bejel, *Gay Cuban Nation* (Chicago: University of Chicago Press, 2001); Ian Lumsden, *Machos, Maricones, and Gays: Cuba and Homosexuality* (Philadelphia: Temple University Press, 1996); and Allen Young, *Gays under the Cuban Revolution* (San Francisco: Grey Fox, 1981).

15. Judith Butler, *Bodies That Matter: On the Discursive Limits of "Sex"* (New York: Routledge, 1993), 124.

16. This, of course, is José Esteban Muñoz's term. See José Esteban Muñoz, *Disidentifications: Queers of Color and the Performance of Politics* (Minneapolis: University of Minnesota Press, 1999), 7.

17. Karl Marx, *A Critique of Political Economy*, vol. 1 of *Capital*, trans. Ben Fowkes (1976; rpt. New York: Penguin, 1992), 164.

18. Gayatri Spivak, "Scattered Speculations on the Question of Value." Hereafter cited in the text.

QUEER STUDIES, MATERIALISM, AND CRISIS

A Roundtable Discussion

Christina Crosby, Lisa Duggan, Roderick Ferguson, Kevin Floyd, Miranda Joseph, Heather Love, Robert McRuer, Fred Moten, Tavia Nyong'o, Lisa Rofel, Jordana Rosenberg, Gayle Salamon, Dean Spade, Amy Villarejo

This roundtable was conducted by e-mail from June 2009 to August 2010. We divided participants into three groups, with each group responding in staggered fashion to the prompts. In this way, group 2 was able to see group 1's responses before they sent in their own. Group 3 was able to see the responses of groups 1 and 2. Through this process, we were able to not only include a remarkably large cluster of participants but also allow for the possibility of dialogue between groups. Group 1 consisted of Roderick Ferguson, Kevin Floyd, and Lisa Rofel. Group 2 included Heather Love, Robert McRuer, Fred Moten, and Tavia Nyong'o. Group 3 was Christina Crosby, Lisa Duggan, Miranda Joseph, Gayle Salamon, and Dean Spade.
—Jordana Rosenberg and Amy Villarejo.

Jordana Rosenberg and Amy Villarejo: We'd like to begin with a deliberately open-ended question, to take the pulse of queer studies today. We'd like to know where participants are coming from and heading toward in terms of their orientation to political-economic questions. We've collected a number of possible problematics with which to engage, based on our sense of where queer studies is headed, and how it might best seize on the interconnections between sexuality studies and the legacies of Marxism and historical materialism. Here we ask you to reflect on how a queer hermeneutics can be brought to bear on any of the following: economic crises past or present, the value-form, class and class struggle, capitalist moder-

GLQ 18:1
DOI 10.1215/10642684-1422170
© 2011 by Duke University Press

nity (broadly conceived), periodization, the aesthetic mediation of economic contradiction, exploitation and toil, globalization and theories of space, racism as the
privileged instrument of capital accumulation, secularization, and the narration of
modernity.

Kevin Floyd: I've been thinking about this rather startling reengagement with utopia in queer studies and about how to understand it in relation to the neoliberal
horizon queer studies has been thinking, and thinking against, for some time now.
If articulations of hetero- and homonormativity clarified a queer perspective on the
privatizing capacities of "rights" within a 1990s neoliberalism (e.g., Lauren Berlant, Michael Warner, Lisa Duggan), what's striking is both the increasingly global
horizon of the queer account of neoliberalism in the years since and its elaboration of an explicitly militarized and routinely racist post-9/11 violence (e.g., Martin Manalansan, Chandan Reddy, Jasbir Puar, Anna Agathangelou). This shift in
queer thought seems to resonate with Giovanni Arrighi's argument that in recent
decades the United States has more forcefully asserted its global policing power
precisely in defense of its apparently diminishing financial power.

So where does one get off talking about utopia? Established queer questions about temporality have also become questions about utopia — not simply in
the welcome appearance of José Muñoz's book on utopia but also in the book's
disagreement with anti-utopian interlocutor Lee Edelman.[1] The category of utopia
is indeed central to both of these positions, positions that share a refusal of what
Edelman would rightly call the "narcissistic" future to which a certain neoliberal
normativity wants to take those of us it would rather not just lock up. If it's difficult
to conjure any positive blueprint for a qualitatively different future (though Muñoz
bravely does this, in idealist terms he lays out with refreshing forthrightness), one
can at least embrace negativity, the destruction of the present. (But then for Theodor Adorno, on whom Edelman heavily leans, negativity and utopia tend to converge. Is *No Future* really a crypto-utopian polemic dressed up in the Lacanian
drag of an anti-utopian polemic?)

This engagement with utopia seems symptomatic of a moment in which
capital's colonization of the future appears both unassailable, as a familiar neoliberal narrative would have it (hence the "impossibility" of Edelman's "wager"),
and (as Muñoz suggests) transparently violent in a way that may suggest the opposite: accumulation's radical fragility. Marxism has read crisis both ways; queer
studies seems to be doing the same.

Lisa Rofel: Keywords for global capitalism: value, need, profit, exploitation, universal, uniform. Keywords for a queer hermeneutics: unstable boundaries, unstable

identities, bodies that speak worlds, heterogeneity, abjection. And desire. Brought to bear on global capitalism (and its attendant crises), a queer hermeneutics, especially one that is based in a postcolonial, postnationalist politics, leads us to grasp global capitalism not as a universal, unified phenomenon but as heterogeneous, interconnected practices whose coherence and universalism are asserted in the Euro-American metropoles but undone by the "difference," the specific histories and unequal positionings of the postcolonies. This queer hermeneutics allows us to move beyond the instrumental/affective dichotomy that has plagued analyses of capitalism, a dichotomy that ironically is itself one of the main products of capitalism. This queer hermeneutics allows us to see that the value-form lies not just in material objects but in bodies deemed differentially worthy of a valuable life, that capitalism is about needs but also about desires (which are not the same), that desires take myriad forms and are materialized in the relationship between eroticism and the mundane labor it takes to get through life. A queer hermeneutics that takes seriously the need to analyze how boundaries are shored up over and against what they try to exclude will refuse to draw the border of queer studies within the framework of the United States for considering the question of how to value queer lives. The assumption of the American nation-state as the realm that signifies a universal capitalism, within which we demand rights, assert the importance of queer lives, and otherwise challenge discourses of power, supports the ideology that America can address itself without reference to its empire. A postcolonial, postnationalist queer studies refuses such inadvertent collusion with American empire.

Rod Ferguson: When I started considering Marxism's potentials and limits, I was a graduate student in sociology. And in that discipline Karl Marx was one-third of a godhead completed by Max Weber and Émile Durkheim. My encounter with Marx was part of sociology's own exclusions around race, gender, and sexuality. It wasn't until I read Lisa Lowe's *Immigrant Acts: On Asian American Cultural Politics* that I began to imagine a way to use Marxism as something other than as a vehicle for those exclusions. As an undergraduate at Howard University, I was well aware of revolutionary nationalism's rearticulation of Marxism to account for racial domination. But it really wasn't until *Immigrant Acts* that I began to think about Marxism and intersectionality together.

Around that same time there were these interesting confluences taking place at UC San Diego—the crystallization of a materialist and critical-race feminism led to a large degree by Lowe, a comparative and theoretically attuned ethnic studies spearheaded by George Lipsitz, a deliberately reinventive queer studies called for by Judith Halberstam, and an emergent queer diaspora/queer of color formation developed by Gayatri Gopinath who was at UCSD on postdoc and Chandan Reddy who was dissertating there from Columbia. In the midst of all of this, it occurred to me that there might be an opportunity to rearticulate Marxist theories of the "totality of social relations" to account for these confluences. It was also a way to provide an alternative historical materialism, one that was alternative to the canonical exclusions of Marxism. For me the potential that queerness holds for Marxism still lies in re-posing the question of totality.

Fred Moten: I just returned home from a conference titled "Rethinking Racial Capitalism." The gathering was inspired by the conceptual force of Cedric Robinson's great book, *Black Marxism: The Making of the Black Radical Tradition* (Zed Books, 1983), in which he elaborates the notion of racial capitalism. That notion requires us to think of racism not as capitalism's instrument but as its condition of possibility. Robinson's work, in this regard, is conceptually parallel to Michel Foucault's late lectures on race, racism, and race war, as well as those on the abnormal and "the birth of biopolitics," all of which partly comprise working notes for the project of a history of sexuality. I've been trying to consider blackness — an "ontological totality," in Robinson's words, that is preserved by way of self-generated rupture and expansion — as a matter for thought, as well as the object of a politico-erotic claim, for those of us who are trying to live in a different way. That thought and that claim depend on a radical intellectual inhabitation of the general field of sociality-in-differentiation that calls capitalism into existence as a mode of accumulation set to work by regulative desire. They are animated by the interinanimative relation that structures the history of sexuality and the history of raciality, within which sexual-racial capitalism emerges and within which, in Foucault's words, "life constantly escapes." As a matter of course, knowledge of this fugitive mode of life, this runaway inherence, this unvalued and invaluable self-care of/in the undercommons, is unimaginable outside the radical (thought of the) outside that is queer hermeneutics or, as I also like to call it, black studies. I think it has many other names as well.

Heather Love: I want to call attention to primarily US-based queer writing that focuses on the lived realities of class and race. One key moment in this tradition is Cherríe Moraga's discussion of "queer attack" in her 1981 dialogue with Amber Hollibaugh. ("If you have enough money and privilege, you can separate yourself from heterosexist oppression. You can be sapphic or somethin, but you don't have to be queer.") I would also point to early work in deviance studies, pulp, Audre Lorde's *Zami*, Dorothy Allison's fiction and essays, Leslie Feinberg's *Stone Butch*

Blues, Eileen Myles's *Chelsea Girls*, Cathy Cohen's 1996 piece "Punks, Bulldaggers, and Welfare Queens," and Eli Clare's *Exile and Pride*. Along with recent scholarship on working-class and rural queer life (by Mary L. Gray, Scott Herring, Richard T. Rodriguez, Nadine Hubbs, Lisa Henderson, and others), queer working-class narratives have allowed me to think about my own class trajectory. For those of us for whom queer studies was a route to upward mobility, these texts are crucial. In their reflexivity and their emphasis on the everyday realities of exile, they get at the shame of being an outsider and at the shame of becoming an insider.

I want to recall a queer tradition that focuses on the lived experience of structural inequality. I realize that this might position me at the margins of a discussion that focuses on capital (rather than class as a dimension of social and psychic life). It's also true that I probably have less to say about crisis than about making do and getting by. Because of its emphasis on everyday life and intimate experience, the tradition I am pointing to can seem to lack a revolutionary horizon. But for me this refusal of the choice between revolution and capitulation is what makes this tradition queer.

Robert McRuer: One of the most interesting things about queer theory's engagements with Marxisms of late is the extent to which they cite/site disability and impairment, which often seem to be everywhere in queer theory without being named as such. Over and over, the queer theory we seem to want—one that provides some account of capitalist modernity, neoliberalism, or globalization—is concerned with the invalidated and unthinkable, with figures that are sick, infected, deranged, addicted, scarred, wounded, or traumatized.

Yet at times the figuration of disability in queer theory functions a lot like that of the racialized sex worker in Roderick Ferguson's *Aberrations in Black*. From liberal, Marxist, and anticolonial perspectives alike, Ferguson stresses, she marks the excesses of capitalism but cannot, supposedly, occupy a site from which a critique of capital might be launched. Building on Ferguson, we might note that a range of critiques of capital, again running the spectrum from liberal to revolutionary, figure disability as the sign of capitalism gone wrong while also conjuring up a naturalized able-bodiedness that should follow either its reform (for liberals) or eradication (for Marxists and other revolutionaries). Queer and crip reworkings of Marxism might more effectively speak to each other across their shared desire to not simply straighten that which is bent, and might thereby recognize the multiple locations where transnational crip/queer alliances function as sites for imagining a necessarily disabled world—meaning an inhabitable, sustainable, livable world. Even as various critics, for instance, responded to the Haitian earthquake by again simply metaphorizing Haiti's "crippled" position in the global economy (often using visual invocations of new amputees to make that point), cross-ability alliances on and off the island were imagining a different embodied future by critiquing the ongoing exploitation of Haiti while securing wheelchairs for use in the altered terrain.

Tavia Nyong'o: Marriage equality can seem to take place on an entirely different plane from the tax revolt and survivalist politics of the Tea Party. The latter's noxious social attitudes aside, might there not be a common adaptation to the rigors of a risk society? Both assume "personal responsibility," managing the anxiogenic prospects of a looming future of greater insecurity, lower resilience, and flailing health. These are the "no futures" many of us ponder when we ponder capitalism's death drive. Rather than a "haven in the heartless world," is marriage now woven into the fabric of the market's magic carpet, taking us along for the same wild ride?

Against Love (Pantheon, 2003), Laura Kipnis's brilliant and hilarious polemic, was written before the economic collapse. But her sharply observed demolition of our hypocritical attitudes toward fidelity remains prescient. Thinly disguised beneath magazine-friendly prose is a sound sociological treatise on how we govern ourselves through the very ideals and practices taken to comprise individuality and freedom. The problem with marriage is not the sexism, Kipnis insists, nor even the homophobia. The problem is the *love*, the nigh impossible impositions of which prep us for the masochistic demands of life under capitalism. Much as it always seems, from within a financial bubble, that the laws of capitalism have been repealed and that this time wealth will just keep magically growing, so does it seem within the heady throes of a love affair or new marriage that human nature, or the law of averages, has been finally proved irrelevant, and this particular time, for this particular couple, everlasting fulfillment really is at hand. Shorn of these fantasies—of wealth without work, of reciprocity without end—what less compromising demands would we be impelled to make on society, the state, and indeed, ourselves?

The question of intimate politics—as many queer commentators have shown—resists an instant, rhetorical fix. We cannot simply reject the ideologies of romantic love and companionate marriage for their complicities with contemporary capitalism. It is this very relationship of complicity that makes capitalism (sometimes) survivable. This complicity relates to what Jodi Dean, after Slavoj Žižek, calls "the decline of symbolic efficiency" in contemporary capitalism.[2]

Dean argues that the advanced industrial democracies are increasingly unable to support a stable set of terms for political debate, as those very terms become increasingly the subject of interminable contestation.

In the Lacanian analytic Dean adopts, a decline in symbolic efficiency is accompanied by a resurgence of the imaginary, aggressive dimension of politics. The public inquisitions into politicians' marital infidelity are examples of such aggressive and hypocritical fantasy, as if the stability of our union depended on theirs. Kipnis turns the table on such moralism by daring to speculate that adulterous politicians might be living out the experiments in public intimacy we are too timid to embrace ourselves. And while the noxious men who champion homophobia in public — and privately surf over to rentboy.com to hire "baggage handlers" — are not secretly allies, wouldn't the movement be weaker without their regular recurrence, and the delicious reminder of shared frailties and urgencies their exposure brings?

As much as many hope gays will change the institution of marriage for the better, may we not present the alternative reality that queers will probably do marriage no better than anyone else? We need new anthems for the gay divorcée, new tributes to the failures, *mésalliance*, and complicated legal entanglements we have already entered in our experiments with the public vow. Tracey Thorn's tender lament, "Oh, the Divorces" (*Love and Its Opposite*, 2010), tracks the social and psychic cost not only of the decline of the symbolic efficiency of marriage but also of the excessive inflation of marriage as a public front behind which, it turns out, "we wanted more all along." The song works as an immanent critique of the alienated sociality within which we negotiate other people's lives as presentiments of our own fate, the personal becoming, as Lauren Berlant says, "juxtapolitical." "No one gets off without paying the ride" is a line from Thorn's song, but it could also be a graffiti scrawled on a wall in Athens, or anywhere else ordinary life has been turned upside down by the global slump and its bill past due. Which is everywhere.

Miranda Joseph: As the other contributors to this discussion have already demonstrated, queer studies does its work, contributing to diverse and sometimes conflicting projects, with allies across interdisciplinary humanities and social science scholarship. This intention/effort toward "radical intellectual inhabitation of the general field of sociality-in-differentiation" (Moten) leads us to grasp capitalism "as heterogeneous, interconnected practices" (Rofel). So, when we take up the current "crisis," we define our object of analysis rather differently than the mainstream media (and many academic colleagues as well). We do not see a *financial* crisis, narrowly defined in time and space as a crisis of the financial system, nor can we speak in any uncomplicated way of "mainstreet," nor do we assess "the problem" as some of our behavioral science colleagues might, as a matter of the irrationality of individual decision making. On the contrary, we see that people have been engaged in diverse struggles, over time (not in one particular crisis moment), to make viable lives, to cobble together resources that enable fulfillment of—and occasionally resistance to—norms. We see the ways those efforts have made them available for exploitation and invited them to exploit others. It is in that context, then, that we bring some specifically "queer" tools to bear. For instance, Kevin Floyd's recent book, *The Reification of Desire* (University of Minnesota Press, 2009), directs us to the changing articulations of gender and desire that would attend adjustments to the mode of accumulation provoked by the current crisis. And I'm trying to put Lee Edelman's effort to claim, as queer antifuturists, nineteenth-century hoarders and money fondlers such as Scrooge and Silas Marner (before their redemption by the child, of course) in conversation with popular critiques of the "irresponsible" present-orientation of contemporary investment bankers. The behavior of the bankers might very well be understood to disrupt a variety of norms inseparable from heteronormativity, such as the "moral" responsibility to not "walk away" from an underwater mortgage (see Brent T. White, "Underwater and Not Walking Away: Shame, Fear and the Social Management of the Housing Crisis," 2009) and thus from a home that figured (in) a gendered, raced, sexualized American Dream.

Christina Crosby: I am thinking of John Ruskin, famous in Victorian Britain for his writing on art and architecture, and infamous for his writing on political economy. As an erstwhile enthusiastic Evangelical believer, Ruskin's work is at the intersection of religious ethics and the secular sciences of wealth and society. He makes manifest what Victorian doxa disavows, that a Protestant religious tradition is intertwined with what is imagined as the (moral) value-free discipline of economics.

In demonstrating this collusion, Ruskin's texts tend toward the writerly, gathering a rhetorical force that in his political economy bursts into an efflorescence of allegory. His Evangelical training called him to interpret this world as a figure for another, first in the symbolic economies of the Bible, then in heterodox allegories that perversely seek to be true to this world.

Ruskin's allegories may be illuminated by Walter Benjamin's reading of the intimacy between allegory and the commodity-form of value. For Benjamin, allegory is a systematic overnaming that mutes things only to make them speak more clearly the truths of the allegorist. Like the commodity, then, in allegory "the meaning can be replaced for another at any time. . . . Thus in the commodity, the allegorist is in his element. . . . [Yet]. . . [i]n the soul of the commodity, which gives the illusion of having made its peace in its price, a hell rages."[3] Mute and mournful, or raging, things remain for Benjamin beyond their allegorical existence or their life as commodities, never making their peace with abstraction. Beyond the devilish alienation of allegorizing and commodification, one can glimpse another possibility, as in the "palpable" relation of a collector to the objects collected, which are renewed in the collection that is "always somewhat impenetrable, and at the same time uniquely itself."[4] In Ruskin the violence inherent in the commodity-form of value is rendered as a rhetorical event. Yet there is more than the simple repetition of that violence, and that more is Ruskin's perverse desire for justice. When the interpretive dictates of typological reason fail him, allegorical reason finds meanings beyond the properly legible. In staying true to allegory, Ruskin both appropriates whatever is at hand, conscripting it to represent immaterial values, and also elevates and honors the mundane world and those he finds there. His terrific struggle against doctrinal political economy is illustrative of one of the most tightly sutured and vociferously disavowed relationships of Calvinist secularism, that of religious ethics and orthodox economic theories of value.

La lutte continue. The world we inherit from Victorian Britain is more degraded, more violent, a degradation and violence laid down by industrial capitalism and morphed into our post-Fordist nightmare. Ruskin's work is for me worth reading both as a symptomatic instantiation of that violence and an effort to endow the world with precious meaning adequate to its beauty.

Dean Spade: It's awful to see the process by which various gender and sexual eccentricities that have been sites of resistance and disruption are rehabilitated through liberal equality, recognition, and inclusion rubrics to become fertile spaces for calls to criminalization, standardized family formation, and military occupation. It is painful to watch various sites of grassroots mobilization eclipsed by funder-driven nonprofits articulating "LGBT" politics as a site for building white power. It is complex work that queer and trans scholars and activists engage in the face of these losses, work that must also occur while we navigate the impact that imprisonment, deportation, unemployment, loss of public benefits, the destruction of public education, and other conditions are having on the day-to-day lives of queer and trans people. Part of that work is to account for how the incorporation and deployment of sexual and gender excesses occurs, to analyze the investments in whiteness and capitalism that already belonged to various gay and lesbian ways of life and to gay and lesbian studies and politics that make them available for such adoptions. Another part is to interrogate our alternatives, to examine how they also produce politics of truth that require standardization, normalization, and the identification of internal enemies. This requires producing methods of self-critique and perpetual reflection best modeled by women of color feminism and visible in some prison abolition–focused queer and feminist work today as well. When practices of stateness centered on slavery and genocide perpetually emerge as an exile logic that is constitutive of our very psyches, thinking outside it may in fact be impossible. The impossibility of the other politics and ways of knowing we propose, the attempt to hold them lightly yet practice them urgently, is a struggle of this work. There is something about the practices of marginal queer and trans life that informs this work in all its impurity, something in the grief that has always been central to queer and trans life that is one of its most necessary tools. A queer hermeneutics gives us a depth of field for comprehending these pervasive reiterations of stateness and its regimes of violence, even those articulated in the name of the queer.

Gayle Salamon: In the middle of *Humanism and Terror* (Beacon Press, 1969), Merleau-Ponty says this about Marxism: "The foundations of Marxist politics are to be found *simultaneously* in the inductive analysis of the economic process and in a certain intuition of man and the relations between men." Marxist politics is grounded simultaneously in two different places—economic processes and relations between men—and relies on both induction and intuition. To the first: attention to those economic processes seems to be a particularly vital force in queer theory right now, as in David Eng's recent proposal that closer attention to the workings of capital, and the ways in which surplus value is differentially extracted from subjects of color, might return "queer" to critique and some of the political promise from which it has in recent years become unmoored. That second foundation—intuition—is a bit hazier, but I think a politics is located there, and there might be something useful to our collective musings here, even beyond the inadvertent queerness in his formulation of "relations between men."

I am very interested in Heather Love's suggestion we need to address "the lived experience" of inequality as well as its structure. The importance of spatiality in Love's intervention resonates for me with the importance of space and orientation in Sara Ahmed's *Queer Phenomenology* (Duke University Press, 2006), and I wonder how we might think about spatiality in this context alongside what we might think of as the temporal turn in queer studies, with the important work of Edelman, Halberstam, Muñoz, and Freeman, among others. It seems to me as if these two different ways of considering intractable inequality that Merleau-Ponty proposes—the structural and the experiential, or what we might even call the phenomenological—might offer important interdependent foundations for thinking about contemporary formations of queerness and class. I think Heather is right to suggest that we don't yet have a readily available language for describing class inside and outside queer theory. How might we talk about a lived experience of class, or even class abjection, that can be simultaneously shared and neglected by more dominant narratives without engaging in precisely the same kind of identity politics that it has always been queer theory's task to dismantle?

Lisa Duggan: In the United States in particular, the neoliberal economic reason of state managers in both the Republican and the Democratic Parties is under attack from angry, uncivil Tea Partiers and others who loudly insist that economic decisions are politically loaded and who denounce the Wall Street bailout as stridently as they do health care reform. Where is the Left? While liberals call for a return to reason and civility, perhaps the queer Left especially might have something more provocative to say about political feeling?

Scholars, artists, and activists who collaborate under the umbrella of "Public Feelings" groups in Chicago, Austin, and New York (so far) draw from queer theories and politics to make a double move. We work to expose the cynical or reactionary deployment of feeling in public life, from sentimentality to fury—sometimes under the cloak of political rationality, sometimes as an open seduction into reactionary mobilizations. At the same time, we hope to acknowledge the feelings engaged in and through public life and bring them into debate and deployment in and for the Left. I am thinking of the wide-ranging work of Lauren Berlant, José Muñoz, Janice Gould, Jasbir Puar, Fred Moten, Miranda Joseph, Ann Cvetkovich, Sandra Soto, Janet Jakobsen, and Ann Pellegrini among many others.

I think it is useful to note that the current queen of libertarian reason, and touchstone for the Tea Party Right in the United States, Ayn Rand (whose novel *Atlas Shrugged* is now again enjoying runaway sales), based her eroticized capitalist heroes on a historical example of masculine sociopathy. In her published journals, she praises the figure on whom she based the earliest incarnation of her heroic type—the serial killer William Hickman, tried and imprisoned for the kidnapping and dismemberment of twelve-year-old Marian Parker. Her favored slogan, "What is good for me is right," was attributed to Hickman. From Hickman's mouth to Wall Street's ear. Across the globe, this connection illuminates the affective roots of the rationalized devastations of neoliberal capitalism, as neo-imperial plunder and slaughter as well as theft and exploitation.

For the second move I join José Muñoz along with the Feel Tank in calling for humor, more effective than earnest outrage in so many (not all) circumstances. Here I invite *GLQ* readers to join the more than five thousand members of the Cocktail Party, a barstool-roots movement for left-wing urban homosexuals and those who love us, on Facebook.

Rosenberg and Villarejo: We've got such a wealth of tributaries to follow here! Perhaps it would be best, rather than having to select any one in particular, to try to get at a methodological question that underpins all of these rapprochements between queer studies and Marxism/political economy/historical materialism. That question is the status of totality for queer thought, and, following Roderick Ferguson, we believe now may be a moment in which we might "re-pos[e] the question of totality." If totality has seemed an obstacle in brokering connections between queer methodologies and those of historical materialism, we may be at a point at which that obstacle is breaking down. Specifically, in the wake of identity politics, as we forcefully interrogate some of the presumptions of identity-based sexuality studies, have we opened the way to a new conceptualization of totality, a rapprochement with what had at one point appeared most unqueer to queer studies? We explore some of these questions at greater length in the introduction to this volume, but for now we'd like to hear how the participants have come to navigate these methodological alignments.

Floyd: Can one "re-pos[e] the question of totality" without implicating oneself in an imperial, American universalism? Lisa Rofel suggests that this is a dicey proposition. Must we choose between characterizing global capitalism as either heterogeneous or unified? An old problem still very much with us, as I take several of the earlier interventions in this roundtable to suggest: the problem of grasping the ways in which capitalism's gendered, racialized, sexualized violence is inseparable from (as effect? as condition of possibility? as both?) capitalism's simultaneous identity and nonidentity with itself.

Does re-posing the question of totality mean doing something queer studies hasn't yet done? Or does it mean reframing, rearticulating "the potential that queerness holds for Marxism and has held for Marxism for a while now," as Ferguson intimates with the crucial word "still"? Doesn't it mean thinking what Moten calls "the general field of sociality-in-differentiation" from a point of view which is queer precisely in its refusal of the identitarian vocabularies with which sexuality has been normatively understood? Thinking totality would appear to be one of the things queer studies has been doing at least since the opening lines of *Epistemology of the Closet* (Duke, 1990), at least since Warner's introduction to *Fear of a*

Queer Planet (Minnesota, 1993). And is this not what it does when that dizzyingly broad field called "neoliberalism" becomes one of its defining horizons?

If queer studies has struggled against what Ferguson rightly calls "the canonical exclusions of Marxism," perhaps one of its untapped lessons is that one struggles against totality only by struggling with it. I take the practice of thinking totality to be a necessarily critical effort to grasp a social field as unified precisely in its disunity. Such efforts are limited by definition; Marx, Lukács, and Adorno all insist in their various ways that this kind of conceptual mapping will be defined as much by what it excludes as by what it includes — that presumptions of bird's-eye-view omniscience are ultimately caricatures of this critical practice, which doesn't mean that thinking totality can ever fully avoid turning into its own caricature.

One way queer studies might re-pose the question of totality is to reconsider totality's necessary relation to "exclusion." How does one hold unity and differentiation, identity and nonidentity, in one's head at the same time? One answer is: stumblingly, inadequately.

Ferguson: In Marxist traditions, totality has been a way to theorize the heterogeneity of both social relations and critical formations and to propose relationships between subjects and objects. The trouble is that those theorizations have oftentimes secreted really troubling universalisms, universalisms that themselves become genres of identity politics. On the more favorable side, totality began as a broad attempt to appreciate social and epistemic heterogeneity.

One promising aspect of the notion is its scavenger and interdisciplinary nature. I remember how encouraged I felt as a grad student when I read Lukács's *History and Class Consciousness*, particularly his use of the category "totality" to argue against specialization. That was tremendously important to me as someone who was struggling to do interdisciplinary work and attempting to reinvent familiar objects. If totality is about the reinvention of the object, as Lukács argued, then we might think of Christina's revision of John Ruskin and Lisa Rofel's "queer hermeneutics" as falling within that domain of reinvention.

In addition, the question of totality, as Jordana and Amy pose it in their introduction, partly begs us to consider the critique of identity *as well as* the politics of identity that has often undergirded the term *totality*. In *History and Class Consciousness*, Lukács deploys the concept of totality as a critique of identity, writing that "the category of totality does not reduce its various elements to an undifferentiated uniformity, to identity." To do so would be to deny the dynamism of dialectical relationships. At the same time, in terms of the history of Western

Marxism, "totality" has been a vehicle for the identity politics of the West. In many ways, it was revolutionary nationalist, women of color, and postcolonial scholars who provided powerful rebuttals to that Eurocentrism. And in doing so, those folks worked to produce other notions of totality not purchased through Eurocentrism.

Queer of color and queer diasporic work has an analogous history with queer studies. In queer studies there was both a critique of identity and what Martin Jay calls a "doggedly consistent Eurocentrism."[5] What a lot of us were trying to do and have been trying to do since is point to the invisible maneuvers of identity precisely in those critical formations that presume that they have transcended identity — formations that, in the presumption of removal, have only contracted with discourses of transcendence. We can't help but "do" totality, so best to know how we're doing it.

Rofel: Lukács poses the question of totality to account for the pervasiveness of bourgeois modes of consciousness that went well beyond the immediate capitalist relations of production. Christina Crosby's reading of Ruskin helps us in this regard. A queer hermeneutics desiring a radical future that, as Fred Moten puts it so well, means "knowledge of this fugitive mode of life, this runaway inherence," leads us back to this question of how to think and act in the multiple. I follow Stuart Hall and Rod Ferguson in naming this question one of articulation and intersectionality in order to allow for temporal contingencies.

Heather Love reminds us of the specificities of affect: the so-called crisis, she implies, is clearly a middle-class experience that for others is just the same old "making do and getting by." The public sentiments that Lisa Duggan and others have so presciently named seem to me to be symptomatic of the insecurity of the white-dominated US Empire along with a post-9/11 highly regulative public life bent on endlessly recuperating that empire. The kinds of articulations I seek include not just an invocation of the global but a queer interrogation of global geopolitics as Petrus Liu calls for in "Why Does Queer Theory Need China?": "There transnationally formed, nonterritorially organized power relations are rich sites to be mined for a queer theory that emphasizes that 'the subject' is always barred, incomplete, and opaque to itself." If we are to take seriously the point that "our" worlds in the United States have intimate imbrications with those places pressed into service for the US empire, then we must include in our analytic maps that what is "queer" is constantly expanded, supplemented, and revised by those "others" in Asia and elsewhere whose queerness has also been intimately wrapped up with the United States. The queer subject is a transnational encounter. I read the utopia in queer theory that Kevin Floyd has so incisively honed in on to include the importance of empire to the way queer theory veers from emphasizing how life gets taken over by the norm to highlighting how life manages to escape. This kind of theoretical veering needs to be at the center of the question of articulation.

McRuer: If totality is a way to theorize the heterogeneity of both social relations and critical formations and to propose relationships between subjects and objects (Ferguson) or "a necessarily critical effort to grasp a social field as unified precisely in its disunity" (Floyd), it seems to me that this nuanced conversation about totality might be glossed by Dean Spade's earlier comments on "rehabilitation." Dean describes the ways that queer and trans activists have attempted to think totality by constantly mobilizing sites of "resistance and disruption." These productive sites of excess are, in turn, continually domesticated by bourgeois universalisms, through what Dean calls "liberal equality, recognition, and inclusion rubrics."

Queer theorists have rightfully noted the ways that gay marriage is particularly useful for these rehabilitative processes. Consider, for instance, Arnold Schwarzenegger's comments following the August 4, 2010, court ruling that Proposition 8 (which banned same-sex marriage in California) was unconstitutional: "For the hundreds of thousands of Californians in gay and lesbian households who are managing their day-to-day lives, this decision affirms the full legal and protections and safeguards I believe everyone deserves." It probably goes without saying that the gay and lesbian "management" of day-to-day lives that the Governator invokes is a far cry from what Heather Love describes as "making do and getting by." The bright new gay day invoked by this pronouncement—saturated as it is with universalizing homonationalism—obscures how California is indeed arguably leading the way to the future, but a future of degradation rather than dignity. At the time of Schwarzenegger's statement, in fact, disabled activists had camped out for much of the summer in a tent city on a traffic island in Berkeley that they dubbed "Arnieville." Their camp—a site of resistance and disruption—deliberately redeployed the degradation of "Hooverville" shantytowns from the Great Depression and was intended to protest massive cuts to In-Home Supportive Services (IHSS) and Medi-Cal, along with other programs that elderly, disabled, and poor people depend on. Schwarzenegger did not issue any official pronouncements on Arnieville but did deploy state power to arrest twenty-two activists who took the protest to Sacramento.

I bring forward this localized example, first, to think about how queer and trans and crip (there are many other names, as Fred Moten suggests) attempts to think totality get rehabilitated into recognizable and obfuscating sentiments, and, second, to note the ongoing labor of theorists in multiple locations (including traffic islands) re-posing the question of totality and struggling with the exclusions necessarily generated by those processes.

Moten: Marxism was always animated by this other thing, which was not (a) subject, that it was trying to regulate and disavow. All of Immanuel Kant's ambivalence about the constitutive/disruptive force of the imagination is intensified in Marx, re-intensified in Vladimir Lenin, Lukács, Adorno (its racial and sexual determinations more elaborate and surreptitious, given in sharp relation to certain dangerously informal, form-making and form-breaking, lumpen disabilities until this other thing starts to speak so loudly on its subalternative frequencies that the regular music turns off); and the palpable wrench and rush one feels at having read, let alone at having attempted to address, Kevin Floyd's question—the founding question of our public/private tryst—is all bound up with our implication in the extended romance with that ambivalence. I wonder if a kind of break is made possible if we try to break a little something off that question. On the one hand, "where does one get off talking about utopia?" On the other hand, where does one get off? Where in the world does one get off? In what world does one get off? Is there another world in which we can get off? Is there another world, here, that bears a chance, and bodies forth having taken that chance, to get off of—in having gotten off in—this one, which is more and less than that? Isn't this where the question of totality becomes the question of utopia? Appositions and repositions of that mutually emergent fold are generally asked of and by those who have been posed. They're about what Trane referred to, in an expression of the queerest possible desire, as the opposite. They proliferate in the most beautifully unnatural way: one has to be off—which is to say get off—in the world just to ask, as if one were more and less than that. That old interplay of regulation and disavowal often seems to interdict such curiosity, its erotic, world-making errancy, which is what I take Muñoz's point to be. This other thing wants all or nothing at all.

Spade: I've been hung up for a while on the problem that Foucault identifies at the end of his March 17, 1976, lecture. I think about this as a problem for utopic endeavors: how state racism is inherent to the "mechanisms of biopower that the development of society and State ha[ve] been establishing since the eighteenth century."[6] Such endeavors seek redistribution. In fact, much of what I have been thinking about for a while has been how the increased centrality of legal strategy in gay and lesbian politics (and the emergent formation of a disappointing trans politics that is sometimes assumed to follow in its footsteps) has been a part of what Lisa Duggan aptly described as "neoliberal 'equality' politics — a stripped down, nonredistributive form of 'equality' designed for global consumption during the twenty-first century, and compatible with continued upward distribution of resources."[7] I've been looking at how the production of demands for formal legal equality sustains conditions of maldistribution and wondering if and when law reform campaigns ever can be useful tactics in resistance strategies whose demands (e.g., prison abolition, the end of immigration enforcement) entail the abolition of the American legal system itself which has protected and maintained a racialized-gendered distribution of property since its inception.

The problem that Foucault raises requires that we take our critical examination of how the projects of standardization, normalization, and distribution that constitute stateness always include state racism and apply it to anticapitalist formations with redistribution demands. If we understand all projects of redistribution to produce forms of stateness, and state racism to be inherent to those projects, what might a trans politics envision when we dream of alternatives to neoliberalism? Andrea Smith suggests a need to think about more just forms of governance, and to imagine "visions of nation and sovereignty that are separate from nation-states."[8] I find myself asking what we might see from the vantage point of a trans politics centered on an understanding of racialized-gendered subjection and a critique of liberation projects that embraces failure and excess while demanding attention to the material conditions of existence and the distribution of life chances. What methods of inquiry and intervention might such a politics develop?

Love: Sedgwick engaged the problem of totality in *Epistemology of the Closet* through her discussion of universalizing and minoritizing discourses of sexuality. I would like to suggest the salience in this context of another important (but less often cited) theoretical framework: the distinction between descriptive and prescriptive approaches to sexuality elaborated in Gayle Rubin's 1984 essay "Thinking Sex." Rubin makes the distinction in the context of a defense of sexology and sex research, which, she argues, are characterized by "abundant detail . . . and a well-developed ability to treat sexual variety as something that exists." Because of their focus on description and taxonomy, these fields can "provide an empirical grounding for a radical theory of sexuality more useful than the combination of psychoanalysis and feminist first principles to which so many texts resort."[9]

Rubin's brief against prescriptive "first principles" has not been taken up in queer studies; in fact, the radicalism of the field has in part been defined by its anti-empiricism and by its explicitly ideological and partisan character. But Rubin suggests that radicalism might consist, for example, in making space for the existence of sexual minorities. The descriptive tendency in queer studies and politics is, to my mind, too often obscured. But it is there. You can see the workings of this impulse in *Epistemology*, even or especially in the axioms. What is the first of Sedgwick's first principles? "People are different from each other."[10]

The question of totality must be routed through more sustained reflection on the distinction between the prescriptive and the descriptive; ultimately a shift toward description and inclusion would be an important development in the field. To play this out in terms of the question of identity: whatever we think of identity, whether or not we believe in it or approve of it, it continues to exist, to shape our experience, to affect our life chances, and so on. We need an account of identity that makes space for it, and not merely in the hygienic realm of strategy, either. I would never want to lose the utopian and aspirational aspects of the field of queer studies. But as Rubin has taught us, radicalism is not only about making a new future, it is also about making space for what is.

Crosby: I am reminded here of the penultimate sentence of Gayatri Spivak's "Can the Subaltern Speak?": "Representation has not withered away," which is surely a position as important as ever to defend, for it reminds those of us trained in the humanities that humanity lives in language, and that we must remain sharply vigilant of that condition to which all are subject.[11] Differently.

"I am still very unwell, and tormented between the longing for rest and lovely life, and the sense of this terrific call of human cry for resistance and of human misery for help, though it seems to me as the voice of a river of blood which can but sweep me down in the midst of its black clots, helpless."[12] John Ruskin made the ethical decision to answer this call. The economic cycle of overproduction → crisis → overproduction created both untold wealth and its equivalent or more in misery. The fertile inventiveness of finance capital as it developed over the nineteenth century reminds us that value is representational all the way down. The barred subject of capital, $, cannot know itself and imagines a world in which self-valorizing value is the alpha and omega, world without end. Not so Ruskin's impassioned, eccentric, ethical, and deeply patriarchal utopian impulses remind us that another world is possible.

Ruskin is a subject "barred, incomplete, and opaque to itself" (Lisa Rofel, quoting Petrus Liu), his desires incoherent and obliquely expressed. The cascading details of his writing, while a furious denunciation of the present, are also glimpses of something excitingly different from the world I know and despair of. *Capital* remains indispensable, in its dialectical analysis of the world capital makes. I don't think, however, that Marxist concepts alone allow us to address the rhetorical effects of Ruskin's tropes as we are turned by their logic, sometimes finding a drearily familiar and oppressive fantasy and sometimes a world where the everyday has been irradiated with joy. Taking up once more the question of totality, wherein all the remains of the day are impressed with the logic of capital, is both appealing in its explanatory power and unappealing for the same reason. My education in aesthetics urges on me the importance of writing, wherein is sedimented both the complexity of the past and intimations of lives not yet lived. I like what José Muñoz has to say: "Often we can glimpse the worlds proposed and promised by queerness in the realm of the aesthetic . . . a forward dawning futurity."[13]

Joseph: I asked my upper-division undergraduate class at the University of Arizona: "Are you following the economic crisis, do you pay attention to news stories about it?" One student responded that she was overwhelmed with the details and couldn't really get a handle on what was going on. It struck me that she was in need of what used to be called "an analysis." While the phrase *an analysis* might suggest that one always already knows what one thinks, I would like to hear it instead as connoting a necessarily open framework, one that is, crucially — like *totality* — a thought of relationality.

The possibility of "an analysis" is under direct frontal attack here in Arizona. While SB 1070, Arizona's anti-immigration law, has received the bulk of national attention, we are also dealing with HB 2281, the so-called anti–ethnic studies law, which its promoters have portrayed as intended to shut down a particular high school Mexican American studies program in the Tucson Unified School District. But its language augers a broader effort to bar access to thinking relationality: "The Legislature finds and declares that public school pupils should be taught to treat and value each other as individuals," and prohibits "any classes that . . . advocate ethnic solidarity."[14] The threat is not usually so explicit. The spaces and times for relational thought usually just get swamped by the flood of resources — material, institutional, cultural — that flow in support of the specialized bourgeois knowledge production, the production of one-sided knowledge in service to capital accumulation, against which Lukács wrote.

Our task then is not only to defetishize and queer those dominant knowledges — reading the complex and open totality of relations out of which they emerge — but also to offer an alternative orientation, to make another sense, so that we have allies in the fight for the space/time to have this thought.

Duggan: Empire, neoliberalism, capitalism. These are deeply interrelated large-scale phenomena, but they are not the same thing. US empire may be on the rapid exit ramp now, while neoliberal policies are being retrenched in a long twenty-first century to follow Giovanni Arrighi's long twentieth. Though we may be right on the mark in noting the "end of empire," we may be much too optimistic when we use the phrase *late capitalism*.

From a queer studies perspective, our analyses of the mutually constituting politics of class, race, gender, sexuality, nationalism, religion, and disability will shift with the scale, time frame, and location of the political economic framework through which we focus our work. If we focus too consistently and relentlessly at the broadest time/space scale, we will risk missing significant variations and moments of contest in specific times and places. This is the danger that Timothy Mitchell warns us against when he argues that "capitalism" may be too systematic a concept to capture the history of colonialism, or that, according to J. K. Gibson-Graham, is the underrated importance of the persistence of noncapitalist forms of production and exchange. This is the direction that even David Harvey points us toward when he analyzes "neoliberalism" as a double phenomenon—both a utopian theory of unregulated global markets and a pragmatic political rule regime for installing and maintaining regional, national, or local oligarchies. When we write about neoliberal sexual politics, about which of these neoliberalisms do we write? If we focus, blinkered, on specific times and places, as some historians and anthropologists do, we can radically misunderstand the stakes of our political and scholarly engagements.

So perhaps it makes more sense to speak of provisional, shifting, totalities? Moving beyond the Marxist notions of the relative autonomy of culture, or the contingent hegemony of regimes of state power, might we consider the usefulness of shifting frames for historical, political analysis? I like to think of queerness, for instance, as a kind of promiscuous relational experimentalism. Thinking queerly about the history and future of capitalism is a search for Fred Moten's fugitive modes of life existing, both doomed and prescient, among the fractures of totalities past and present.

Notes

1.   José Esteban Muñoz, *Cruising Utopia: The Then and There of Queer Futurity* (New York: New York University Press, 2009); Lee Edelman, *No Future: Queer Theory and the Death Drive* (Durham, NC: Duke University Press, 2004).

2. Jodi Dean, *Democracy and Other Neoliberal Fantasies* (Durham, NC: Duke University Press, 2009).

3. Max Pensky, *Melancholy Dialectics: Walter Benjamin and the Play of Morning* (Amherst: University of Massachusetts Press, 1993), 167, quoting Benjamin, *GS*, 5: 466.

4. Walter Benjamin, "Unpacking My Library," in *Illuminations*, trans. Harry Zohn (New York: Schocken, 1968), 63.

5. Martin Jay, *Marxism and Totality: The Adventures of a Concept from Lukács to Habermas* (Berkeley: University of California Press, 1986), 5.

6. Michel Foucault, *Society Must Be Defended: Lectures at the College de France, 1975–76,* (New York: Picador, 2003), 242.

7. Lisa Duggan, *Twilight of Equality: Neoliberalism, Cultural Politics and the Attack on Democracy* (Boston: Beacon, 2004), xii.

8. Andrea Smith, "American Studies without America: Native Feminisms and the Nation State," *American Quarterly* 2008, 312.

9. Gayle Rubin, "Thinking Sex: Notes for a Radical theory of the Politics of Sexuality" in *Pleasure and Danger: Exploring Female Sexuality*, ed. Carole S. Vance (London: Pandora, 1992), 284.

10. Eve Kosofky Sedgwick, *Epistemology of the Closet* (Berkeley: University of California Press, 1990), 22.

11. Gayatri Chakravorty Spivak, "Can the Subaltern Speak?" in *Marxism and the Interpretation of Culture*, ed. Cary Nelson (Urbana: University of Illinois Press, 1988), 308.

12. John Ruskin, *Unto This Last* (New York: Dutton, 1907), viii.

13. José Muñoz, *Cruising Utopia: The Then and There of Queer Futurity* (New York: NYU Press, 2009), 1.

14. Sandra K. Soto and Miranda Joseph provide a full reading of the working of the law in "Neoliberalism and the Battle Over Ethnic Studies in Arizona," *Thought and Action: The NEA Higher Education Journal*, Fall 2010: 45–56.

CODA:
THE COST OF GETTING BETTER

Suicide, Sensation, Switchpoints

Jasbir K. Puar

There are many things lost in the naming of a death as a "gay youth suicide."
In what follows, I offer a preliminary analysis of the prolific media attention to
gay youth suicides that began in the United States in the fall of 2010. I am interested in how this attention recalls affective attachments to neoliberalism that
index a privileged geopolitics of finance capitalism. I have been struck by how
the discourses surrounding gay youth suicide partake in a spurious binarization of
what I foreground as an interdependent relationship between bodily capacity and
bodily debility. These discourses reproduce neoliberalism's heightened demands
for bodily capacity, even as this same neoliberalism marks out populations for
what Lauren Berlant has described as "slow death" — the debilitating ongoingness of structural inequality and suffering.[1] In the United States, where personal
debt incurred through medical expenses is the number one reason for filing for
bankruptcy, the centrality of what is termed the medical-industrial complex to
the profitability of slow death cannot be overstated.[2] My intervention here is an
attempt to go beyond a critique of the queer neoliberalism embedded in the ten-
dentious mythologizing that "it gets better" by confronting not only the debilitating
aspects of neoliberalism but, more trenchantly, the economics of debility. If the
knitting together of finance capitalism and the medical-industrial complex means
that debility pays, and pays well, then the question becomes, how can an affective
politics move beyond the conventional narratives of resistance to neoliberalism?

GLQ 18:1
DOI 10.1215/10642684-1422179
© 2011 by Duke University Press

The Cost of Getting Better

To begin, I pose two queries: one, what is contained in the category of sexuality? Two, what kinds of normative temporal assumptions are produced through the "event" of suicide? As a faculty member of Rutgers University in New Jersey, where a student, Tyler Clementi, committed suicide after videos of him having sex with a man were circulated by his roommate and another student, I want to provide better context for the local circumstances of his death. All three students (Clementi, Dharun Ravi, and Molly Wei) were living on Busch campus in Piscataway, New Jersey, already codified as the campus for science/premed "geeks" (some might say sissies). Busch is also racially demarcated as the "Asian" campus, an identity rarely disaggregated from geek at US colleges. Clementi's suicide has predictably occasioned a vicious anti-Asian backlash replete with over-determined notions of "Asian homophobia" and predictable calls to "go back to where you came from," as seen in numerous online articles. Commenting on the biases of the criminal justice system against people of nonnormative race, ethnicity, and citizenship, a press release from a Rutgers organization called Queering the Air notes that Garden State Equality (a New Jersey LGBT advocacy group) and Campus Pride (a national group for LGBT students) have demanded the most severe consequences for Ravi and Wei, prosecution for hate crimes, maximum jail time, expulsion without disciplinary hearing, and that "18,000 people endorse an online group seeking even more serious charges—manslaughter."[3]

It seems imperative that the implications of two "model minority" students from a wealthy New Jersey suburb who targeted an effete, young, queer white man be considered beyond convenient narratives of the so-called inherent homophobia within racialized immigrant communities. Is it possible to see all three students involved as more alike—all geeks, in fact—than different? Instead of rehashing that old "gaybashers are closet cases" canard, perhaps there is a reason to destabilize the alignments of "alikeness" and "difference" away from a singular, predictable axis through "sexuality." A letter recently circulated by Queering the Air claims that Clementi's death is the second suicide by an LGBTQ student since March and that four of the last seven suicides at Rutgers were related to sexuality.[4] What, then, is meant here by "related to sexuality"? I am prompted by Amit Rai's reformulation of sexuality as "ecologies of sensation"—as affect instead of identity—that transcends the designations of straight and gay and can further help disaggregate these binary positions from their racialized histories.[5]

Missing from the debate about Clementi's suicide is a discussion about the proclivities of young people to see the "choice" of Internet surveillance as a mandatory regulatory part not only of their subject formations but of their bodily habits and affective tendencies. For these youth, so-called cyberstalking is an integral part of what it means to become a neoliberal (sexual) subject. Think of the ubiquity of sexting, applications like Grinder, Manhunt, DIY porn, and cellphone mass circulation of images—technologies that create simultaneous sensations of exposure (the whole world is watching) and alienation (no one understands). These cyborgian practices constitute new relations between public and private that we have yet to really acknowledge, much less comprehend. "Invasion of privacy" remains uncharted territory for jurisprudence in relation to the Internet. But more significantly, to reiterate Rai, the use of these technologies impels new affective tendencies of bodies, new forms of attention, distraction, practice, and repetition. The presumed differences between "gay" and "straight" could be thought more generously through the quotidian and banal activities of sexual self-elaboration through Internet technologies—emergent habituations, corporeal comportment, and an array of diverse switchpoints of bodily capacity.

If signification and representation (what things mean) are no longer the only primary realm of the political, then bodily processes (how things feel) must be irreducibly central to any notion of the political. Clementi's participation in the testimonial spaces of the chat room to detail his roommate's invasion of his "privacy" and Clementi's use of Facebook for the explanatory "suicide note" reflect precisely the shared continuities with his perpetrators through ecologies of sensation. Accusations of "homophobia," "gay bullying," and even "cyberbullying" fail to do justice to the complex uptake of digital technologies in this story.

The apparently sudden spate of queer suicides is also obviously at odds with the claims of purported progress by the gay and lesbian rights movement. As noted by Tavia Nyong'o, Dan Savage's sanctimonious statement "it gets better" is a mandate to fold oneself into urban, neoliberal gay enclaves: a call to upward mobility that discordantly echoes the now-discredited "pull yourself up by the bootstraps" immigrant motto.[6] (The symbolism of Clementi's transit from central New Jersey to the George Washington Bridge that connects northern New Jersey to upper Manhattan is painfully apparent.) Part of the outrage generated by these deaths is based precisely in a belief that things are indeed supposed to be better, especially for a particular class of white gay men. As I argue in my op-ed in the *Guardian*, this amounts to a reinstatement of white racial privilege that was lost with being gay.[7] Savage has also mastered, if we follow Sarah Lochlain Jain on the "politics of sympathy," the technique of converting Clementi's injury into cultural capital, not only through affectations of blame, guilt, and suffering but also through those of triumph, transgression, and success.[8]

Affective Politics: States of Capacity and Debility

The subject of redress and grievance thus functions here as a recapacitation of a debilitated body. To make my second and related point, then, I want to shift the registers of this conversation about "queer suicide" from pathologization versus normativization of sexual identity to questions of bodily capacity, debility, disability, precarity, and populations. This is not to dismiss these queer suicides but to ask what kinds of "slow deaths" have been ongoing that a suicide might represent an escape from. It is also to "slow" the act of suicide down—to offer a concomitant yet different temporality of relating to living and dying. Berlant moves us away from trauma or catastrophe, proposing that "slow death occupies the temporalities of the endemic" (756). Slow death occurs not within the timescale of the suicide or the epidemic but within "a zone of temporality . . . of ongoingness, getting by, and living on, where the structural inequalities are dispersed, the pacing of their experience intermittent, often in phenomena not prone to capture by a consciousness organized by archives of memorable impact" (759). In this nonlinear temporality, for it starts and stops, redoubles and leaps ahead, Berlant is not "defining a group of individuals merely afflicted with the same ailment, [rather] slow death describes populations marked out for wearing out" (760–61n20). That is, slow death is not about an orientation toward the death drive, nor is it morbid; rather, it is about the maintenance of living, the "ordinary work of living on" (761).

In the context of slow death, I ponder three things. First, what does it mean to proclaim "it gets better," or "you get stronger"? Second, why is suicide constituted as the ultimate loss of life? Third, how can we connect these suicides to the theorization of debility and capacity? David Mitchell's moving invocation of disability "not as exception, but the basis upon which a decent and just social order is founded," hinges on a society that acknowledges, accepts, and even anticipates disability.[9] This anticipatory disability is the dominant temporal frame of both disability rights activism (you are able-bodied only until you are disabled) as well as disability studies. As the queer disability theorist Robert McRuer writes, "It's clear that we are haunted by the disability to come."[10] Disability is posited as the most common identity category because we will all belong to it someday, as McRuer's comment implies. Yet, as David Mitchell and Sharon Snyder argue, disability is "reified as the true site of insufficiency."[11] But Berlant's formulation of slow death implies that we might not (only) be haunted by the disability to come but also disavow the debility already here.

Berlant argues that "health itself can then be seen as a side effect of successful normativity" (765). Therefore, to honor the complexity of these suicides, they must be placed within the broader context of neoliberal demands for bodily capacity as well as the profitability of debility, both functioning as central routes through which finance capital seeks to sustain itself. In my current book project, "Affective Politics: States of Capacity and Debility," I examine these heightened demands for bodily capacity and exceptionalized debility. Capacity and debility are seeming opposites generated by increasingly demanding neoliberal formulations of health, agency, and choice — what I call a "liberal eugenics of lifestyle programming" — that produce, along with biotechnologies and bioinformatics, population aggregates. Those "folded" into life are seen as more capacious or on the side of capacity, while those targeted for premature or slow death are figured as debility. Such an analysis re-poses the questions: which bodies are made to pay for "progress"? Which debilitated bodies can be reinvigorated for neoliberalism, and which cannot? In this regard, Savage's project refigures queers, along with other bodies heretofore construed as excessive/erroneous, as being on the side of capacity, ensuring that queerness operates as a machine of regenerative productivity. Even though post-structuralist queer theory critically deploys registers of negativity (and increasingly negative affect) in reading practices primarily deconstructive in their orientation, such a figuration of queer theory has emerged from a homeostatic framework: queer theory is already also a machine of capacity in and after the cybernetic turn. Bioinformatics frames — in which bodies figure not as identities or subjects but as data — entail that there is no such thing as nonproductive excess but only emergent forms of new information.[12] This revaluing of excess/debility is potent because, simply put, debility — slow death — is profitable for capitalism. In neoliberal, biomedical, and biotechnological terms, the body is always debilitated in relation to its ever-expanding potentiality.

What I am proposing, then, is also an intervention into the binaried production of disabled versus nondisabled bodies that drives both disability studies and disability rights activism. Even as the demands of ableism weigh heavy and have been challenged by disability scholars and activists, attachments to the difference of disabled bodies may reify an exceptionalism that only certain privileged disabled bodies can occupy. While the disability rights movement largely understands disability as a form of nonnormativity that deserves to be depathologized, disability justice activists seek to move beyond access issues foregrounded by the Americans with Disabilities Act as well as global human rights frames that standardize definitions of disability and the terms of their legal redress across national locations. They instead avow that in working-poor and working-class communities of color, disabilities and debilities are actually "the norm." Thus a political agenda that disavows pathology is less relevant than a critique of the reembedded forms of liberal eugenics propagated by what they call the medical-industrial complex and its attendant forms of administrative surveillance. Such work suggests that an increasingly demanding ableism (and I would add, an increasingly demanding disable-ism—normative forms of disability as exceptionalism) is producing nonnormativity not only through the sexual and racial pathologization of certain "unproductive bodies" but more expansively through the ability or inability of all bodies to register through affective capacity.

What disability justice activists imply is that slow death is constitutive to debility, and disability must be rethought in terms of precarious populations.

The distinctions of normative and nonnormative, disabled and nondisabled do not hold up as easily. Instead there are variegated aggregates of capacity and debility. If debility is understood by disability justice activists to be *endemic to* disenfranchised communities, it is doubly so because the forms of financialization that accompany neoliberal economics and the privatization of services also produce debt as debility. This relationship between debt and debility can be described as a kind of "financial expropriation": "the profit made by financial institutions out of the personal income of workers is a form of financial expropriation, seen as additional profit generated in the realm of circulation."[13] Given the relationship of bankruptcy to medical care expenses in the United States, debt becomes another register to measure the capacity for recovery, not only physical but also financial. Debility is profitable to capitalism, but so is the demand to "recover" from or overcome it.

From Epistemological Corrective to Ontological Irreducibility

I am proposing, then, a methodology that inhabits the intersections of disability studies, the affective turn, and theories of posthumanism—all fields of inquiry that put duress on the privileging of (able-bodied) subject formation as a primary site of bodily interpellation. The affective turn, as I interpret it, signals intellectual contestation over sites of struggle, whose targets are now the following: social constructionism (reinvigorated interrogation of biological matter that challenges both biological determinism and also performativity), epistemology (ontology and ontogenesis), psychoanalysis (trauma rethought as the intensification of the body's relation to itself), humanism (the capacities of nonhuman animals as well as inorganic matter, matters), and agency (the centrality of cognition and perception as challenged by theories of sensation). The modulation and surveillance of affect operates as a form of sociality that regulates good and bad subjects, possible and impossible bodily capacities. Here affect entails not only a dissolution of the subject but, more significantly, a dissolution of the stable contours of the organic body, as forces of energy are transmitted, shared, circulated. The body, as Brian Massumi argues, "passes from one state of capacitation to a diminished or augmented state of capacitation," always bound up in the lived past of the body but always in passage to a changed future.[14]

This understanding of capacity and debility entails theorizing not only specific disciplinary sites but also broader techniques of social control, marking a shift in terms from regulating normativity (the internalization of self/other subject formation) to what Michel Foucault calls regularizing bodies or what has been designated "the age of biological control."[15] In the oscillation between disciplinary societies and control societies, following Foucault's "security regimes" and Gilles Deleuze's "control society," the tensions have been mapped out thusly: as a shift from normal/abnormal to variegation, modulation, and tweaking; from discrete sites of punishment (the prison, the mental hospital, the school) to preemptive regimes of securitization; from inclusion/exclusion to the question of differential inclusion; from self/other, subject/object construction to micro-states of subindividual differentiation; from difference between to difference within; from the policing of profile to patrolling of affect; from will to capacity; from agency to affect; from subject to body.[16] And finally, and I believe most importantly, there is a shift underway, from Althusserian interpellation to an array of diverse switchpoints of the activation of the body.

What does it mean to rethink disability in terms of control societies? The particular binary categorization of dis/abled subjectivity is one that has many parallels to other kinds of binary categorizations propagated — in fact, demanded — by neoliberal constructions of failed and capacitated bodies. Therefore we cannot see this binary production as specific only to the distinction of disabled versus nondisabled subjects; all bodies are being evaluated in relation to their success or failure in terms of health, wealth, progressive productivity, upward mobility, enhanced capacity. And there is no such thing as an "adequately abled" body anymore. However, it is precisely because there are gradations of capacity and debility in control societies — rather than the self/other production of being/not being — that the distinction between disabled and nondisabled becomes fuzzier.

As an example, Nikolas Rose maintains that depression will become the number one disability in the United States and the U.K. within the next ten years. This expansion of depressed peoples will not occur simply through a widespread increase of depression but through the gradation of populations. In other words, it will occur not through the hailing and interpellation of depressed subjects — and a distinction between who is depressed and who is not — but through the evaluation and accommodation of degrees: to what degree is one depressed?[17] One is already instructed by television advertisements for psychotropic drugs such as "Abilify," claiming that "two out of three people on anti-depressants still have symptoms" and offering a top-off medication to add to a daily med regime. Through this form of medical administration, bodies are (1) drawn into a modulation of subindividual capacities (this would be the diverse switchpoints); (2) surveilled not on identity positions alone but through affective tendencies, informational body-as-data, and statistical probabilities — through populations, risk, and prognosis; (3) further stratified across registers of the medical-industrial complex: medical debt, health insurance, state benefits, among other feedback loops into the profitability of debility.

How the disaggregation of depressed subjects into various states, intensities, and tendencies will change the dimensionality of disability remains an open prospect, but at the very least it forces recognition of the insufficiency of disability as a category. The disability at stake is an affective tendency of sorts as well as a mental state, and as such challenges the basis on which disability rights frames have routed their representational (visibility) politics. A field that has been dominated by the visibility of physical disabilities is acknowledging the scope and range of cognitive and mental disabilities. This recognition, in turn, has challenged the status of rational, agential, survivor-oriented politics based on the privileging of the linguistic capacity to make rights claims. Why? Because the inability to "communicate" functions as *the* single determinant of mental or cognitive impairment (thereby regulating the human/animal distinction), thus destabilizing the centrality of the human capacity for thought and cognition.

In an effort to open up capacity as a source of generative affective politics rather than only a closure around neoliberal demands, I briefly return to Gayatri Spivak's "Can the Subaltern Speak?," perhaps unfashionably so.[18] In the context of disability studies, this question becomes not only a mandate for epistemological correctives but a query about ontological and bodily capacity, as granting "voice" to the subaltern comes into tension with the need, in the case of the human/animal distinction, to destabilize the privileging of communication/representation/language altogether. The ability to understand language is also where human/nonhuman animal distinctions, as well as human/technology distinctions, have long been drawn, and here disability studies, posthumanism, and animal studies may perhaps articulate a common interest in a nonanthropomorphic, interspecies vision of affective politics. Posthumanism questions the boundaries between human and nonhuman, matter and discourse, technology and body, and interrogates the practices through which these boundaries are constituted, stabilized, and destabilized. (The burgeoning field of animal studies is thus also a part of the endeavor to situate human capacities within a range of capacities of species as opposed to reifying their singularity.) If, according to posthumanist thinkers such as Manual DeLanda and Karen Barad, language has been granted too much power, a nonanthropomorphic conception of the human is necessary to resituate language as one of many captures of the intensities of bodily capacities, an event of bodily assemblages rather than a performative act of signification.[19]

Our current politics are continually reproducing the exceptionalism of human bodies and the aggrieved agential subject, politics typically enacted through "wounded attachments."[20] Without minimizing the tragedy of Clementi's and other recent deaths, dialogue about ecologies of sensation and slow death might open us up to a range of connections. For instance, how do queer girls commit suicide? What of the slow deaths of teenage girls through anorexia, bulimia, and numerous sexual assaults they endure as punishment for the transgressing of proper femininity and alas, even for conforming to it? What is the political and cultural fallout of recentering the white gay male as ur-queer subject? How would our political landscape transform if it actively decentered the sustained reproduction and proliferation of the grieving subject, opening instead toward an affective politics, attentive to ecologies of sensation and switchpoints of bodily capacities, to habituations and unhabituations, to tendencies, multiple temporalities, and becomings?

Notes

Thanks to Elena Glasberg, Dana Luciano, and Jordana Rosenberg for close readings, and to Tavia Nyong'o, Eng-Beng Lim, Ashley Dawson, and Richard Kim for feedback on an earlier version of this article, "Ecologies of Sex, Sensation, and Slow Death" published in *Social Text* on November 27, 2010.

1. Lauren Berlant, "Slow Death (Sovereignty, Obesity, Lateral Agency)," *Critical Inquiry* 33 (2007): 754–80. Hereafter cited in the text.

2. See David Himmelstein et al., "Medical Bankruptcy in the United States, 2007: Results of a National Study," *American Journal of Medicine* 122 (2009): 741–46.

3. "Justice Not Vengeance in Clementi Suicide," Queering the Air, October 19, 2010 (URL no longer working).

4. Queering the Air, e-mail message to author, October 1, 2010.

5. Amit Rai, *Untimely Bollywood: Globalization and India's New Media Assemblage* (Durham, NC: Duke University Press, 2009).

6.   Tavia Nyong'o, "School Daze," September 30, 2010, bullybloggers.wordpress
     .com/2010/09/30/school-daze/.

7.   "In the Wake of It Gets Better," *Guardian*, November 16, 2010, www.guardian.co.uk/
     commentisfree/cifamerica/2010/nov/16/wake-it-gets-better-campaign?showallcom
     ments=true#comment-fold.

8.   Sarah Lochlann Jain, *Injury: The Politics of Product Design and Safety Law in the
     United States* (Princeton: Princeton University Press, 2006), 24.

9.   David Mitchell, Keynote Plenary (Annual Meeting, Society for Disability Studies,
     Temple University, June 2010).

10. Robert McRuer, *Crip Theory* (New York: New York University Press, 2007), 207.

11. David Mitchell and Sharon Snyder, *Cultural Locations of Disability* (Chicago: Univer-
     sity of Chicago Press, 2006), 17.

12. See, e.g., Eugene Thacker, *The Global Genome* (Cambridge: MIT Press, 2006);
     Kaushik Sunder Rajan, *Biocapital: The Constitution of Postgenomic Life* (Durham,
     NC: Duke University Press, 2006).

13. Sam Ashman, "Editorial Introduction to the Symposium on the Global Financial Cri-
     sis," *Historical Materialism* 17 (2009): 107.

14. Brian Massumi, "Of Microperception and Micropolitics: An Interview with Brian
     Massumi," *Inflections*, no. 3 (2008): 2.

15. Michel Foucault, *"Society Must Be Defended": Lectures at the Collège de France,
     1975–76*, ed. Mauro Bertani and Alessandro Fontana, trans. David Macey (New
     York: Picador, 2003); and Ian Wilmut, Keith Campbell, and Colin Tudge, *The Second
     Creation: Dolly and the Age of Biological Control* (Cambridge, MA: Harvard Univer-
     sity Press, 2001).

16. Michel Foucault, *Security, Territory, Population: Lectures at the Collège de France,
     1977–78*, ed. Michel Senellart, trans. Graham Burchell (New York: Picador, 2009);
     Gilles Deleuze, "Postscript on Control Societies," in *Negotiations* (New York: Colum-
     bia University Press, 1997).

17. Nikolas Rose, "Biopolitics in an Age of Biological Control" (lecture, New York Uni-
     versity, New York, October 15, 2009).

18. Gayatri Chakravorty Spivak, Can the Subaltern Speak?," in *Marxism and the Inter-
     pretation of Culture*, ed. Cary Nelson and Larry Grossberg (Basingstoke: Macmillan
     Education: 1988), 271–313.

19. Manuel DeLanda, *A New Philosophy of Society: Assemblage Theory and Social Com-
     plexity* (London and New York: Continuum, 2006); Karen Barad, "Posthumanist Per-
     formativity: Toward an Understanding of How Matter Comes to Matter," *Signs: Jour-
     nal of Women in Culture and Society* 28 (2003): 801–31.

20. See Wendy Brown, "Wounded Attachments," *Political Theory* 21 (1993): 390–410.

QUEER MEDIA LOCI:

Israel/Palestine

*W*e are pleased to follow our inaugural feature "Queer Media Loci: Bangkok" by staging *GLQ*'s return to the Israel/Palestine region.[1] "Festival Exoticism: The Israeli Queer Film in a Global Context" by Jewish Israeli media scholars Boaz Hagin and Raz Yosef represents Queer Media Loci's second effort "to present a cross-sectional analysis of queer media in terms of production, exhibition, and reception at a specific location, and to an international readership interested in queer scholarship."[2] Unlike the previous survey approach to digital media in Thailand, Hagin and Yosef chose instead to home in on the positioning of queer Israeli cinema abroad and its effects on the Israeli mediascape. By interrogating on a micro-level how some queer Israeli films are financed and marketed to the global film festival circuit and art cinema markets, the authors present specific case studies that sketch out, on a macro-level, the complex and contradictory dynamics among state propaganda, self-representation and othering, and the queer resistance to these forces within Israel that together shape the production, reception, and exhibition of queer media of, within, and outside the region.

Some readers may notice the reversal of nations in our title from the recent *GLQ* special issue on the region. This "switch" signals that this contribution was written by two Jewish Israeli citizens analyzing primarily queer Jewish Israeli media productions. Hagin and Yosef highlight this position as part of their own queer media locus, as well as their unease with this position of privilege, by writing in a self-reflexive manner about their circumscribed viewpoint from within the region.[3] Their "self-othering" performance about the self-othering of queer Israeli festival films then becomes a self-reflexive, if always uncomfortable, locus. As Gil Z. Hochberg, the guest editor for the *GLQ* issue on the region, noted in her introduction: "To write about queer politics in the context of Palestine/Israel is to be in an uncomfortable position. It is to reside in a discursive and political field fraught with contradictions and dominated by passionate controversies and disputes."[4]

We look forward to seeing how Hagin and Yosef's intervention in discourses about the queer media practices of this locus will contribute to the "passionate controversies and disputes" about queer politics and media in the context of Israel/Palestine. We thank the authors for contributing such a thought-provoking entry to the Queer Media Loci series and continue to work on upcoming, developing contributions focused on Hong Kong, Brazil, India, Vietnam, Africa, and Eastern Europe.

—Ming-Yuen S. Ma and Alexandra Juhasz

Notes

1. See Gil Z. Hochberg, ed., "Queer Politics and the Question of Palestine/Israel," special issue, *GLQ* 16, no. 4 (2010).
2. Ming-Yuen S. Ma and Alexandra Juhasz, introduction to Queer Media Loci Series, *GLQ* 17 (2011): 167.
3. As noted in the *GLQ* special issue, one effect of the Israeli government's increased militarization of the region is increased difficulty in mobility and communication by Palestinians, especially within the occupied territories. Given Queer Media Loci's aim to present "on the ground" perspectives from a locus, it makes the solicitation and presentation of Palestinian perspectives from the region all the more difficult.
4. Gil Z. Hochberg, "Introduction: Israelis, Palestinians, Queers: Points of Departure," in "Queer Politics and the Question of Palestine/Israel," special issue, *GLQ* 16 (2010): 511.

DOI 10.1215/10642684-1501702

FESTIVAL EXOTICISM

The Israeli Queer Film in a Global Context

Boaz Hagin and Raz Yosef

Israel's Bel Ami

In 2009 Manhattan-based Lucas Entertainment announced that it was releasing the first gay "adult production" shot entirely on location in Israel with an all-Israeli cast, *Men of Israel* (dirs. Michael Lucas and mr. Pam). The film's website explains that this "groundbreaking event" and "landmark in the history of Israel and in the evolution of adult entertainment" has two aims: not only to represent the "sexually arousing" and "tanned and chiseled muscle hunks" of Israel for whom "it came naturally to perform with such raw sexual passionate [sic]" but also to allow Israel to "play a lead visual character as a country with rich history and a wide range of natural beauty." It assures us that "Israel has a number of sites and destinations to lure any tourist to book a flight."[1] According to the website, the film's codirector Michael Lucas hopes that through the film's dual adulation of the raw attractiveness of the men "in their remarkable natural environment" and of Israel itself—which not only offers an orientalist fantasy of passionate rawness but is also, according to him, "a truly progressive, multicultural society"—he will be able to parlay the film's success into a tourist boom for Israel as the Eastern European gay pornography company Bel Ami did for that region.[2]

The film's double role as gay pornography and tourist advertisement is hard to miss. At times the roles harmonize and resonate. In one segment, the camera tilts up from the groin of an aroused man on a balcony overlooking Tel Aviv–Jaffa to the erect skyscrapers of the city's skyline. In another, the men discuss in Hebrew their decision to switch sexual position (because of one of the men's discomfort), adding a local, authentic ingredient to the film while also making sure the non-Hebrew-speaking potential tourists are less likely to suspect that their performance is not quite raw and natural.

The two functions cohere less smoothly at other moments, for example, when some of the men insist on announcing their imminent ejaculation in English, with a heavy Israeli accent. The filmmakers sometimes prefer extreme long shots that are better at highlighting the scenic vistas than the attractiveness of the men, or they include both the men and sprawling beaches in the same frame, resulting in awkward compositions. Furthermore, no lighting arrangement seems to capture both Israel's exotic scenery and the men together, resulting either in overexposed backgrounds or low-key illumination schemes that form bizarre chiaroscuro effects, underexposing the men's bodies or leaving them as mere silhouettes.

Men of Israel and its Internet paratext are a blunt yet emblematic example of queer representations in Israeli cinema. While not always aimed at expanding tourism explicitly, many queer Israeli films nonetheless cater to the viewpoints and expectations of non-Israelis implicitly. Like the rhetoric of *Men of Israel*'s public-ity, queer representations in Israeli cinema are sometimes perceived as "natural" performances symptomatically expressing Israeli society, but are also a mélange of Israel as an orientalist paradise for tourism and an allegedly progressive West-ern haven in the Middle East, selected and deliberately engineered for foreign viewers.

We were somewhat troubled after being asked to write a contribution on Israel/ Palestine for the Queer Media Loci series. How could we present all facets of queer media in an entire — not particularly stable, homogenous, or peaceful — region, and can and should we, as Jewish Israeli citizens, purport to present Palestin-ian experiences? Moreover, as queer scholars who have written critically about Israeli cinema, society, and politics, would we want to be in a position in which we represent or even defend Israel or Israeli cinema? After all, isn't Judith Butler boycotting us? We felt that the essay puts us in the uncomfortable position that is all too familiar from our encounters with scholars or cinephiles from abroad in which it is assumed that, being from Israel, or in presenting certain aspects of Israeli cinema, we are representing and defending the country and its films, and in which we are judged for not being critical enough — or sometimes for being too critical — of them.

We address our unease with the scope of the project and our circumscribed viewpoint from within the region by concentrating on our field of expertise — Israeli cinema. Additionally, this essay focuses on the expectations for and percep-tions of queer Israeli cinema (and its accompanying scholarship) abroad. Indeed, we suspect that one reason that we were asked to write this contribution has to do with the success and increased visibility in recent years in the United States and other world markets of films from Israel and Palestine that feature queer rep-resentations. Part of our uneasiness has to do with the positioning of these films in world cinema. We argue that the recent success of these Israeli films can be understood not only in relation to the historical junctures in our region — as they are frequently described in scholarship on the topic — but also in relation to a wider, global network in which they were funded and distributed, which disrupts their belonging to the very region they supposedly represent. We suggest that this can offer a fruitful framework for analyzing queer representations in Israeli cinema and can complement the existing work that usually places the films within the context of Israel and Palestine. In this sense, *Men of Israel* can prove extremely educational.

A Nation Like All Others

Extant literature on gay, lesbian, and queer representations in Israeli cinema has frequently tied it to other realms of culture and society in the region. According to these studies, the political project of Zionism — liberating the Jewish people and creating a nation like all other nations — was intertwined with a longing for the sexual redemption and normalization of the Jewish body. In the anti-Semitic scientific-medical discourse of the late nineteenth century, the male Jewish body, for example, was associated with disease, madness, degeneracy, sexual perversity, and femininity, as well as with homosexuality. This pathologization of Jewish male sexuality also entered the writings of Jewish scientists and medical doctors, including Sigmund Freud.[3] Zionist thinkers such as Theodor Herzl and Max Nordau were convinced that the invention of a stronger, healthier, heterosexual "Jewry of Muscles" would not only overcome the stereotype of the Jewish male as a homosexual but also solve the economic, political, and national problems of the Jewish people. Unlike the passive, ugly, femme, Diasporic Jewish male, the new Zionist man would engage in manual labor, athletics, and war, becoming the colonialist-explorer in touch with the land and with his body. This notion of a new Jewish masculinity became the model for the militarized masculine Sabra — the native-born Israeli.

These aspects of the Zionist project resulted in excluding gays and lesbians from Israeli society. At the end of the 1980s and into the 1990s, a major shift in social attitudes and governmental policy occurred when a series of legal and social struggles of the Aguda, the Association of Gay Men, Lesbians, Bisexuals and Transgender in Israel, led to a degree of civic legitimacy for gays and lesbians in the central institutions of Israeli society — the army, family, and motherhood — that define the limits of membership and participation in the Israeli collectivity.[4] The association's members fought to expand their civic rights and the right of representation of sexual preference, and criticized the absence and marginalization of gays and lesbians in Israeli society (including media representations). The successes of these struggles promoted the visibility of gay men and women in mainstream media, as well as allowed for the rise of an urban queer culture that confidently took its place within the heterosexual national consensus. Emphasis was placed on the "normality" of the community's members and their being "good citizens."[5]

Israeli and pre-state Zionist cinema can be understood within these contexts. Early pro-Zionist propaganda films reflect the heterosexualizing aspirations of the movement by displaying the gender-normative Sabra and redemptive potential of the land. Some later films are more critical of Zionism and introduce other variations. The cinematic works of Amos Gutman and Eytan Fox are often singled out as reflecting and contributing to the increased visibility of gay people in Israeli culture. Both filmmakers tried in different ways to deconstruct Zionist heterosexual masculinity and to offer a new imagery of homosexual social existence. However, they are also very different in their perspectives on gay identity. Gutman shows an obvious contempt for "politically correct," idealized, and sanitized depictions of (homo)sexuality; refuses to provide consensual images of either gay or straight sex; and explicitly associates male (homo)sexuality with power and domination, violence, and death. Fox's films, on the other hand, represent an attempt of the dominant Israeli gay culture to join the national heterosexual collectivity, such as the Israeli army.[6]

This article offers a framework for understanding queer representations in Israeli cinema in the last decade without limiting their context to Zionism or Israel/Palestine. Instead, it suggests that we consider queer Israeli films within the phenomenon of "world cinema." As Thomas Elsaesser notes, these films in many cases, and certainly in the Israeli one, rely on a modification of the way European national cinemas of the 1970s and 1980s were financed by state-funded support schemes and cultural subsidies. In contemporary world cinema, however, this model extends beyond nationally representative cinema, and it now facilitates film production and distribution across the globe.[7] Like other examples in world cinema, many Israeli films are in fact transnational coproductions, relying not only on local film funds and investments by Israeli television channels but also on European coproduction funds and presales to television channels like the Franco-German ARTE.

It is not only the financing and production of "Israeli" films that problematize their regional or national identity. By the 1980s, after a period of post–World War II domestic crisis and global weakness, Hollywood reemerged as the world's premier provider of mass entertainment with blockbusters, new marketing techniques, and powerful global distribution cartels (308).[8] By then, many national popular film industries had collapsed, and their viewers had moved to television and video rental circuits (489). Hollywood's multinational conglomerates have since held a firmly established position in the global entertainment sector and over the world's cinema markets (499). Israel is no exception, with local productions gaining substantially less viewers than Hollywood blockbusters.[9] Some Israeli films can become relatively successful at the Israeli box office, sometimes, but not always, following their success in international festivals. Other films do poorly in the domestic market; some are derided by local critics for being simplistic and superficial "festival films."[10]

Who, then, are world cinema films, including Israeli ones, made for? Elsaesser describes a second global distribution system that functions in addition to the Hollywood commercial industry and other cinema industries such as Bollywood—the network of international film festivals. It is here that many world cinema films find an audience. In addition, some festivals offer production funds, development money, or a talent campus with workshops and platforms for collaborations.

The festivals hold a "clearing house function" for distributors of minority interest films that have attracted critical plaudits or have won prizes (88, 504), and "act collectively as a distribution system . . . effectively select[ing] each year which films will fill the few slots that art-house cinemas or the dedicated screens of the multiplexes keep open for the minority interest cinema" (91). In festivals, films can gather the cultural capital and critical prowess necessary for further exhibition so that "no poster of an independent film can do without the logo of one of the world's prime festivals, as prominently displayed as Hollywood productions carry their studio logo" (87).

World cinema films, then, cater to the needs of the festival circuit and foreign viewers, a fact that influences and is even reflected in their subject matter. Elsaesser notes world cinema's attention to globalization and to national and subnational identities. Questions of "underdevelopment, exclusion, racism, genocide, poverty, and of the clash between traditional ways of life and the impact of globalization, modernity, and Western habits or lifestyles" play a major role in world cinema, as do "the constructions of gender and ethnicity, family values and religion, concepts of good and evil, state authority and censorship, and the role/oppression of women in traditional societies" (509). In addition, Elsaesser discerns the festivals' interest in topical areas and international hotspots—two positions that Israel/Palestine has been filling for many years—as well as their receptivity to various groups and causes, including queer issues (504, 100). World cinema is often driven by an "ethnographic outlook." Its dramatizations of conflicts between tradition and modernity, hegemony and the margins, global and local, Westernization and indigenization take place through "self-othering" or "self-exoticization" in which, according to Elsaesser, "the ethnic, the local or the regional expose themselves, under the guise of self-expression, to the gaze of the benevolent other" so that like the participant observer of anthropology, world cinema might be presenting "the mirror of what the 'native' thinks the other, the observer wants to see" (510).

The Israeli films that have achieved significant success in world markets seem to bear out Elsaesser's account. They deal with topical and political issues in the region or in Israeli society—such as the Israeli-Palestinian conflict, wars, and the Holocaust and its aftermath (which seem to be perennially topical in the Academy Awards and in European film festivals). They self-exoticize conflicts around ethnic and familial identities (such as Georgian Jews in Dover Koshashvili's *Late Marriage* [2001] and *Gift from Above* [2003]), or communities that resist Westernization, such as ultraorthodox Jews in *Ushpizin* (dir. Giddi Dar; 2004) and *My Father, My Lord* (dir. David Volach; 2007).[11]

As already noted, festivals are receptive to queer content, and a vast network of international lesbian and gay film festivals are entirely devoted to queer films. In the competition over coproduction funds and the attention of festival programmers, a film can gain points by offering a combination of Israeli self-othering and gay characters, thus adding a gay twist to the familiar Israeli formula or providing an exotic locale to revitalize otherwise worn-out gay narratives. For example, *Walk on Water* (dir. Eytan Fox; 2004), an Israeli-Swedish coproduction boasting the logos of major film festivals such as Berlin and Toronto on its DVD cover, features a bromance between a macho and heterosexual Israeli Mossad assassin whose parents were Holocaust survivors and a gay German who is the grandson of a Nazi criminal whom the Israeli assassin is sent to kill.[12] *The Bubble* (dir. Eytan Fox; 2006), which won multiple prizes, including at the Berlin International Film Festival and many gay and lesbian film festivals, focuses on a gay love story between an Israeli reserve soldier and a Palestinian who becomes a suicide bomber after struggling with being gay in a traditional society.[13] *The Secrets* (dir. Avi Nesher; 2007), an Israeli-French coproduction and an official selection at the Toronto Film Festival, tells of two young ultraorthodox women who fall in love, while they and the viewers discover the joys of ritual bathing in the nude in a Mikveh.[14] *Eyes Wide Open* (dir. Haim Tabakman; 2009), an Israeli-German-French coproduction and an official selection at the Karlovy Vary, Toronto, and Cannes film festivals, tells of two men in an ultraorthodox Jewish community in Jerusalem who have an affair while they and the viewers discover the joys of ritual bathing in the nude in a spring outside the city.[15]

Figure 1. Two ultraorthodox men fall in love in *Eyes Wide Open* (dir. Haim Tabakman; 2009). Courtesy of New American Vision

In the case of the double exoticization of queer characters in Israeli films, we can discern a tendency to view the societies depicted through the lens of Western liberal individualism, and in particular, gay liberation. That other societies might have their own forms of nonheterosexual desires and conducts remains unimaginable in many of these films. Thus, as Elsaesser argues, self-othering can "stand in the way of encountering the otherness of the other" (509).[16] When the individualist gay liberation discourse is combined with Israeli self-othering—notably ultraorthodox communities, wars, and the Israeli-Palestinian conflict—the result can be a story of self-realization and liberation of Westernized and Westernizing gays that is often contrasted with the tragedy of others who are unable to break away from their repressive society and achieve Western liberal gay identity.

Several scholars have shown that Fox's work, in particular, has adhered to this positive view of gay liberal identity and has displayed a tendency to eliminate all those who deviate from it.[17] Fox's internationally successful *Yossi and Jagger* (2002), for example, tells of two gay officers serving near the Lebanese-Israeli border. It promotes an image of gay men as handsome, straight-acting army officers who can be incorporated into a military framework as "respectable homosexuals" and is careful to avoid any lingering ideas or images that might offend a West-

Figure 2. *Yossi and Jagger* (dir. Eytan Fox; 2002) promotes an image of gay men as handsome, straight-acting army officers who can and should be assimilated into mainstream normalcy. Courtesy of Lama Productions

ern liberal audience or in any way question the view that homosexuality can and should be assimilated into mainstream normalcy. The film is particularly careful to fend off the possibility that the boundaries between homosexuality and hetero-sexuality are permeable, especially in the army, and downplays anal penetrative sex between men. Moreover, the officer who comes closest to challenging the film's sexual conformist politics — by an uncompromising demand that he and his lover come out of the closet — is killed during a military operation at the end of the film, burying his potentially subversive identity in a heroic death and dismissing his troubling presence in the film.[18]

Similarly, Avi Nesher's *Secrets* seems unable to imagine any alternatives to a Western individualist gay identity. Its protagonist is the precocious and reserved young daughter of a rabbi who falls in love with another young woman at a Jewish women's seminary. In the film, the option of a gay identity in secular society is never shown and the L-word is never uttered. Moreover, the protagonist claims that she never even dreamed that such a love or attraction was possible. Nevertheless, she seems to discover and embrace gay liberation quickly on her own: she refuses to marry her fiancé, leaves her father's house, suggests to the woman she loves that they move in together and create a home, resents the latter's implication that they or she might not be "normal" or is violating Jewish laws (she decides that only men are forbidden by Jewish law to have sex with a member of their own gender)—all but directly demanding ultraorthodox Judaism to endorse and perform lesbian marriage. These films have managed to secure funding and international distribution not only by means of double exoticization but also by reducing the otherness of the other for a liberal Western audience.

Gay Vampires and Orthodykes

While in many cases a sensible strategy, or simply a good prognosticator of which films will attain funding and successful global distribution, the self-othering that Elsaesser describes is not mandatory or ubiquitous.[19] There are Israeli feature films that refuse to follow this formula. Some, for example, take place in a civilian Westernized secular milieu where characters who are not straight can frequently be encountered. There is a young lesbian struggling within a dysfunctional family in the drama *Things behind the Sun* (dir. Yuval Shafferman; 2006) and a young woman who is suspected by the other characters of being gay in the horror film *Rabies* (dir. Ahron Keshales and Navot Paposhaddo; 2010). None of these characters needs to confront centuries of religious oppression, fundamentalist Muslim terrorists, ultraorthodox rabbis, or ethnic tensions or to resolve the Israeli-Palestinian conflict, take part in blood-soaked battles, or work through the trauma of the Holocaust. In principle their stories could have taken place in many other places around the globe. Lacking this strong self-othering ingredient, many of these films are not enjoying the same success in major festivals and awards as some other Israeli films. Although some of these films can be successful in Israel, there is a good chance that many non-Israeli readers are less familiar with them than with the films mentioned earlier.[20]

However, there is not a clear-cut dichotomy between self-othering festival films made for export and domestically consumed films in which queer representations are common and normalized. Elsaesser's framework suggests further options. Some films, he writes, "are made for the festival circuits and rarely if ever reach other screens" (76). Indeed, short films or extremely low-budget or no-budget fringe productions stand virtually no chance of ever transcending the festival circuit. They are thus free to ignore or subvert the self-othering formula that is the sine qua non for further distribution in art houses and dedicated multiplex screens. Many Israeli gay-themed short student films, for example, which are marginal both in the local film culture and in the major festivals, take place in a Westernized urban secular milieu in which coming out or being gay is a nonissue. The films frequently deal with relationships and love, and sometimes toy with gay

Figure 3. What begins as yet another Israeli film about a gay soldier coming to terms with his sexuality ends up challenging the obviousness of gay liberation and the attractiveness of Tel Aviv's nightlife in *Watch over Me* (dir. Mysh [Rozanov]; 2010). Photograph by Nimrod Shapira. Courtesy of Mysh

and lesbian stereotypes from within the gay community, such as lesbians' supposed predilection for codependent relationships and gay men's supposed difficulty with emotions and monogamy. In *Whatever It Takes* (dir. Adi Halfin; 2004), for example, a woman tries to prevent her girlfriend from leaving her to study abroad by feigning a coma, and in *A Word* (dir. Yoav Inbar; 2010) a gay man is incapable of telling his boyfriend he loves him.

Particularly interesting in this context are films that take up the self-othering festival film formula and the individualist gay liberation narrative only to reject or subvert it. The short film *Watch over Me* (dir. Mysh [Rozanov]; 2010) begins as what appears to be yet another typical story of a gay soldier in the Israeli army struggling to come to terms with his sexuality, not unlike Fox's short *Time Off* (1990) and his later *Yossi and Jagger. Watch over Me* begins with Eitan, a young soldier about to complete his training in an elite commando unit. He is given one-day leave and told to go out with two other soldiers who have already completed their training. They go to a bar in Tel Aviv, where one of them picks a fight with a man distributing leaflets advertising a gay party, who makes a pass at him and flagrantly checks Eitan out. The two soldiers tell Eitan to go and kill the gay man at the completion of his training. Eitan refuses, claiming that it is blatantly illegal to kill an Israeli citizen. He runs away, finds the gay man, and tells him he is in danger because the other soldiers want to kill him. Eitan promises to watch over him, and they end up on the beach, where they take their clothes off, enter the water, and start kissing. Eitan then knocks him down and bites him, revealing vampire fangs and supernatural black eyes as the musical score pays homage to the theme of *Buffy the Vampire Slayer*. Sitting by the shore next to the corpse, wearing his uniform again, he is joined by the other two men from the unit, and they exchange racist and homophobic banter. He is told that he is now part of the unit and is awarded a pin—vampire wings surrounding two wooden stakes—and he looks into the camera with a wicked smile.[21] The film's blunt metaphor obviously suggests that the homophobic and racist Israeli army makes soulless bloodthirsty monsters of its recruits and that its deadly violence cannot be contained and will return to claim civilian lives in places like Tel Aviv. At the same time, however, it suggests that the gay liberation narrative is far from universal and that a young man, when given the choice, might prefer the exhilarating thrills of killing for the army to the peaceful life of gay parties in secular left-wing Tel Aviv. This provocative and politically incorrect stance not only rejects the standard festival film formula of gay liberation, but as the allusion to *Buffy the Vampire Slayer* attests, also signals a preference for forging an alliance with Hollywood's pop culture (and its own nonnormative queer potential, in the case of *Buffy*), which is frequently viewed as the "bad Other" against which the festival/art house circuit defines itself.[22]

The fifty-two-minute documentary *Keep Not Silent* (dir. Ilil Alexander; 2004) seems to take up the usual self-exoticizing festival film formula, but at the same time rigidly maintains the otherness of its subjects and does little to bring a Western gaze closer. It deals with three lesbian women in the ultraorthodox community of Jerusalem who are part of the "Orthodykes" group. The film refuses to offer any easy or obviously preferable option for the women. Unlike the readings of Jewish law by the protagonist of *The Secrets*, a meeting between a rabbi and one of the three women early on in the film makes it clear that in the world depicted in this film, the prohibitions on same-sex intercourse and marriage in orthodox Jewish law definitely do apply to women. Furthermore, the film refuses any trajectory that suggests increasing integration of the Jewish orthodox and lesbian aspects of the women's lives, and certainly not any benefits to their coming out.

Keep Not Silent can be contrasted with the extremely successful American-Israeli-French feature-length documentary *Trembling before G-d* (dir. Sandi Simcha DuBowski; 2001), which follows the lives of Hassidic and Jewish orthodox gay and lesbian people who try and to some degree manage to integrate these two aspects of their lives. They encounter friendly orthodox rabbis, including one who is gay, who are willing to listen and learn if not quite condone homosexuality. Judaism in *Trembling* is largely portrayed as a lifestyle that consists of ethnic food, songs, fond childhood memories, family celebrations, and the interspersing of Yiddish phrases when talking, in which gay and lesbian people can partake, and which can be a warm home to return to or remain within. In *Keep Not Silent*, by contrast, the ultraorthodox community is mainly shown as a stifling constraint that dictates every aspect of people's lives, and the women choose to join it or remain within it exactly for this reason while rejecting the widespread Western reasoning that puts the individual at the center.

While *Trembling* was experienced by its participants and viewers as a positive learning experience that can empower a shift from shame to pride, as well as other forms of positive self-transformation (including losing weight!), it is difficult to imagine *Keep Not Silent* being interpreted in these ways.[23] Only one of the women comes out, and she is shunned by her parents; she is shown crying several times in the film, including at the ceremony in which she exchanges vows with her partner, because they do not accept her. Another woman, a mother of ten, says that if people knew she was a lesbian it would be harmful not only to her but also to her children whose lives would be ruined: other children would refuse to play with her children, they would not come to her house, and her children would not be allowed to stay in school. The woman who uses the alias "Ruth" in the film and is a mother of six became religious at the age of sixteen because she wanted a "regular life" after realizing that she loved women. In the film, she explains how her eldest daughter went to a social worker and claimed that her mother was a lesbian who was neglecting her children, which resulted in that daughter's leaving home to live with a foster family.

Most strikingly, *Keep Not Silent* refuses to endorse a Western individualist trajectory and continuously challenges notions of a coherent, unified, and knowable self. Ruth's husband claims he does not judge her, her girlfriend says she does not want to hear about her sex life with her husband, and Ruth says to her son that in her head she has two completely separate worlds—one with her girlfriend and one with her husband and children. She then tells her son that she understands that he cannot comprehend her experience. Values such as the importance of individuality and being faithful to oneself are repeatedly contrasted with other values

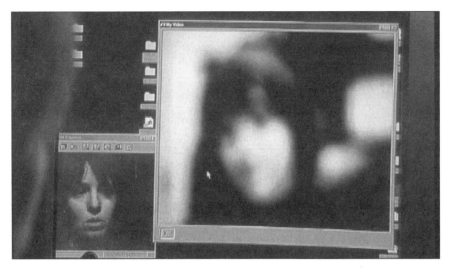

Figure 4. The windows on a computer screen in *Keep Not Silent* (dir. Ilil Alexander; 2004) show the director's face clearly (bottom left), while keeping the object of the documentary out of focus and ultimately undecipherable at the end of the film. Courtesy of Ilil Alexander

in the film, such as marrying and having children who study the Torah, choosing to remain part of a historical continuum of two thousand years of Jewish heritage in which lesbian relationships are unequivocally prohibited, or rejecting the modern world even if it means remaining single, childless, and showing total devotion to Jewish orthodoxy in other ways. The women in the film are shown to prefer these "other" options.

Whereas *Trembling* managed to work around the need for anonymity of some of its participants, focusing on expressive hands and mouths, or staging highly aestheticized vignettes of Jewish celebrations such as Shabbat dinner with stylized silhouettes that mask the identity of the queer participants, *Keep Not Silent* uses the need for anonymity to visually create an unbridgeable distance between the viewers and the women, a viewpoint reflected in much of what the interviewees say in the film. The film begins with a woman who uses the alias "Miriam-Esther" and who is only interviewed through a computer video chat in which her face is out of focus. Her first words, which also open the film, are "I want to make sure that you can't identify me . . . it's blurred enough so that you can't really see who I am." All we see is a blurred face on one window on a computer monitor, next to another window in which we see the director's face clearly. At times the camera zooms in on Miriam-Esther's face, mocking the documentary convention of creating intimacy, since the low-resolution image of her face becomes increasingly abstract and inhuman as the camera zooms in closer. *Keep Not Silent* ends with a pride parade in Jerusalem picketed by ultraorthodox Jews holding signs denouncing the "blasphemy." Across the street, keeping her distance from both camps, is an orthodox woman seen from behind, perhaps one of the anonymous participants in the film. In the soundtrack we hear Miriam-Esther explain that the world is complex, lives are complex, and *kedushah* (holiness) is complex and has not yet been revealed. The scene then cuts to Miriam-Esther wearing a rainbow head kerchief and apparently smiling, as far as the still-blurred image can show. Unlike the self-exoticizing films that reduce the otherness of their subjects to a Western film festival audience and embrace Western liberal individualism and gay liberation, *Keep Not Silent* leaves us with a feeling that we have encountered irreducible otherness. Neither the viewers nor the women and their friends and families have a firm grasp of their situation or identities; to themselves and to others they remain fragmented and opaque. Although *Keep Not Silent* contains all of the necessary ingredients for a run-of-the-mill self-exoticizing festival film, it ultimately does not bring its subjects any closer to an outsider's gaze.

In conclusion, the highest profile films with queer characters from our region are a part of the wider phenomenon of world cinema, in which local and regional issues are self-exoticized for the gaze of the other. To be sure, there is still considerable work to be done in analyzing the films, as there is considerable flexibility within the formula of self-othering and extensive diversity between the films.

Our discomfort at writing about Israeli-Palestinian media partly results from this context in which the films are always already entangled in an outsider's point of view and often represent what Israeli filmmakers think the Western film festival circuit expects from them. But our discomfort is also a result of our own complicity in this dynamic: we and other scholars are part of a similar self-othering, in which we are happy to submit to highly regarded English-language academic journals and publishers texts that contextualize these same high-profile films within the politics and history of our region while ignoring their self-exoticizing moment.[24] Perhaps taking up Michael Lucas's pornographic *Men of Israel* as a lens through which to study selections at Cannes and Berlin is our way to be better aware and to begin to question the self-othering demanded from us as gay Middle Eastern film scholars. The video, which promised a tourist boost for the nation, has certainly proven itself highly effective, or at the very least prophetic. In 2010, the year following the release of *Men of Israel*, there was a 26 percent rise in visitor arrivals in Israel, which broke an all-time record.[25]

Notes

This research was supported by the Israel Science Foundation (grant No. 133/10).

1. *Men of Israel*, homepage, Lucas Entertainment, www.menofisraelxxx.com (accessed February 17, 2011).

2. Men of Israel, "About," homepage, Lucas Entertainment, www.menofisraelxxx.com/index.php/about/ (accessed February 17, 2011).

3. On this topic see, e.g., Sander L. Gilman, *Freud, Race, and Gender* (Princeton: Princeton University Press, 1993); Daniel Boyarin, *Unheroic Conduct: The Rise of Heterosexuality and the Invention of the Jewish Man* (Berkeley: University of California Press, 1997); Michael Gluzman, "Longing for Heterosexuality: Zionism and Sexuality in Herzl's *Altneuland*" [in Hebrew], *Theory and Criticism* 11 (1997): 145–63.

4. For instance, the 1988 repeal of Israel's antisodomy law; forbidding discrimination in the workplace based on sexual tendencies; the first sitting of the Knesset that dealt with homo-lesbian issues in 1993; a Supreme Court of Justice decision in the case of Yonatan Danilowitz, an El-Al air steward, who demanded that the airline recognize his boyfriend as a partner. For a more detailed description, see Lee Walzer, *Between Sodom and Eden: A Gay Journey through Today's Changing Israel* (New York: Columbia University Press, 2000); Amit Kama, *The Newspaper and the Closet: Israeli Gay Men's Communication Patterns* [in Hebrew], (Tel Aviv: Hakibbutz Hameuchad Publishing House, 2003), 40–45. On this issue, see Aeyal Gross, "Sexuality, Masculinity, Military, and Citizenship: Gay Military Service in IDF in Comparative View," [in Hebrew] *Pelilim* (2000): 95–183.

5. As Walzer writes, "The Aguda was pursuing a very mainstream strategy and image at that time—demonstrating that gays and lesbians are 'just like everyone else,' serving in the military, and living in committed long-term relationships" (*Between Sodom and Eden*, 41).

6. On Israeli cinema in this context, see Raz Yosef, *Beyond Flesh: Queer Masculinities and Nationalism in Israeli Cinema* (New Brunswick: Rutgers University Press, 2004). For further discussion of the work of Gutman and Fox and their reception, see chapter 5.

7. Thomas Elsaesser, *European Cinema: Face to Face with Hollywood* (Amsterdam: Amsterdam University Press, 2005), 502–3. Hereafter cited in the text.

8. "Hollywood" is commonly used as shorthand for the international media and entertainment conglomerates that are not necessarily US owned and conduct only some of their business, production, and postproduction in or around Hollywood. Many of them still employ the classic Hollywood studio names as brands for some of their productions and distributions.

9. The box-office leader for 2010 in Israel was *Avatar* (dir. James Cameron; 2009); limiting 2010 box-office figures to films released that year, of the ten box-office leaders in

admissions, eight were not Israeli films. See blog.orange.co.il/cinemascope/?p=5769 (accessed February 17, 2011). In 2009 *Ice Age: Dawn of the Dinosaurs* (dir. Carlos Saldanha and Mike Thurmeier; 2009) and *Up* (dir. Pete Docter and Bob Peterson; 2009) topped the charts in Israeli movie theaters, with only one Israeli film reaching the top ten (blog.orange.co.il/cinemascope/?p=3046 [accessed February 17, 2011]). Figures are for admissions and not grosses, which Israeli distributors do not make public. Ticket prices for 3-D films are higher, and it is therefore likely that Israeli films, none of which were released in 3-D, would not have ranked higher had the figures been for grosses rather than admissions.

10. On the negative reception in Israel of one such film, see Boaz Hagin, "Male Weeping as Performative: The Crying Mossad Assassin in *Walk on Water*," *Camera Obscura*, no. 68 (2008): esp. 105–7.

11. Examples of Israeli films that received a nomination for an Academy Award in the best foreign-language film category include: *Ajami* (dir. Scandar Copti and Yaron Shani; nominated in the 2010 awards) depicts Jewish-Arab violence and conflicts; *Waltz with Bashir* (dir. Ari Folman; nominated in the 2009 awards) deals with the traumatic memories of Israeli soldiers during the first Lebanon war including the massacre in the Sabra and Shatila Palestinian refugee camps and a reference to the Holocaust; and *Beaufort* (dir. Joseph Cedar; nominated in the 2008 awards) tells of the evacuation of an Israeli post at the end of the first Lebanon war. For further discussion of contemporary Israeli cinema, see Raz Yosef, *The Politics of Loss and Trauma in Contemporary Israeli Cinema* (New York: Routledge, 2011).

12. It was also screened at the Boston Jewish Film Festival and Outfest.

13. The film won prizes at the Dublin Gay and Lesbian Film Festival, Durban International Film Festival, the GLAAD Media Awards, Outfest in Los Angeles, Miami Gay and Lesbian Film Festival, Torino International Gay and Lesbian Film Festival, and the Inside Out Lesbian and Gay Film and Video Festival in Toronto. See www.imdb.com/title/tt0476643/awards (accessed February 17, 2011).

14. It was additionally an official selection at the Stony Brook Film Festival and won best feature at the Jackson Hole Film Festival and Audience Choice Award at the Los Angeles and New York Israeli Film Festival. See the film's official website, www.montereymedia.com/theatrical/films/secrets_the.html (accessed February 17, 2011).

15. It was also awarded the best first feature prize at the Palm Springs International Film Festival. See the film's official website, www.eyeswideopenfilm.com (accessed February 17, 2011).

16. Gay liberation discourse has been dominant in substantial portions of Israeli Hebrew-language secular media. It is even possible to construct a triumphalist local history from invisibility (or "symbolic annihilation") to the growing visibility and normalcy of gay, lesbian, and queer representations in the Hebrew-language secular media in Israel. See Amit Kama, "From *Terra Incognita* to *Terra Firma*: The Logbook of the

Voyage of Gay Men's Community into the Israeli Public Sphere," *Journal of Homosexuality* 38, no. 4 (2000): 133–62.

17. This has frequently been read in light of Israeli society's mainstream gay politics, which might help contextualize Fox's point of view, but does little to explain the astounding success of his films abroad and their accessibility to audiences who know little about internal Israeli politics.

18. Raz Yosef, "The National Closet: Gay Israel in *Yossi and Jagger*," *GLQ* 11 (2005): 283–300. Similarly, Fox's later *The Bubble* seems unable to break out of the confines of a gay Western liberal point of view. As Raya Morag shows, employing a critical reading of Joseph Massad's work, this tragic gay romance between an Israeli and a Palestinian contains absolutely no representation of the gay Palestinian man's process of sexual maturity within his own society. The only viable alternative to the Palestinian conservative heterosexual lifestyle, as far as the film shows us, is passing as a Jewish Westernized gay Israeli in Tel Aviv under the supervision and guidance of gay Israelis. Moreover, the suicide terrorist attack at the end of the film is presented as an act not of a radical fundamentalist Muslim as it is commonly perceived in Israeli society but, according to Morag, of a person who despairs of ever being able to live as a proud gay in his own Arab society. There seems to be no alternative to Western gay liberation. See Raya Morag, "Interracial (Homo) Sexualities: Post-Traumatic Palestinian and Israeli Cinema during the al-Aqsa Intifada (*Diary of a Male Whore* and *The Bubble*)," *International Journal of Communication* 4 (2010): 932–54. On *The Bubble* and Fox's conservative gay politics in his other works, see also Rebecca L. Stein, "Explosive: Scenes from Israel's Gay Occupation," *GLQ* 16 (2010): 517–36.

19. As already noted, there is no immediately discernible correlation between the success of these films on the festival circuit and their success or lack thereof on Israeli screens.

20. Google Scholar offers eighty-two results for Eytan Fox and zero for Yuval Shafferman, Ahron Keshales, or Navot Paposhaddo (accessed February 17, 2011). There is, of course, also a chance that initially they will stand out in the festival circuit exactly because they refuse to adhere to the usual formula of self-othering expected from Israeli films. Similarly, on Israeli television shows—whose primary audience is local—queers enjoy high visibility and normalcy. Queer people are frequently found on-screen (and behind the scenes) in fiction, documentary series and television films, news, talk shows, and reality shows (both as participants and as hosts and judges). In many cases they are not considered any more exotic than characters who embody heteronormative standards. Presumably, the assimilationist liberal gay viewpoint has been successful, at least among decision makers in the Israeli Hebrew-language secular media, and queer characters are no longer considered as exotic on Israeli television as are members of other minorities, such as ultraorthodox Jews or Arabs.

21. The pin is a variation on the pins awarded to Israeli military paratroopers and pilots,

which have wings on them, and particularly on the pin of Shayetet 13, an elite naval commando, which actually does have bat wings on it, but no wooden stakes.

22. As Elsaesser notes, national and "art/auteur" cinema are both defined around American cinema as the significant bad Other (*European Cinema*, 16). We are grateful to the editors of MIR for pointing out the significance of the queer following of *Buffy*. A similar choice against the festival film—both as gay liberation self-othering and as hostile to Hollywood genres—can be found in the short *Reset* (dir. Yair Peri; 2010), which offers a time-travel story, in which two twenty-five-year-old men find themselves back in high school. They initially believe it is a chance to relive the night in which they kissed and became a couple, but then realize that coming out this young was a mistake for one of them and ruined his life. They decide that this is an opportunity to reset their lives and, in stark contrast to films that embrace a gay liberal narrative and depict the misery of those who do not, realize that it would be better to not come out of the closet as they had originally done when in high school.

23. According to *Trembling on the Road* (dir. Sandi Simcha DuBowski; 2003), the featurette included in the *Trembling before G-d* DVD, since the film was made one participant, Leah, has chosen to reveal her name and face that were obscured in the original film; Michelle, another participant, says she lost 130 pounds and gained a smile on her face and a feeling of strength and pride thanks to her appearance in the film.

24. A point also noted by Elsaesser in his own career, in which he came to the United States to study American cinema and found himself teaching German cinema. See Thomas Elsaesser, "Stepping Sideways," *Cinema Journal* 49 (2009): esp. 122–23.

25. Israeli Central Bureau of Statistics, press release, January 4, 2011, www.cbs.gov.il/www/hodaot2011n/28_11_005b.pdf.

DOI 10.1215/10642684-1422188

COMING TO TERMS

Homosexuality and the Left in American Culture

Aaron Lecklider

Bohemian Los Angeles and the Making of Modern Politics
Daniel Hurewitz
Berkeley and Los Angeles: University of California Press, 2007.
xii + 367 pp.

Free Comrades: Anarchism and Homosexuality in the United States,
1895–1917
Terence Kissack
Oakland, CA: AK Press, 2008. 229 pp.

Claude McKay, Code Name Sasha: Queer Black Marxism
and the Harlem Renaissance
Gary Holcomb
Gainesville: University Press of Florida, 2009. xiv + 288 pp.

The Reification of Desire: Toward a Queer Marxism
Kevin Floyd
Minneapolis: University of Minnesota Press, 2009. 270 pp.

In 1989 John D'Emilio was invited to participate in a *Journal of American History* roundtable considering "the challenges that people with different identities, commitments, and agendas have brought to research and teaching in American history." D'Emilio, a scholar who exerted a formative influence on LGBT historiography and helped form the Gay Academic Union (GAU), considered what distin-

GLQ 18:1
DOI 10.1215/10642684-1422197
© 2011 by Duke University Press

guished the study of sexuality from other contentious historical subjects. "Radicalism is a perspective that can be brought to the study of any historical topic," D'Emilio offered; "by contrast, gayness has been relatively marginal and marginalized for much of the American experience."[1] Though he acknowledged that both radicalism and sexuality were central concerns within the historical profession, D'Emilio suggested how studying sexuality brought special problems that required a particular historical approach and presented unique challenges for gays working within the academy.

One year earlier, the writer, novelist, and influential activist Sarah Schulman had offered a decidedly different, yet strikingly parallel, comment on the relationship between radicalism, homosexuality, and current scholarship to a conference of the Socialist Scholars. In a talk presented at their 1988 meeting, Schulman provocatively assessed the Left's engagement with homosexuality. "The left has never come to terms with the passion of homosexuality," Schulman declared, "and AIDS cannot be adequately discussed if you cannot say 'ass-fucking.'" The blindness of the Left to the AIDS crisis, which Schulman attributed to the "straight men of the left, who are willing to march for every nation in struggle in the world, [but] will not walk into a room full of queers and make a stand with them," revealed the impossibility of forging a radicalism that responded to homosexuality while refusing to acknowledge, describe, and come to terms with its passions.[2]

In both episodes, distinct though they might have been, the relationship between sex and the American Left was treated as a site of potential cross-pollination that was frustrated by either the failure of the Left to bring lesbians and gay men into the conversation or the inconceivability of a productive relationship between homosexuality and radicalism as similarly unstable categories of minoritized identity. Despite their divergence, for both D'Emilio and Schulman the relationship between radicalism and sexuality represented a potentially fruitful site of valuable intersection, conceptual overlap, and productive interplay that also illustrated a series of missed historiographical opportunities and interpretive dead ends.

In the two decades between today's new historiography and D'Emilio's and Schulman's engaging observations on sex and the Left, scholarly interest in bringing radicalism into conversation with sexuality has appeared in fits and starts. Though there is hardly an extensive literature on sexuality and the Left, interest appears to be on the upswing. Four recent books by scholars representing a range of academic orientations have introduced themes and tenacious arguments poised to shake up our understanding of the relations between sexuality and radicalism. Though they build on the contributions of several generations of scholarship, this new crop of scholars moves toward defining queer leftist studies, and together these authors suggest constructive avenues for mapping future studies of queer communities, culture, and politics in the United States.

The growing attentiveness to sexuality in the historiography of the Left might be attributed to several scholarly shifts. First among these is the cultural turn within studies of the "Old Left" that took root in the 1980s and 1990s, a development that expanded scholars' archives to include novels, paintings, plays, and songs, and also writers, artists, actors, and performers. That these professions, for much of the twentieth century, were especially hospitable to queer women and men is a matter of historical record.[3] At the same time, particularly in the Depression-era Communist Party, US culture workers carved a path within the Left that respected the centrality of the organizational leadership of the CP while allowing individuals freedom to move in more independent directions.[4] It is unsurprising, therefore, that a significant number of mid-twentieth-century leftist culture workers were either homosexual or had well-known same-sex affairs; the list includes Will Geer, Josephine Herbst, Ella Winter, Marc Blitzstein, Henry Wadsworth Longfellow Dana, Willard Motley, and Agnes Smedley.[5]

The first generation of literary scholars studying American leftist writers in the 1950s was willing to challenge the anticommunism of their time by reassessing communism in the United States as having a multifaceted cultural influence, but they did not extend such revisionist interpretation to their readings of homosexuality.[6] In 1956 Walter Rideout offered a largely uncontested interpretation of homosexuality and the Left: "For the proletarian novelist," Rideout determined, "homosexuality came to stand arbitrarily as a convenient, all-inclusive symptom of capitalist decay."[7] This simplistic interpretation, as indebted to the repressive context of America's lavender scare as it was to an actual reading of radical fiction, shaped historiography on the literary Left; this despite the fact that homosexuality was a prominent subject treated with great subtlety in proletarian novels such as H. T. Tsiang's *Hanging in Union Square* (1935) and throughout James T. Farrell's *Studs Lonigan* trilogy published between 1932 and 1935.

The advent of sexuality studies in the 1980s provided an initial opportunity for scholars' coming to terms with sex and the Left. The publication of *Powers of Desire: The Politics of Sexuality*, coedited by Ann Snitow, Christine Stansell, and Sharon Thompson in 1983, introduced a dazzling collection of essays that defined the field, and the editors were hardly reticent about their leftist allegiances and materialist analyses.[8] The editors discussed "sex and socialism" and dissected the relationship between the Old Left and "sexual rebellion." Though they diminished the Old Left's contributions to sexual politics as being defined by "sexual restraint," they acknowledged in a contradictory aside that "fragments of evidence indicate that [Communist] party members, especially the women, had a loose reputation" (19). Though these essays did not fully exhaust the meeting of sexual and radical studies, the significance of a materialist methodology for one of the most influential volumes creating sexuality studies should not be discounted.

The influence of women's history on the academy made it similarly impossible for scholars studying American radicalism to ignore the relationships among gender, sex, and the Left. Rosalyn Baxandall's 1993 essay "The Question Seldom Asked: Women and the CPUSA," which appeared in a defining volume of revisionist history on the Communist Party in the United States, *New Studies in the Politics and Culture of U.S. Communism*, detailed a complicated and uneven history of exclusion and resistance shaping women's experiences in the CP and influencing the shape of the organized Left.[9] This essay contributed to a growing literature that took women's involvement in the Old Left seriously and challenged interpretations that considered women's experiences as marginal, exceptional, and lacking agency. Paula Rabinowitz's work as author of *Labor and Desire: Women's Revolutionary Fiction in Depression America* (1991) influenced a generation of literary scholars looking at gender and sexuality in radical working-class fiction.[10] Rabinowitz did not shy away from interrogating the sexual politics of proletarian fiction, noting of lesbianism in such work that "most women's revolutionary fiction intertwines the two tropes — sex and strikes — by conflating the narratives of desire and history," and she carefully read lesbianism in works by authors such as Herbst and Gale Wilhelm.[11]

Key figures in scholarship on the left found it impossible to ignore these new critical directions and produced work that followed the inroads of sexuality studies. Alan Wald, a historian of the literary Left, resisted any Marxist interpretation that diminished the importance of racial, ethnic, gender, and sexual identities in favor of a class analysis. Wald's second book, *The Revolutionary Imagination* (1983), profiled two poets, one of whom was the bisexual John Wheelwright, incorporating details about sexuality in his analysis.[12] His two-thirds-complete trilogy of books on US literary communism, published in 2002 and 2007, features important discussions of queer leftist writers including Willard Motley and William Rollins.[13] Wald's work has moved beyond a discussion of the biographical details of leftists who might have had homosexual proclivities to ask more in-depth questions, inquiring into how the form and politics of the proletarian novel have shaped its queer representations.

Much of the important work on the cultural Left was made possible partly by the opening up of studies of US radicalism to include actors and participants who did not necessarily join the Communist Party. In Michael Denning's influential 1992 study of the "laboring of American culture," *The Cultural Front*, complicated figures who moved in and out of the Left, fellow travelers who were sympathetic to the goals of the Left but skeptical about political parties, and bohemians, renegades, and iconoclasts whose leftist sympathies were as much a product of antagonism toward dominant Americanism as they were a expressions of a Marxist critique, were treated as no less significant to the building of a leftist "cultural front" than was the leadership and rank and file of the CPUSA.[14] Such interest in an increasingly amorphous leftist identity muddled the distinction drawn by such scholars as D'Emilio between radicalism as politics and homosexuality as identity, the latter of which confronted the struggle, at least within the academy, of "neither access nor entry but rather coming out and staying in."[15] If the chief distinction between studying radicalism and gay communities was, for D'Emilio, the distinction between battling for entrance and the process of being known in the first place, Denning's work outlined a new historiographic emphasis upon identifying leftists within and outside the Communist Party and exploring the negotiated meanings and uses of the Left for radicals of many stripes.

It is not mere coincidence that the radical lifestyle detailed in *The Cultural Front* (drinking in cafés, writing operas, hanging out on street corners, and becoming recognizable to one another) parallels the historicizing of gay male identity in George Chauncey's now-classic *Gay New York*, a book that appeared two years after Denning's.[16] Chauncey's research foregrounded the working class in relation to the formation of New York's sexual communities and considered figures who did not belong to sexual identities that corresponded with contemporary sexual taxonomies.[17] Though Chauncey worked within a Foucauldian framework, his attentiveness to interclass conflict over sexual definition, practices, and surveillance borrowed liberally from the new working-class studies. Gay New York, in Chauncey's study, was always already in the process of becoming and was defined as much by social practices and contested cultural meanings as it was by a singular set of identities or behaviors.

In the ensuing years since Chauncey's work redefined the methods, questions, and scholarly models used to study US sexual identities, three strains have dominated new scholarship in queer studies. First, community-based studies have reflected both the diversity of LGBT experiences and confirmed certain historical shifts over the twentieth century.[18] These studies have complicated the definition of sexual identities, interrogated the meanings of exclusion within LGBT communities, and foregrounded both the important work accomplished through LGBT cooperation and the effects of gender, patriarchy, and heteronormativity on homosexual subcultures and political organizations. Second, queer theory continues to dominate humanities scholarship, both in LGBT studies and in the academy at large. Finally, the new queer studies has foregrounded a critique of neoliberalism that, while often shunning the history of the American Left as a model for new political engagement, has been willing to adopt an anticapitalist position and to espouse the legitimacy of Marxian analytic categories for understanding both queer communities and politics under late capitalism.

Within community-based studies, following Chauncey's and Denning's approach, the parallel (and occasionally overlapping) work being done in sexual and radical political communities is striking, though there is little acknowledgment among either set of scholars that the other community was active in the same time and place. Though the voluminous literature on communism and homosexuality in urban spaces has established enough points of contact and intersection to unequivocally establish that queer and leftist individuals must have been aware of one other, the critique of metronormativity that has generated one of the most significant historiographical shifts in studies of US sexual communities, spearheaded by such scholars as John Howard, Judith Halberstam, and Scott Herring, mirrors the shift within studies of the Left from the Harlem of Mark Naison's *Communists in Harlem during the Depression* (1983) to the rural spaces of Robin Kelley's Alabama communists.[19] The imagining of communities outside the protective space of the city has forced scholars of both sexuality and the Left not only to redefine what counts as a legitimate political community but also to expand their archives to accommodate the decentralized practices and identities found outside urban subcultures.

Queer theory has opened a space for thinking about the Left or, more accurately, for Marxist interpretations of sexuality, yet also has tended to favor a Foucauldian framework that looks with suspicion on Marxist categories. The specter of Marxism has emerged in uneven and sometimes unpredictable ways. Yet one need only look at the groundbreaking scholarship in José Esteban Muñoz's *Disidentifications*, published in 1999, or Rosemary Hennessey's *Profit and Pleasure* from 2000 to find a careful engagement with Karl Marx.[20] Queer of color critique, an increasingly influential and predominant strain within queer theory, has been at the vanguard of this return to Marxist categories and materialist analysis.[21] Muñoz's most recent book, *Cruising Utopia: The Then and There of Queer Futurity*, resuscitates Marxist critic Ernst Bloch to herald a reinvigorated queer politics.[22] Finally, attacks on neoliberalism have auspiciously imagined the need to affirm queer identity by foregrounding this queer of color analysis while also directly confronting the excesses of late capitalism. In 2004 Lisa Duggan's

Twilight of Equality? offered a significant volley in this direction by directly confronting neoliberalism, tolerance, and homonormativity, and Jasbir Puar dissected homonationalism in *Terrorist Assemblages* (2007), similarly taking on conservative strains within lesbian and gay communities.[23] This leftist orientation within contemporary queer studies has a rich history of its own. In 1975 Jonathan Ned Katz organized a Marxist study group for "GAU expatriates" that studied classic texts including Marx's *German Ideology* and Friedrich Engels's *Origins of the Family, Private Property, and the State.* Among those in attendance was D'Emilio, whose *Sexual Politics, Sexual Communities* was shaped by his realization as part of this group that Marxism "left ample room for issues of culture and consciousness, matters of great significance in the construction of a gay historical literature."[24]

Despite the undercurrent of interest in thinking about homosexuality in relation to the Left, until recently few texts took as their primary analysis historicizing and theorizing this relationship. Yet in the past several years several prominent books have appeared that directly address sexuality and the Left in complicated ways, opening up the field to new lines of inquiry and revisiting older categories and models.[25] Among the most interesting of this recent crop is Daniel Hurewitz's *Bohemian Los Angeles and the Making of Modern Politics.* Published in 2007, Hurewitz's book brings together a community-based study, focusing specifically on Edendale (later known as Silver Lake) in Los Angeles, with a comprehensive reexamination of the concept of identity in shaping modern sexual politics. Hurewitz's research is immediately appealing for the range of known characters who passed through Edendale between the 1910s and the 1950s: his community includes such familiar figures as the female impersonator Julian Eltinge, Mattachine founder Harry Hay, ONE cofounder Dale Jennings, and the avant-garde composer John Cage. Yet Hurewitz's study offers far more than a dynamic profile of a community that fostered art, communism, and homosexuality in seemingly equal and inextricable measure (though this might have been enough). Perhaps most vitally, Hurewitz argues that this milieu fostered the stirrings of a modern politics grounded in "an interior realm of personality, essence, and identity" (5) that would dominate the political and sexual landscape for decades to follow. By historicizing the very foundations of identity in the twentieth-century United States, Hurewitz offers a convincing recasting of the narratives of sexual and radical politics that makes homosexuality and communism mutually constitutive and historically connected. Disrupting a narrative of sexual politics that places identity at the center of an exclusively post-1960s movement, Hurewitz shifts the period of sexual identity politics earlier while claiming that a gay political movement emerged in large measure because of the intersections between sexual, artistic, and leftist communities. "Ultimately," Hurewitz argues about homophile activists, "their politicization of sexual identity was directly influenced by the debates about the abstract notions of 'self' and 'politics' carried on by their neighboring artists and leftists" (11).

Hurewitz's study begins before gay identity emerged as a political category. Using Eltinge as a local case study, Hurewitz demonstrates how he was initially able to perform as a female impersonator while retaining his identity as a heterosexual man who went largely unquestioned. By the 1920s such a bifurcated identity was being fundamentally challenged, yet far from being a foregone conclusion the meanings of sexual identities at this time remained in flux. "While audiences laughed at male effeminacy in the 1900s and 1910s," Hurewitz writes, "increasingly they began to believe that the hidden truth of male effeminacy was homosexuality; sexual desires constituted something fundamental" (75). Artists contributed to this growing conception of identity as a basis for community as they "transformed Edendale into a place where self-expression itself could be the mark of identity and the potential basis of a community" (113). Finally, Communists formed communities based on identity and lifestyle; membership in the party offered "an emotionally rich, politically significant identity that rested on the deep bonds of community." As would become a central tenet of the second-wave feminists and sexual liberationists decades later, Communists demonstrated "how personal passion and political action could be meaningfully intertwined to inspire action" (186).

One dynamic that Hurewitz identifies as central in the shift toward an identity-based politics in Edendale was the ongoing interest among leftists in the racial antagonisms simmering in Los Angeles. As Communists drew analogies between racial, ethnic, and other forms of identity during the 1930s and 1940s, the politics of wartime Los Angeles confirmed a growing consensus on the left that "racial group politics constituted a model for all politicized identities" (190). Hurewitz details how Japanese American removal, anti-Mexican violence, and racially discriminatory hiring practices elicited a response by Communists that precipitated an invigorated anticommunism in Los Angeles, which was in turn met with the notion that "social minorities . . . had the right to resist discrimination and demand some version of self-rule" (228).

By the time Mattachine was formed in 1951, features borrowed from artistic and communist communities and ethnic and racial minority struggles crystallized into a modern political organization advocating for civil rights. Members assumed the expression of "inner lives and desires" as central to their identities; and the analogous lessons of "distinct, politically identified, and active racial groups became a key model for the Mattachine founders" (237). Mattachine represented an archetype for modern politics, and Hurewitz suggests this would have been impossible without the cross-pollination of the various communities he discusses in Edendale. Though Harry Hay still features as a central figure in Hurewitz's story of the origins of gay rights, "Mattachine was equally the child of Edendale, where Hay lived and where he experienced the same conjunction of artistry and leftist politics that defined the neighborhood" (237).

Hurewitz's energetic, creative study moves scholarship on sexuality and the Left in significantly new directions. Among his major contributions, Hurewitz makes it impossible to discuss the origins of the homophile movement without taking into account the role of earlier political communities in shaping its organizational structure. His interpretation of the formation of modern politics through his attentive consideration of identity also bears the potential to radically reshape our understanding of recent LGBT political movements. By thinking about modern politics rooted in questions of identity rather than fragmented political programs, Hurewitz is able to more or less avoid confronting the exclusions of homosexuality as a topic (and, in many cases, homosexuals themselves as people) from the work of the Communist Party, creating a usable past within social movements that might otherwise be excluded from the narrative of LGBT history. His book should inform scholars of sexuality and radicalism in equal measure, and his attentive focus on Los Angeles should also appeal to urban historians interested in the dynamic intersectional processes that cities allow.

Terence Kissack's *Free Comrades* foregrounds the organizational commitments of prominent anarchists and asks how their political affiliations informed their ideas about sexuality. Noting the apparent absence of an activism centered on homosexuality in the United States during a period of the early twentieth century when many such groups appeared in northern Europe, Kissack suggests that within the English-language anarchist movement, "there was, in fact, a vital, engaged, political discussion of homosexuality" (3). Informed by movements in Europe, American anarchists incorporated a tentative acceptance of homosexuality into a political program that "insisted that there should be no external authority governing people's personal or public associations; all 'desires, tastes, and inclinations' should be respected and given room to flourish" (5). Anchored in a fundamental distrust of government intrusion in personal and individual lives, anarchists were uniquely positioned to foster a dissident politics of homosexuality that was both visible and influential in its embrace of same-sex love.

Kissack's concern is with "public pronouncements" by anarchists about homosexuality. To this end, his book is structured around individuals within the anarchist movement who explicitly commented on, theorized, or celebrated homosexuality. He studies anarchist responses to Oscar Wilde and Walt Whitman particularly closely, and special attention is reserved—unsurprisingly given her prominent position in both the movement and scholarship—for Emma Goldman. Kissack's discussion of Wilde examines how anarchists leapt to Wilde's defense after his sensationalized trial and imprisonment, in some cases even publishing Wilde's work when the scandalized network of mainstream American publishers would not touch it. Wilde was an attractive figure to anarchists because of his philosophical sympathies with some aspects of anarchism, and also as a "symbol of the anarchist struggle to transform society" through "sexual freedom, personal liberty, [and] the freedom from coercion by the state" (67). Similarly, Whitman was taken up for his public homosexuality and commitment to espousing freedom; he "both inhibited and enabled different anarchist sex radicals to speak out on the moral, legal, and social status of same-sex love" (95).

Other figures in Kissack's book were more directly associated with anarchism in the United States. Alexander Berkman, for example, was imprisoned for his attempted political assassination of Henry Frick; while in prison for this crime, Berkman assembled his *Prison Memoirs of an Anarchist*, a text Kissack claims "is one of the most important political texts dealing with homosexuality to have been written by an American before the 1950s" (102). Berkman's acknowledgment of same-sex love in prison as an ordinary matter and his willingness to present homosexual subjects with dignity and compassion mark a profound counterpoint to the surveillance and regulation of homosexuality in the United States outside his prison walls.

Kissack's research demonstrates persuasively why broadening studies of homosexuality to include voices on the left frustrates historiographical claims that organized LGBT politics began only with the 1950s homophile movement. His work reminds scholars that the fact that American political organizations did not form to specifically address homosexuality until that time should not be taken to mean that political responses to homosexuality were nonexistent. This is an important intervention. Yet it is disappointing that Kissack explains away the dearth of African American anarchists as a by-product of southern racism and suppression of radicalism, a claim that diminishes the long history of black radicalism in the United States (including in the South) and the courageous interracialism of other leftist organizations, while also pushing aside the too-frequent failures on the left to truly commit to racial justice. It seems quixotic to recover and celebrate a political movement for its advances in sexual politics while diminishing the consequences of its racial exclusions.

Kissack is also curiously sectarian in his wholesale dismissal of the CPUSA as having turned back the clock on advancing homosexual politics. When Communism appears in his work, Kissack summarily discounts the "profoundly antifeminist sexual politics of Stalin and his admirers," an analysis that smacks of factional smear and suggests a historiographical consensus where one does not exist (169). Still, Kissack's work connecting homosexuality with anarchism has broad implications for scholars working on the history of sexuality and the Left. His book offers further evidence that homosexuality was taken up as a matter of political concern well before the Stonewall uprisings and that members of the Old Left acknowledged sexual diversity, and his mining of the historical archive reminds us that the notion of political silence about homosexuality speaks as much to the gaps in historiography as it does to actual conditions in the past. His book makes it impossible to think about anarchism outside its sexual politics.

Gary Holcomb's *Claude McKay, Code Name Sasha* turns the theoretical dial up a notch, training his critical eye on McKay, a complicated figure who was publicly aligned with both homosexuality and the Left. Coming from a literary-critical perspective, Holcomb emphasizes close readings of several important works of fiction and the autobiography by McKay to position his work as of interest to scholars "who are invested in rethinking ways in which race and leftist politics intersect with sexual dissidence" (xi) and rereads McKay's oeuvre to demonstrate how his "black Marxism cannot be disentangled from his queer resistance" (12). Central to Holcomb's study is his theorization of "queer black Marxism," a political and aesthetic category Holcomb invokes to both articulate the contributions to the history of sex and the Left McKay foregrounded in his work and to highlight the connections between McKay's historical moment and our own. "Some of the earliest expressions of queer counterspeech," Holcomb writes, "are present in McKay's black radical leftist writings" (12).

Claude McKay, Code Name Sasha mines McKay's work for evidence of his queer black Marxism in the most unexpected places. *A Long Way from Home*, for example, a memoir McKay wrote after he abandoned Communism, becomes in Holcomb's analysis a space where "the filtrate of [McKay's] Marxist intellectual work and sexual dissidence resides" (90). Holcomb is no less skilled at digging into McKay's more-familiar works and mining them for radical content. *Home to Harlem* is reclaimed as "a queer black anarchist manifesto" (92), especially through Jake Brown and Raymond's complicated dialectical relationship where McKay dreams his revolution. *Banjo* constitutes a radically queer text, with McKay as "*agent provocateur*, inciting black proletarian agency through his novels, written for consumption by black readers in the United States" (147). Holcomb devotes a full chapter to McKay's unpublished novel, *Romance in Marseilles.* In this work, which Holcomb refers to as the third text of McKay's "queer black Marxist trilogy," Holcomb finds a nuanced articulation of queerness through the form of a proletarian novel. Holcomb attentively dissects how this "sex novel fuses black proletarianism and dissident black queer rhetorics, bringing politics and the personal together in what is one of the most vital documents of twentieth-century diaspora literature, published or not" (224).

Holcomb's study is also valuable for its contribution to the transnational turn, a shift that can be seen in both studies on the left and in LGBT scholarship. One might explain the recent surge of interest in McKay — "McKay," Holcomb writes in his introduction, "is at last in vogue" — by pointing to his broad, cross-sectional appeal to scholars of the black Atlantic, queers of color, Caribbean and diasporic black identities, the Communist Party, and the Harlem Renaissance (1). Yet the transnational character of both McKay's life and his literary work, much of which hops from place to place and features a motley cast of characters from around the world and without a narrow definition of home, has placed him at the center of transnational queer, black, and leftist studies. "Generally speaking," Holcomb writes, "the McKay currently familiar to the world is an anomalous pastiche of frequently incompatible identities" (3).

Claude McKay, Code Name Sasha recovers a figure from the past as a progenitor of queer black Marxism and presents a riveting personality whose work offers a roadmap for thinking through contemporary theoretical and political roadblocks. "My objective," Holcomb elegantly writes in his summary conclusion, "has been to regenerate lost, dangerous intelligence, to revive the creative efforts of black Marxist modernist writing, to resume our conversations with the dead — these 'priceless treasures sinking in the sand,' to reiterate McKay's vision of 'America' — and to ask what they may communicate to us even now" (232). McKay's work both influenced and was informed by the tremendous expansion of Depression-era proletarian literature at the height of his creative power and by a perverse attraction to radical politics that made it possible for him to refuse state efforts to regulate his sexual desire. It is only through the recent convergence of new discursive possibilities in queer and leftist scholarship that the full breadth of McKay's import can be fully explored in all its dimensions. Holcomb offers both a major contribution to our understanding of queer black Marxism and a compelling model for the sort of work now imaginable for LGBT scholars.

One factor that has foreclosed the kind of bold, creative work found in *Code Name Sasha* is the persistent claim that critical Marxism reduces all social experience to the class struggle, thereby negating Marx's analytic power to articulate anything new about sexual identities or the Left's attraction for queer people. Kevin Floyd's challengingly dense work of queer political theory, *The Reification of Desire*, engages such concerns directly by analyzing Marxist theorists whose work rarely finds its way into scholarship on queer sexualities. For Floyd, the problem of totality is a clear point of entry for considering how queer theory and Marxism have unwittingly covered shared ground and might be developed into a more fruitful site of interchange. Replacing the tendency within Marxist thought to assume "that capital mediates sexuality in relatively consistent, predictable ways," Floyd acknowledges a curious convergence in Marxism and queer theory that hinges on "a common critique of epistemological particularization, a common 'impulse of generalization,' a common emphasis on totality thinking" (9).

Incorporating a twentieth-century historical narrative of Marxism and homosexuality in the United States alongside a sophisticated theoretical apparatus that grapples with the esoterica of Marxist literary and political theory, the most significant Marxian concept for Floyd is that of reification, characterized as a "misapprehension of capitalist social relations" where the historical processes of capitalism are conceived as ahistorical and objectively real (19). Floyd places this process in capitalist development into conversation with the emergence of queerness as "a century-long history of struggle against compulsory heterosexuality, a history that itself is conditioned by capital's internal differentiation of social relations" (20).

One central question lurking behind Floyd's study is how to put his Marxist interpretation alongside the Foucauldian framework that has come to dominate so much of LGBT studies. Here lies a significant convergence of queer theory and Marxism for Floyd: both Foucault and Georg Lukács, though they come to their conclusions through different theoretical apparatuses, note a major "epistemological shift" at the turn-of-the-twentieth century. Reification of desire occurs, in Floyd's interpretation, "as the family is increasingly saturated not only with pathology, but also with commodities, amid the normalized consumption characteristic of an emergent, intensive regime of accumulation, from within capital's emergent distribution of a new sexual knowledge of self" (61). Ultimately, however, Floyd turns away from a wholesale appropriation of Foucault, indicating the limitations of his work that "mystifies the very character of the regime of sexual knowledge he elaborates—specifically, its status as a product of this increasingly complex social division of labor" (41).

Floyd's book offers an important contribution to thinking through the queer Left by offering a persuasive defense of queer Marxism as a theoretical enterprise. The unique contribution of Floyd's work lies in both its theoretical richness and its interpretive potential: reintroducing Marxist categories into discussions of homosexuality offers scholars a useful vocabulary for challenging both the defanged historiographical movement away from a radical queer critique and for addressing the concerns about neoliberalism and homonationalism that such scholars as Lisa Duggan and Jasbir Puar have made the case for foregrounding. Floyd confesses his own motivation also to "nudge Marxism into developing a greater capacity to speak to certain dimensions of social and historical reality powerfully illuminated in queer theory's relatively brief history" (4). As with each of the scholars discussed in this essay, the aspiration to bring discordant political, theoretical, and sexual terms into conversation precipitates Floyd's scholarly inquiry, and his work struggles to find points of intersection between queer studies and Marxist categories. Floyd's provocative and urgent book leaves plenty of opportunities for future scholars to connect his theoretical concerns with historical narratives of the organized Left while offering a surfeit of analysis that is sure to fundamentally reorganize scholarship on both Marxist and queer theory.

Taken together, these four recent studies of homosexuality and the Left point to a cogent new body of literature that centralizes, legitimizes, and convincingly thinks through the relationship between radicalism and queer sexuality. Though they are divergent in their methods, disciplines, and conclusions, these works together organize disparate ideas about sex and the Left into a legitimate subfield within LGBT studies. They build on the significant work of such radical historians as D'Emilio and Katz and history-minded activists such as Schulman. Their work helps explain the roots of queer Left connections and provides convincing directions for mapping the future of queer studies. Though these scholars point toward an audacious new energy and willingness to think through the implications of sex and the Left directly and without apology, they also build on currents that have been simmering within LGBT and leftist historiography for decades. Their work forces us to think critically about both the history we know and the way we write our history. Scholars of sexuality and the Left have much to teach one another, and the vibrant works discussed in this essay give just a hint of how much we can learn from joining these conversations and coming to terms with their shared passions.

Notes

1. John D'Emilio, *Making Trouble: Essays on Gay History, Politics, and the University* (New York: Routledge, 1992), 138; 139.

2. Sarah Schulman, *My American History: Lesbian and Gay Life during the Reagan/ Bush Years* (New York: Routledge, 1994), 185.

3. See, e.g., Michael S. Sherry, *Gay Artists in Modern American Culture: An Imagined Conspiracy* (Chapel Hill: University of North Carolina Press, 2007).

4. The scholarly tendency to privilege participation in the Communist-led Left while discounting the role of the party has been a point of contention for many scholars of the Left, notable among them Geoff Eley, who has decried the new "history of communism with the Communism left out" ("International Communism in the Heyday of Stalin," *New Left Review* 157 [January–February 1986]: 92). See also Bryan D. Palmer, "Rethinking the Historiography of United States Communism," *American Communist History* 2 (2003): 147–52; Barbara Foley, *Radical Representations: Politics and Form in U.S. Proletarian Fiction, 1929–1941* (Durham, NC: Duke University Press, 1993); Andrew Hemingway, *Artists on the Left: American Artists and the Communist Movement, 1926–1956* (New Haven: Yale University Press, 2002); Eric Homberger, *American Writers and Radical Politics, 1900–1939* (Basingstoke, UK: Macmillan, 1986); James Murphy, *The Proletarian Moment: The Controversy over Leftism in Literature* (Urbana: University of Illinois Press, 1991).

5. The relationship between the Communist Party, leftist ideology, and early gay liberation has been expansively discussed in Stuart Timmons's important biography of Harry Hay. See Stuart Timmons, *The Trouble with Harry Hay, Founder of the Modern Gay Movement* (Boston: Alyson, 1990).

6. Daniel Aaron, *Writers on the Left: Episodes in Literary Communism* (New York: Harcourt, Brace and World, 1961); James Gilbert, *Writers and Partisans: A History of Literary Radicalism in America* (New York: Wiley, 1968); Walter Rideout, *The Radical Novel in the United States: Some Interrelations of Literature and Society, 1900–1954* (Cambridge: Harvard University Press, 1956).

7. Walter Rideout, *The Radical Novel in the United States: Some Interrelations of Literature and Society, 1900–1954* (1956; rpt. New York: Columbia University Press, 1992), 174.

8. Ann Snitow, Christine Stansell, and Sharon Thompson, *Powers of Desire: The Politics of Sexuality* (New York: Monthly Review Press, 1983). The formative influence of socialist feminism for opening this discourse was also important. See Zillah R. Eisenstein, ed., *Capitalist Patriarchy and the Case for Socialist Feminism* (New York: Monthly Review Press, 1979).

9. Rosalyn Baxandall, "The Question Seldom Asked: Women and the CPUSA," in *New Studies in the Politics and Culture of U.S. Communism*, ed. Michael E. Brown, Randy

Martin, Frank Rosengarten, and George Snedeker (New York: Monthly Review Press, 1993), 141–62.

10. Charlotte Nekola and Paula Rabinowitz, *Writing Red: An Anthology of American Women Writers* (New York: Feminist Press at the City University of New York, 1987); Paula Rabinowitz, *Labor and Desire: Women's Revolutionary Fiction in Depression America* (Chapel Hill: University of North Carolina Press, 1991).

11. Rabinowitz, *Labor and Desire*, 80.

12. Alan M. Wald, *The Revolutionary Imagination: The Poetry and Politics of John Wheelwright and Sherry Mangan* (Chapel Hill: University of North Carolina Press, 1993).

13. Alan M. Wald, *Exiles from a Future Time: The Forging of the Mid-Twentieth-Century Literary Left* (Chapel Hill: University of North Carolina, 2002); Wald, *Trinity of Passion: The Literary Left and the Antifascist Crusade* (Chapel Hill: University of North Carolina, 2007). Wald also contributed a useful entry on American writers on the left to the online *GLBTQ: An Encyclopedia of Gay, Lesbian, Bisexual, Transgender, and Queer Culture*, www.glbtq.com/literature/am_mawriters_left.html (accessed June 10, 2010).

14. Michael Denning, *The Cultural Front: The Laboring of American Culture in the Twentieth Century* (New York: Verso, 1996).

15. John D'Emilio, "Not a Simple Matter: Gay History and Gay Historian," *Journal of American History* 76 (1989): 139.

16. George Chauncey, *Gay New York: Gender, Urban Culture, and the Makings of the Gay Male World, 1890–1940* (New York: Basic Books, 1994).

17. David Montgomery, *The Fall of the House of Labor: The Workplace, the State, and American Labor Activism, 1865–1925* (New York: Cambridge University Press, 1987); E. P. Thompson, *The Making of the English Working Class* (New York: Pantheon, 1964). Other examples of foundational texts in working-class studies that are relevant here include Kathy Lee Peiss, *Cheap Amusements: Working Women and Leisure in Turn-of-the-Century New York* (Philadelphia: Temple University Press, 1986); and Roy Rosenzweig, *Eight Hours for What We Will: Workers and Leisure in an Industrial City, 1870–1920* (New York: Cambridge University Press, 1983).

18. For a useful overview, see Marc Stein, "Theoretical Politics, Local Communities: The Making of U.S. LGBT Historiography," *GLQ* 11 (2005): 605–25.

19. John Howard, *Men Like That: A Southern Queer History* (Chicago: University of Chicago Press, 1999); Judith Halberstam, *In a Queer Time and Place: Transgender Bodies, Subcultural Lives* (New York: New York University Press, 2005); Scott Herring, "Regional Modernism: A Reintroduction," *Modern Fiction Studies* 55 (2009): 1–10; Herring, "Out of the Closets, into the Woods: 'RFD,' 'Country Women,' and the Post-Stonewall Emergence of Queer Anti-Urbanism," *American Quarterly* 59 (2007): 341–72; Mark Naison, *Communists in Harlem during the Depression* (Urbana: Uni-

versity of Illinois, 1983). Robin D. G. Kelley's *Hammer and Hoe: Alabama Communists During the Great Depression* (Chapel Hill: University of North Carolina Press, 1990) followed the direction gestured toward in Nell Irvin Painter, *The Narrative of Hosea Hudson, His Life as a Negro Communist in the South* (Cambridge: Harvard University Press, 1979).

20. José Esteban Muñoz, *Disidentifications: Queers of Color and the Performance of Politics* (Minneapolis: University of Minnesota Press, 1999); Rosemary Hennessy, *Profit and Pleasure: Sexual Identities in Late Capitalism* (New York: Routledge, 2000). Muñoz's recently published book, *Cruising Utopia*, moves even farther in this direction through an extended consideration of the Marxist philosopher Ernst Bloch (*Cruising Utopia: The Then and There of Queer Futurity* [New York: New York University Press, 2009]).

21. Roderick Ferguson's *Aberrations in Black*, published in 2004, inaugurated both a return to Marx and an attentive theorization of black queer identity. Ferguson urges a disidentificatory historical materialism that responds to Marxist thought by "investigating how intersecting racial, gender, and sexual practices antagonize and/or conspire with the normative investments of nation-states and capital" (*Aberrations in Black: Toward a Queer of Color Critique* [Minneapolis: University of Minnesota Press, 2004], 4).

22. Muñoz, *Cruising Utopia*.

23. Lisa Duggan, *The Twilight of Equality? Neoliberalism, Cultural Politics, and the Attack on Democracy* (Boston: Beacon, 2003); Jasbir K. Puar, *Terrorist Assemblages: Homonationalism in Queer Times* (Durham, NC: Duke University Press, 2007).

24. John D'Emilio, *Making Trouble*, xxxii.

25. Regrettably Martin Duberman's significant contribution to scholarship on queer radicalism was published too recently to be included in this review essay: Martin Duberman, *A Saving Remnant: The Radical Lives of Barbara Deming and David McReynolds* (New York: The New Press, 2011).

ANTHOLOGIZING THE FIELD

Robert Azzarello

Queer Ecologies: Sex, Nature, Politics, Desire
Catriona Mortimer-Sandilands and Bruce Erickson, eds.
Bloomington: Indiana University Press, 2010. 410 pp.

Because of their very nature, anthologies are difficult to write about — so many claims, so many perspectives, so many references to texts still unread, so many histories and projections for the future. In this sense, they mimic what actually happens in an academic field of study, the swirling together of ideas, at least for a moment, around a central post. The difficulty in charting an academic field, like that of reviewing an anthology, is all the more intensified in a book like *Queer Ecologies: Sex, Nature, Politics, Desire* because its aim is to connect *two* fields of study, queer and environmental, two fields that historically have lacked much contact. Bringing together the perceptive insights of thirteen unique writers, the editors, Catriona Mortimer-Sandilands, a professor of environmental studies at York University, and Bruce Erickson, an environmental historian at Nipissing University, make a solid and sustained contribution to the coalescing of two fields that has been over a decade in the making.

But what *is* the connection between queer studies and environmental studies? Because of their very different critical histories and rhetorical protocols — that is, the very different assumptions about the proper domains and political exigencies of their subjects — these two fields may seem very much at odds. One is seen as urban, the other as rural; one is concerned with culture, the other with nature; one tends toward a constructivist epistemology, the other toward objectivism; one studies people, the other studies plants and animals. Mortimer-Sandilands, Erickson, and the other contributors to the volume, however, insist that it is wrong to assume that the two fields are so categorically distinct after all. From the very beginning, queer studies and environmental studies have shared a set of concerns

GLQ 18:1
© 2011 by Duke University Press

that often gets obscured in popular stereotypes of the fields and their practitioners. It is the task of *Queer Ecologies* to identify that set of concerns.

The introductory chapter, coauthored by Mortimer-Sandilands and Erickson, includes several metatextual moments that highlight the central post around which the concerns of the field circulate. The premise is simple enough: "understandings of nature inform discourses of sexuality . . . understandings of sex inform discourses of nature" (2–3). The simplicity of the premise, however, quickly gets more complicated when one follows what the contributors to the volume mean by those elusive terms *sex* and *nature* and — perhaps even more importantly — that crucial verb *inform*. According to Mortimer-Sandilands and Erickson, their aim is twofold: first, to encourage "a sexual politics that more clearly includes considerations of the natural world and its biosocial constitution," and second, to cultivate "an environmental politics that demonstrates an understanding of the ways in which sexual relations organize and influence both the material world of nature and our perceptions, experiences, and constitutions of that world" (5).

The volume is rich with interesting writers making compelling arguments. To name just a few, Stacy Alaimo explores the problematics and pleasures in identifying animals as queer beings; Noël Sturgeon unpacks the importance of reproductive justice in terms of environmental activism; Giovanna Di Chiro identifies the relationships between toxic discourse and sex panic; Rachel Stein writes about the nature poetry of Adrienne Rich and Minnie Bruce Pratt; Diane Chisholm presents a close reading of biophilia and evolutionary theory in Ellen Meloy, a nature writer of the American Southwest. Some of the essays are exceptional; everyone thinking about environmental rhetoric should read Ladelle McWhorter's chapter "Enemy of the Species." What unites all of these essays, besides an interest in all things queer and ecological, is a drive toward interdisciplinarity. The anthology on the whole, however, does seem specifically geared to the humanities and the theoretical social sciences. After reading all the pieces, one wonders how a professional ecologist would write about "queer ecology" and what kind of book *Queer Ecologies* would be if Mortimor Sandilands and Erickson had solicited the work of trained biologists — not as some sort of ultimate authority but as supplementary voice.

Despite this last criticism, *Queer Ecologies* is a welcome addition to the critical scene, joining a handful of texts such as David Bell and Gill Valentine's collection *Mapping Desire: Geographies of Sexualities* (1995) and Noreen Giffney and Myra J. Hird's volume *Queering the Non/Human* (2008), that make concerted efforts to blur the boundaries between the two fields of study.[1] There is also evidence that this type of work is becoming more popular. In a recent issue of *PMLA*, the great *arbiter elegantiarum* of literary-critical habits, Timothy Morton, has written a guest column called "Queer Ecology" (2010) in which he insists on inserting queer theory into environmental studies as an indispensable next step, both philosophically and politically.[2] What will be the long-term impact of this work on academic discourse, on queer persons, and on the environment remains to be seen, but Mortimer-Sandilands and Erickson's anthology will constitute essential reading for future debates on the subject.

Notes

1. David Bell and Gill Valentine, eds., *Mapping Desire: Geographies of Sexualities* (New York: Routledge, 1995); Noreen Giffney and Myra J. Hird, eds., *Queering the Non/Human* (Burlington, VT: Ashgate, 2008).
2. Timothy Morton, "Queer Ecology," *PMLA* 125 (2010): 273–82.

Robert Azzarello is assistant professor of English at Southern University at New Orleans.

DOI 10.1215/10642684-1422206

THE BONDS OF CHOICE

S. Pearl Brilmyer

The Feeling of Kinship: Queer Liberalism and the Racialization of Intimacy
David L. Eng
Durham, NC: Duke University Press, 2010. xiv + 251 pp.

In 1991 the anthropologist Kath Weston coined the phrase "families we choose" to describe queer forms of kinship fashioned as an alternative to the biological family. According to Weston, in gay and lesbian communities in 1980s San Francisco, "Kinship began to seem more like an effort and a choice than a permanent, unshakable bond or a birthright."[1] Now that American notions of marriage and child rearing are shot through with the rhetoric of choice and self-making, does the mantra "families we choose" retain any radical power? Who has been eclipsed in the portrait of the queer family as a contractual unit with state-sanctioned rights to "privacy" and "intimacy"?

Such questions motivate David L. Eng's *Feeling of Kinship*, a critical perspective on the recent surge of appeals for marriage, custody, and inheritance rights from gays and lesbians in the United States. Drawing from a range of theoretical traditions, including legal theory and psychoanalysis, Eng's work brings a transdisciplinary set of questions to bear on what Lisa Duggan has called "the new homonormativity . . . a politics that does not contest dominant heteronormative assumptions, but upholds and sustains them."[2] As Eng argues, inclusionary appeals by gays and lesbians for the right to participate in normative social institutions present "a domesticated version of family and kinship, one predicated on the conjugal family and its Oedipal arrangements as the only legally recognizable and tenable household structure" (31). He calls this turn in queer politics to the petition for rights and recognition before the law "queer liberalism," arguing that the consolidation of queer politics with the "liberal political norms of inclusion" forgets the racial genealogies of oppression and exploitation that made liberalism historically possible. Built on the legacies of slaves and colonized peoples, Eng shows, modern liberalism emerged in the distinction between public and private that rendered intimacy a kind of *property*—the right to which citizens were granted if they conformed to bourgeois notions of privacy and domesticity. The book's central argument is this: the ideals of individual choice, economic self-determination, and the right to privacy driving queer politics of late rely on a rhetoric of colorblindness forgetful of the history and enduring present of racism. As Eng demonstrates, in its conception of citizens as abstract and equal subjects, queer liberalism relegates racial struggle to the historical past, casting the fight for sexual equality as the second round of a fight already won by people of color.

Excavating these histories of "racial forgetting," Eng draws on texts haunted by the feeling that the project of "racial liberation" is far from complete. As an affective historian, Eng gracefully archives the feelings of loss, displacement, and longing of those left behind in queer narratives of freedom and progress. Monique Truong's acclaimed 2003 novel *The Book of Salt* proves the perfect example for Eng in this endeavor, chronicling the forgotten story of Bình, the imagined Vietnamese colonial and household chef of Gertrude Stein and Alice B. Toklas. Putting *The Book of Salt* in conversation with Wong Kar-wai's 1997 film *Happy Together*, in chapter 2 Eng shows how in these texts the queer Asian migrant must perform the "art of waiting," while the modern emerges around him in sync with the tempo of liberal progress and capitalist development. Chapters 3 and 4 analyze the films *First Person Plural* (2000) by Deann Borshay Liem and *History and Memory* (1991) by Rea Tajiri, developing a "poststructuralist account of kinship" that, while heavily indebted to Freudian psychology, theorizes lack in more "highly personalized and alternative forms" (16, 135).

What stands out across the body of *The Feeling of Kinship* is Eng's sustained attention to the issue of transnational adoption, a topic highly underresearched in queer studies, despite its increasing relevance for gay and lesbian parents. This issue proves exemplary for Eng in his attempt to theorize kinship as a structure of feeling *between* the "bonds" of biological relationships and the "effort or choice" of willed ones (to re-cite Weston) — as a network of affects unique to each person's experience of love, loss, and reparation. Transnational adoption, addressed first in chapter 3 in relation to the film *First Person Plural*, forms the basis of chapter 4, a case history cowritten with the psychoanalyst Shinhee Han. These chapters make good on Eng's commitment to "recognizing and responding to the diverse ways in which we now structure and live out our intimate lives" and serve as a call for more psychoanalytic work on the racial and diasporic ties failed by structures like the Oedipus complex (30).

Eng's most exciting contribution to queer studies, however, consists in his transformative reading of the landmark court ruling in *Lawrence v. Texas* (2003), the Supreme Court case championed for its extension of "privacy" to gay "couples" (to use the words of Presiding Justice Kennedy). In chapter 1 Eng draws attention to the little-known racial backstory of *Lawrence v. Texas*, the case lauded as a victory for gays and lesbians for its overturning of the antisodomy ruling of *Bowers v. Hardwick* (1986). Critical of analogies that draw parallels between *Lawrence* and *Loving v. Virginia* — whose 1967 ruling overturned the antimiscegenation statute in Virginia — Eng shows how references within the queer community to *Lawrence* as "our *Loving*" erase the tale of racial trespass and infidelity that drew police to Lawrence's home in the first place. If *Loving* had successfully awarded the right to privacy to interracial couples in 1967, Lawrence and his African American partner might not have attracted the police attention in 1998.

As *The Feeling of Kinship* elegantly demonstrates, a queer liberalism that places faith in a future of legislated equality risks obscuring the present of those relegated to the waiting room of history.

Notes

1. Kath Weston, *Families We Choose: Lesbians, Gays, Kinship* (New York: Columbia University Press, 1997), xv.
2. Lisa Duggan, *The Twilight of Equality: Neoliberalism, Cultural Politics, and the Attack on Democracy* (Boston: Beacon, 2004), 50.

S. Pearl Brilmyer is a PhD candidate in comparative literature at the University of Texas at Austin.

DOI 10.1215/10642684-1422215

FLOCKING TOGETHER

David Greven

Manly Love: Romantic Friendship in American Fiction
Axel Nissen
Chicago: University of Chicago Press, 2009. x + 229 pp.

Looking at works from authors both well-known (Henry James, Mark Twain, William Dean Howells) and less familiar (Bayard Taylor, Bret Harte, and, especially, Theodore Winthrop), Axel Nissen creates an inviting, enveloping world of "manly love" in the literature of the Gilded Age. Students and scholars of this era's literary output with an interest in questions of queer sexuality will find much to value in Nissen's study, especially its careful attention to heretofore obscure as well as more familiar texts.

When he outlines the genre by discussing key, overlapping themes in the literature of romantic friendship, Nissen's work really shines: on the one hand, trademarks include "the emphasis on the erotics of the hand, the allusion to ancient Greece, and the feminization and infantilization of the men involved in a homoerotic relationship" (142); on the other hand, a desire to "create kin" led men to innovative strategies such as marrying their beloved friend's sister. Nissen is wonderfully alert and open to these period-specific customs and sensibilities, and his reading of such works as Harte's story "Tennessee's Partner," Winthrop's largely unknown novel *Cecil Dreeme*, Taylor's *Joseph and His Friend*, and best-selling Confederate author Augusta Jane Evans's *St. Elmo* brims with insights into the different ways that Gilded Age individuals arranged their desiring and affectional lives. Nissen makes the valuable point that creating family ties was a paramount concern for nineteenth-century people, and those who principally desired someone of their own sex faced the challenge of creating kin through nonbiological means.

In a rather, to my mind, dubious but nevertheless noteworthy accomplishment, Nissen makes works by more prominent authors such as James generically similar to the works by lesser lights in this tradition. I say "dubious" because what is particular and meaningful in James becomes, in Nissen's treatment, much more generic. In *Roderick Hudson*, James's first "claimed" and major novel, the relationship between two young men, the slightly older Rowland Mallet and the brash, younger titular artist whom he financially supports in Rome, seems uncannily evocative of a homosexual love affair. Of James's startlingly modern treatment, Nissen asks,

> What are we to say, then, of a novel in which the characters that personify true womanhood and manhood are not irresistibly drawn to each other, choosing rather to attach themselves to the dissipated and the sensual? Where the women turn out to be manly and the men womanly? Where daughters do not necessarily love their mothers and men do not necessarily love the traits in other men that are most manly? Where four characters battle for the role of the heroine of the tale and only two of them are biologically female? Where none of the protagonists are finally united in anything remotely resembling Duffey's ideal of marriage? (100–101)[1]

These are salient questions indeed. But Nissen's answer is that James conforms to the generic constraints of the romantic friendship tradition, rather than that, perhaps, James's own complexity as a novelist and thinker may have contributed to his resistant depiction of sexual matters.

Nissen's treatment of the James novel is characteristic. While he is astutely attentive to the novel's unconventional social dynamics — which in his treatment come to seem quite conventional in the end — he is not a particularly convincing critic of the novel itself. For one thing, his presentation of Mallet, a disquietingly blank character whose control over the artist Roderick Hudson has a disturbing relentlessness, blunts the critical edge of James's depiction. To my mind, James's subject here is how those who can perceive and admire talent in others but cannot share in it themselves sometimes do their best to sabotage the object of their awe. Moreover, this is a novel about failed relationships and intimacies rather than romantic friendship, despite Nissen's determined attempt to place it in that generic tradition.

Overall, Nissen presents the romantic friendship tradition as one he has unearthed, and in many ways this makes sense, as many of the texts here will be unfamiliar to readers. I know that I will be referring to his scrupulous delineation of the romantic friendship tradition as I research and teach these topics. But a discussion of romantic nineteenth-century friendships — which, it should be added, developed out of the ardent cult of romantic friendship in the eighteenth century — has been under way for quite some time, undergirding, as it does, Leslie Fiedler's thesis of "innocent homosexuality." From the 1970s (Carroll Smith-Rosenberg) to the 1980s (Robert K. Martin's study of Herman Melville) and to the present, a sense of the primacy of same-sex relationships in the period has become broadly established. Nissen alternately ignores and overlooks a great deal of the work in this area that has preceded his own.

Most troublingly of all, Nissen (though he is hardly alone) has created a vision of the nineteenth century as a time in which same-gender love, though not sex (which plays a minor role in his account), could flourish without the impediments of sexual classification imposed by the emergent power of psychoanalysis and other "sciences" of sexuality. As a historicist account of nineteenth-century American literature generally has taken hold (and despite Nissen's attempts to problematize historicism, his work falls squarely within its purview), it has been increasingly informed by a shared, broad, hazy, Foucauldian understanding of same-sex desire as a phenomenon that was radically reshaped by the new sexual taxonomies of the late nineteenth century. This view has cast psychoanalysis and "sexuality" as the end point of nineteenth-century romantic friendship and the beginning of a new era of sexual normativity and classifications. Yet the idea that men and women should form close ties, at least before marriage, was quite a compulsory and prevailing notion in the nineteenth century. The compulsory nature of same-sex ties makes their ardent manifestation in romantic fiction somewhat less utopian than Nissen would have it. Moreover, the competitiveness of American life that became only increasingly intense in the Gilded Age needs to be taken into account when we consider the visible erosion of homoaffectionalism in American culture. Indeed, this market competitiveness as well as the development of muscular Christianity and the ever-more prominent emergence of the United States as a imperialistic world superpower in the latter half of the nineteenth century—and all of the attendant transformations of the gendered identity of American citizens—makes nary an impression on Nissen's ultimately anodyne argument. For all of its considerable strengths, the poignant and appealing *Manly Love* takes the study of same-sex love in the nineteenth century a step backward even as it opens up promising new ground.

Note

1. Nissen refers here to Eliza Duffey, whose book *The Relations of the Sexes* (1876) was an attempt, he describes, to "save married and unmarried women alike from the undesirable, even life-threatening sexual passion of husbands and bachelors" (98–99).

David Greven is associate professor of English and chair of the literatures in english department at Connecticut College.

DOI 10.1215/10642684-1422224

About the Contributors

Lisa Marie Cacho is an associate professor in the Latina/Latino studies department and the Asian American Studies Program at the University of Illinois, Urbana-Champaign. Her book *Social Death: Racialized Rightlessness and the Criminalization of the Unprotected* examines the ways in which illegality, criminality, and social death are relationally constituted (forthcoming 2012).

Christina Crosby is professor of English and feminist, gender, and sexuality studies at Wesleyan University. She has long been engaged with poststructuralist feminism and Victorian studies, with publications in both fields. Her current work is focused on theories and practices of embodiment.

Lisa Duggan is professor of social and cultural analysis at NYU. She is the author most recently of *Twilight of Equality: Neoliberalism, Cultural Politics and the Attack on Democracy.*

Roderick A. Ferguson is associate professor and chair of the American studies department at the University of Minnesota, Twin Cities. He is the author of *Aberrations in Black: Toward a Queer of Color Critique* (2004) and is completing a manuscript entitled "The Reorder of Things: On the Institutionalization of Difference," to be published by the University of Minnesota Press.

Kevin Floyd is the author of *The Reification of Desire: Toward a Queer Marxism* (2009). He is associate professor of English at Kent State University, where he teaches courses on Marxism, queer studies, and twentieth-century US literature and culture. His current research is on totality and dialectic in the work of Samuel Delany.

Carla Freccero is professor of literature, feminist studies, and history of consciousness at UCSC. She also directs the UCSC Center for Cultural Studies. Her books include *Father Figures* (1991), *Popular Culture* (1999), and *Queer/Early/Modern* (2006). She coedited *Premodern Sexualities* (1996). Her current book project, on nonhuman animals and figuration, is "Animate Figures."

Boaz Hagin is assistant professor at the Department of Film and Television, Tel Aviv University. He is author of *Death in Classical Hollywood Cinema* (2010) and coauthor with Thomas Elsaesser of "Memory, Trauma, and Fantasy in American Cinema" (in press). His articles appear in *Cinema Journal, Camera Obscura, Journal of Popular Film and Television*, and elsewhere.

Grace Kyungwon Hong is associate professor of Asian American studies and women's studies at UCLA. She is the author of *The Ruptures of American Capital: Women of Color Feminism and the Culture of Immigrant Labor* (2006) and coeditor (with Roderick A. Ferguson) of *Strange Affinities: The Gender and Sexual Politics of Comparative Racialization* (2011).

Janet R. Jakobsen is director of the Center for Research on Women and Ann Whitney Olin Professor of Women's, Gender and Sexuality Studies at Barnard College, Columbia University, where she has also served as dean for faculty diversity and development. She is the author of *Working Alliances and the Politics of Difference: Diversity and Feminist Ethics* (1998). With Ann Pellegrini she is the author of *Love the Sin: Sexual Regulation and the Limits of Religious Tolerance* (2003) and editor of *Secularisms* (2008), and with Elizabeth Castelli she is editor of *Interventions: Academics and Activists Respond to Violence* (2004). Before entering the academy, she was a policy analyst and organizer in Washington, DC.

Miranda Joseph is associate professor of gender and women's studies at the University of Arizona. Her publications include *Against the Romance of Community* (2002) and "Neoliberalism and the Battle over Ethnic Studies in Arizona" (coauthored with Sandra K. Soto) in *Thought and Action: The NEA Higher Education Journal* (2010). Her current project is "A Debt to Society."

Aaron Lecklider is assistant professor of American studies and affiliated faculty in women's studies at the University of Massachusetts Boston. His essays have been published in the *Journal of American Studies* and the *Journal of Popular Music Studies*. He is currently finishing research for a book project titled "Love's Next Meeting: Sex and Radicalism in Twentieth-Century American Culture."

Heather Love is the R. Jean Brownlee Term Associate Professor at the University of Pennsylvania. She is the author of *Feeling Backward: Loss and the Politics of Queer History* (2007) and the editor of a special issue of *GLQ* on the work and legacy of Gayle Rubin ("Rethinking Sex") (2011).

Robert McRuer is professor and deputy chair of the Department of English at George Washington University. He is author of *Crip Theory: Cultural Signs of Queerness and Disability* (2006) and coeditor, with Abby L. Wilkerson, of "Desiring Disability: Queer Theory Meets Disability Studies," a special issue of *GLQ* published in 2003. With Anna Mollow, he is coeditor of the forthcoming anthology "Sex and Disability."

Fred Moten, Helen L. Bevington Professor of Modern Poetry at Duke University, is author of two forthcoming books: "The Feel Trio" (Letter Machine Editions) and "theory of blackness" (Duke University Press).

Tavia Nyong'o is associate professor of performance studies at New York University. He writes on race, sexuality, popular music, and cultural history and is the author of *The Amalgamation Waltz* (2009).

Jasbir Puar is associate professor in the Department of Women's and Gender Studies at Rutgers, the State University of New Jersey. She is the author of *Terrorist Assemblages: Homonationalism in Queer Times* (2007), which won the 2007 Cultural Studies Book Award from the Association for Asian American Studies. Professor Puar has also authored numerous articles that appear in *Gender, Place, and Culture, Social Text, Radical History Review,* and *Signs*. She edited a special issue of *Social Text* titled "Interspecies" (coedited with Julie Livingston, Spring 2011), a special issue of *GLQ* titled "Queer Tourism: Geographies of Globalization" (Fall 2002), and with Patricia Clough, a forthcoming special issue of *Women's Studies Quarterly* on "Viral." She is currently working on a new book project focused on queer disability studies and theories of affect and assemblage.

Lisa Rofel is professor of anthropology at the University of California, Santa Cruz. Her most recent work includes *Desiring China: Experiments in Neo-liberalism, Sexuality and Public Culture* and a coedited special issue of *positions* with Petrus Liu titled "Beyond the Strai(gh)ts: Transnationalism and Queer Chinese Politics," which won the MLA's Council of Editors of Learned Journals' prize for best special issue for 2010.

Jordana Rosenberg is assistant professor of English at the University of Massachusetts Amherst. She is the author of *Critical Enthusiasm: Capital Accumulation and the Transformation of Religious Passion* (2011). Her current project is titled "Apertures of Enclosure: The Form of Dispossession in the Ages of Finance."

Gayle Salamon is assistant professor of English and gender and sexuality studies at Princeton University. Her research interests include phenomenology, feminist and queer theory, psychoanalysis, and visual culture. Salamon is the author of *Assuming a Body: Transgender and Rhetorics of Materiality* (2010) and is currently at work on a manuscript exploring narrations of chronic pain in contemporary memoir.

Dean Spade is an assistant professor at the Seattle University School of Law, teaching administrative law, law and social movements, and poverty law. In 2002 he founded the Sylvia Rivera Law Project, a law collective that provides free legal help to trans, intersex, and gender-nonconforming people who are low-income and/ or people of color and works to build trans resistance centered in racial and economic justice. He is the author of *Normal Life: Administrative Violence, Critical Trans Politics, and the Limits of Law* (2011).

Amy Villarejo holds a joint appointment with the Department of Theatre, Film, and Dance (of which she is currently department chair) and the Feminist, Gender, and Sexuality Studies Program (which she directed from 2004–2007) at Cornell University. She has published widely, including a book on film and cultural studies (*Keyframes*, 2001), on queer documentary (*Lesbian Rule*, 2003), and an introduction to the discipline of cinema and media studies, *Film Studies: The Basics* (2007). More recently, she is the coeditor of a special issue of *GLQ*, "Queer Marxism," and author of a forthcoming monograph on television, "Ethereal Queer."

Meg Wesling is associate professor of literature at the University of California, San Diego, where she teaches courses on US literature, gender studies, and cultural studies. She is the author, most recently, of *Empire's Proxy: American Literature and U.S. Imperialism in the Philippines* (2011) and is working on a book about queer politics and globalization.

Raz Yosef is an associate professor and the chair of the cinema studies BA program at the Department of Film and Television, Tel Aviv University. He is the author of *Beyond Flesh: Queer Masculinities and Nationalism in Israeli Cinema* (2004) and *The Politics of Loss and Trauma in Contemporary Israeli Cinema* (2011). His work on gender, sexuality, ethnicity, and nationalism in Israeli visual culture has appeared in *GLQ*, *Third Text*, *Framework*, *Shofar*, *Journal of Modern Jewish Studies*, *Camera Obscura*, and *Cinema Journal*.

GLQ: A JOURNAL OF LESBIAN AND GAY STUDIES

Subscribe today.

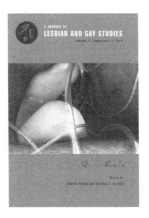

*Ann Cvetkovich and
Annamarie Jagose, editors*

Providing a much-needed forum for
interdisciplinary discussion, *GLQ* publishes
scholarship, criticism, and commentary in
areas as diverse as law, science studies, religion,
political science, and literary studies. Its aim
is to offer queer perspectives on all issues
touching on sex and sexuality.

Recent Special Issues

"Sexuality, Nationality, Indigeneity" (16:1/2)
Daniel Heath Justice, Mark Rifkin, and
Bethany Schneider, special issue editors

"Rethinking Sex " (17:1)
Heather Love, special issue editor

"Queer Bonds" (17:2/3)
Damon Young and Joshua J. Weiner,
special issue editors

Subscription Information

Quarterly
RSS feeds and online access are availble with a print subscription.
Individuals: $38
Students: $24 (photocopy of valid student ID required)

To place your order, visit dukepress.edu/glq.

Keep up-to-date

on new scholarship from this journal.

Email Alerts is a complimentary service that delivers electronic tables of contents straight to your inbox, allowing you to stay current on new scholarship as it is published.

Sign up for free e-mail alerts today at dukejournals.org/cgi/alerts *(no subscription necessary).*

- Complete the free registration process.

- Select your favorite journals to start receiving electronic tables of contents.

DUKE
UNIVERSITY PRESS

For more information about Duke University Press Journals, visit **dukejournals.org**.